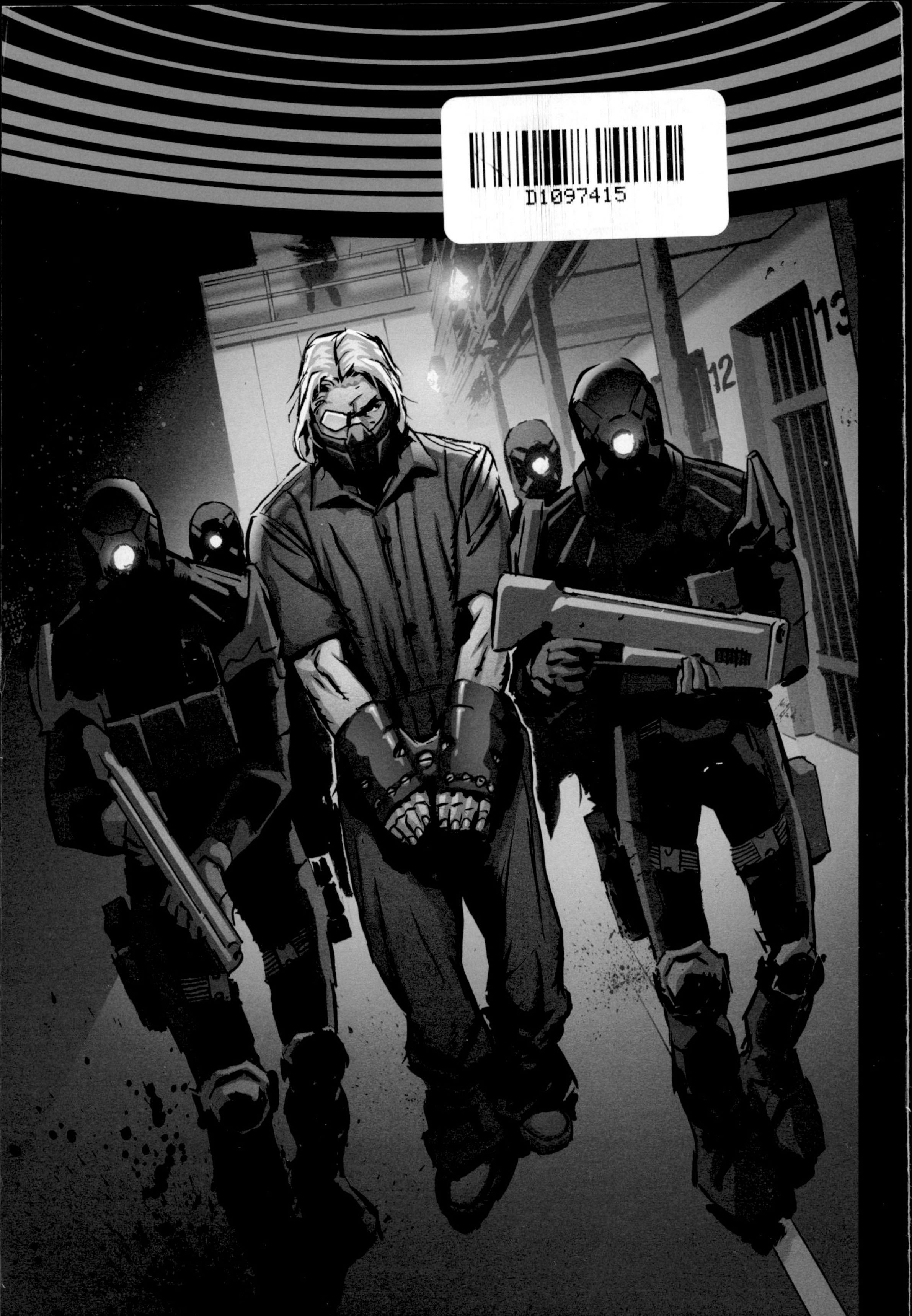
12
13

DEATHSTROKE

VOL.2 THE GOSPEL OF SLADE

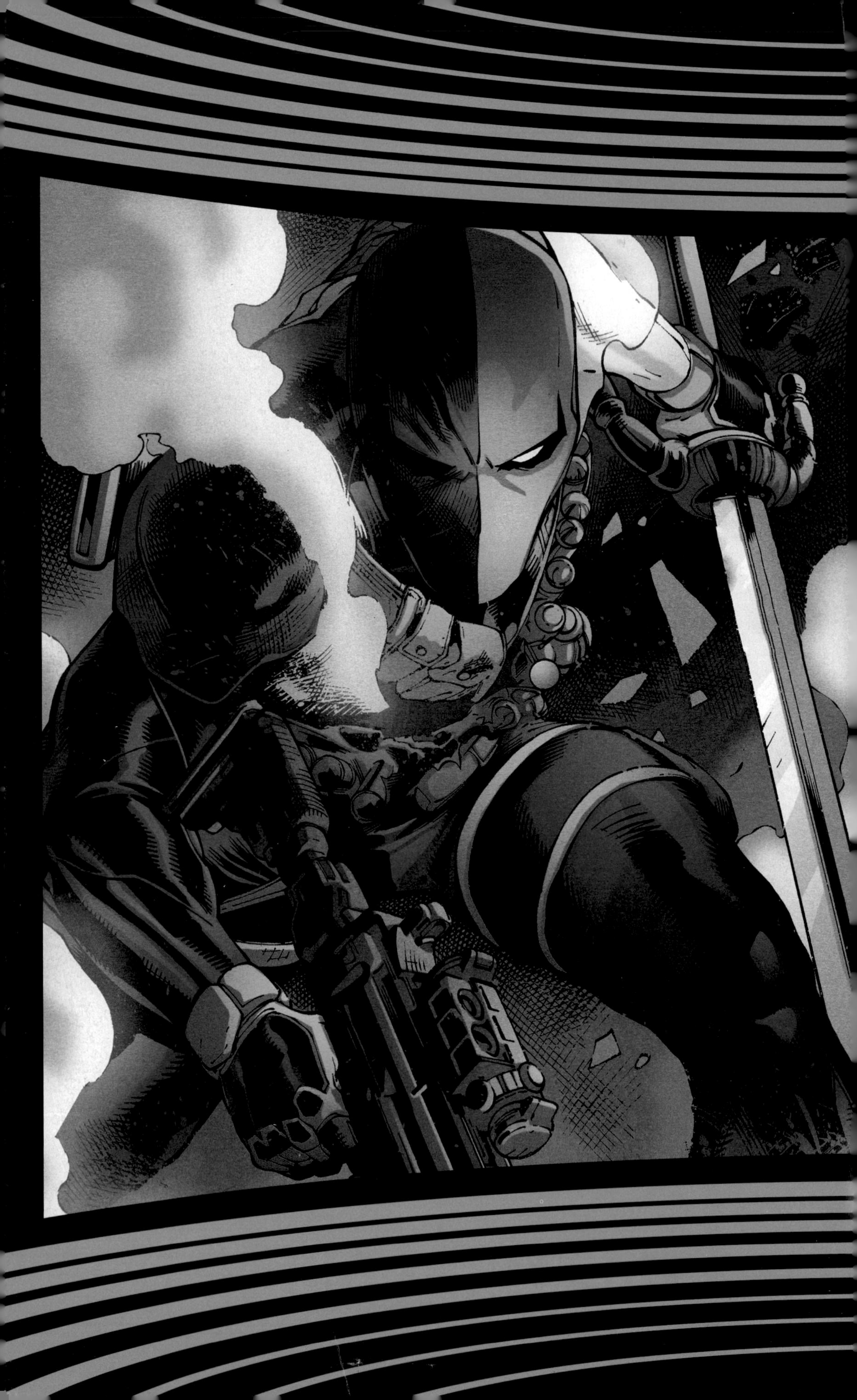

DEATHSTROKE
VOL.2 THE GOSPEL OF SLADE

CHRISTOPHER PRIEST
writer

LARRY HAMA
breakdowns

CARLO PAGULAYAN * CARY NORD * DENYS COWAN
pencillers

JASON PAZ * SEAN PARSONS * CARY NORD * BILL SIENKIEWICZ
inkers

JEROMY COX * HI-FI
colorists

WILLIE SCHUBERT
letterer

SHANE DAVIS, MICHELLE DELECKI and ALEX SINCLAIR
collection cover artists

DEATHSTROKE created by Marv Wolfman and George Pérez

JERICHO created by Marv Wolfman and George Pérez

SUPERMAN created by Jerry Siegel and Joe Shuster
By special arrangement with the Jerry Siegel family

ALEX ANTONE Editor - Original Series ✳ BRITTANY HOLZHERR Assistant Editor - Original Series
JEB WOODARD Group Editor - Collected Editions ✳ LIZ ERICKSON Editor - Collected Edition
STEVE COOK Design Director - Books ✳ MONIQUE GRUSPE Publication Design

BOB HARRAS Senior VP - Editor-in-Chief, DC Comics

DIANE NELSON President ✳ DAN DiDIO Publisher ✳ JIM LEE Publisher ✳ GEOFF JOHNS President & Chief Creative Officer
AMIT DESAI Executive VP - Business & Marketing Strategy, Direct to Consumer & Global Franchise Management ✳ SAM ADES Senior VP - Direct to Consumer
BOBBIE CHASE VP - Talent Development ✳ MARK CHIARELLO Senior VP - Art, Design & Collected Editions
JOHN CUNNINGHAM Senior VP - Sales & Trade Marketing ✳ ANNE DePIES Senior VP - Business Strategy, Finance & Administration
DON FALLETTI VP - Manufacturing Operations ✳ LAWRENCE GANEM VP - Editorial Administration & Talent Relations
ALISON GILL Senior VP - Manufacturing & Operations ✳ HANK KANALZ Senior VP - Editorial Strategy & Administration
JAY KOGAN VP - Legal Affairs ✳ THOMAS LOFTUS VP - Business Affairs
JACK MAHAN VP - Business Affairs ✳ NICK J. NAPOLITANO VP - Manufacturing Administration
EDDIE SCANNELL VP - Consumer Marketing ✳ COURTNEY SIMMONS Senior VP - Publicity & Communications
JIM (SKI) SOKOLOWSKI VP - Comic Book Specialty Sales & Trade Marketing ✳ NANCY SPEARS VP - Mass, Book, Digital Sales & Trade Marketing

DEATHSTROKE VOL. 2: THE GOSPEL OF SLADE

DC Comics, 2900 West Alameda Ave., Burbank, CA 91505.
Printed by LSC Communications, Salem, VA, USA. 6/2/17. First Printing
ISBN: 978-1-4012-7098-8

Library of Congress Cataloging-in-Publication Data is available.

PEFC Certified

Printed on paper from
sustainably managed
forests, controlled
sources

PEFC/29-31-337   www.pefc.org

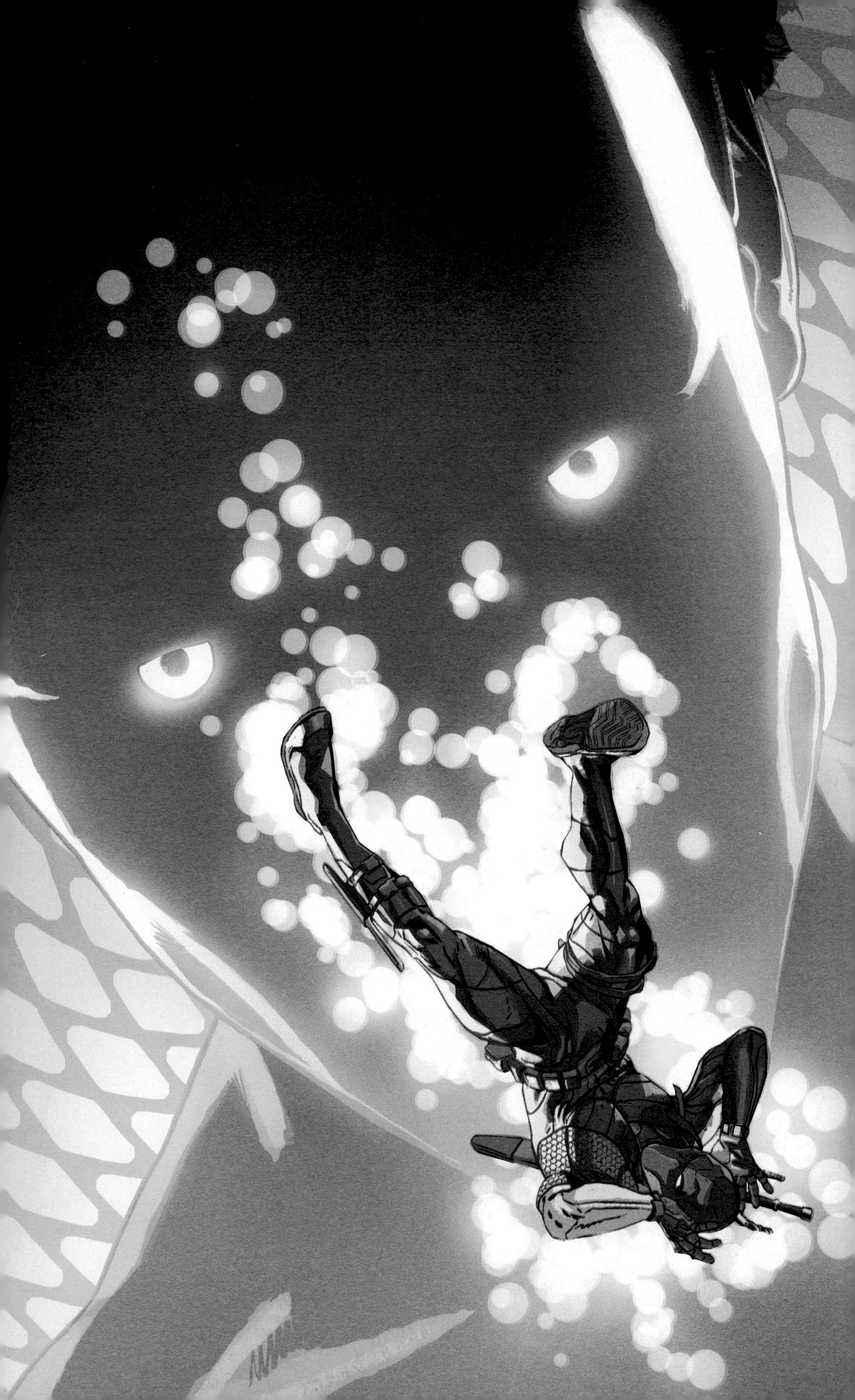

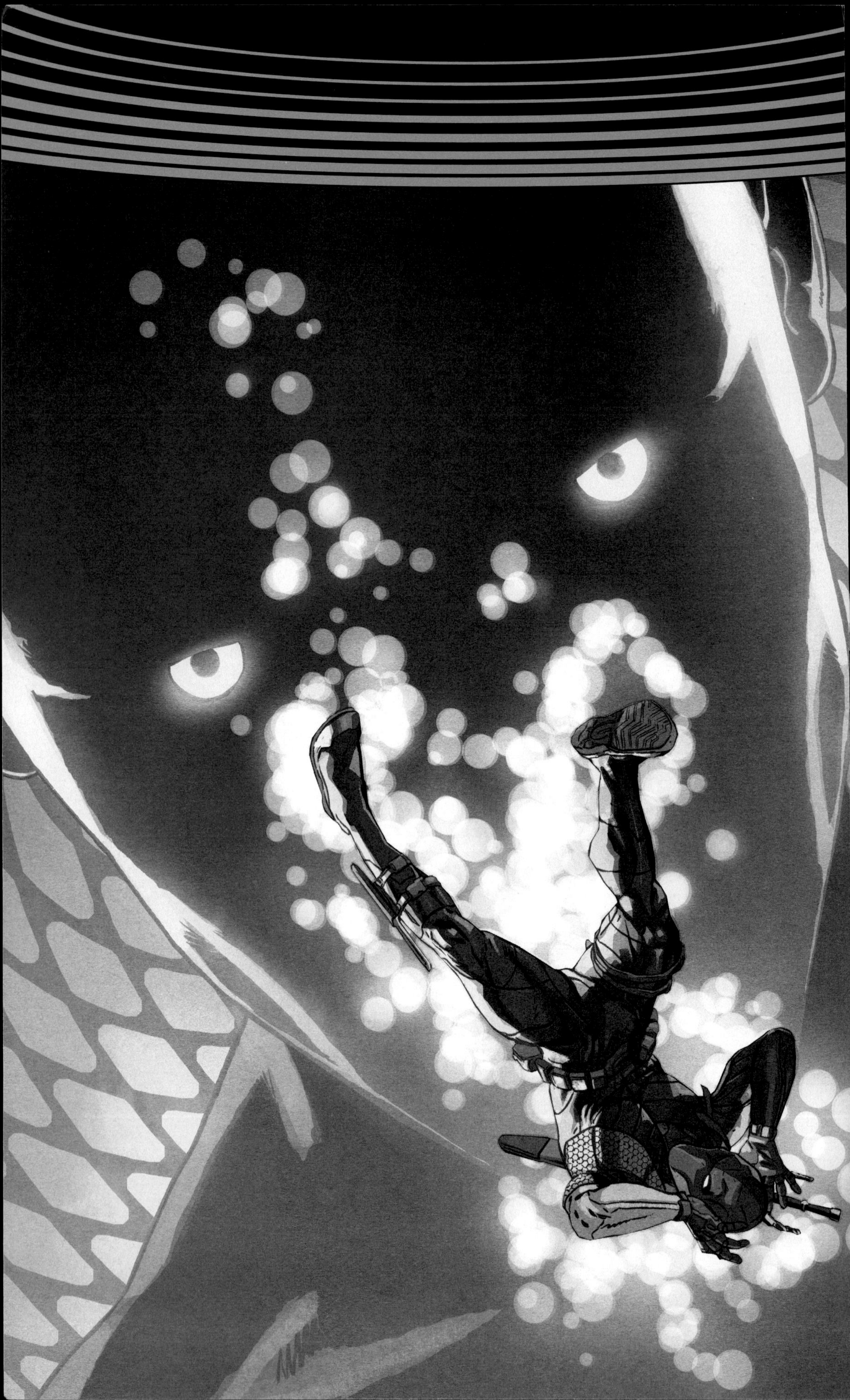

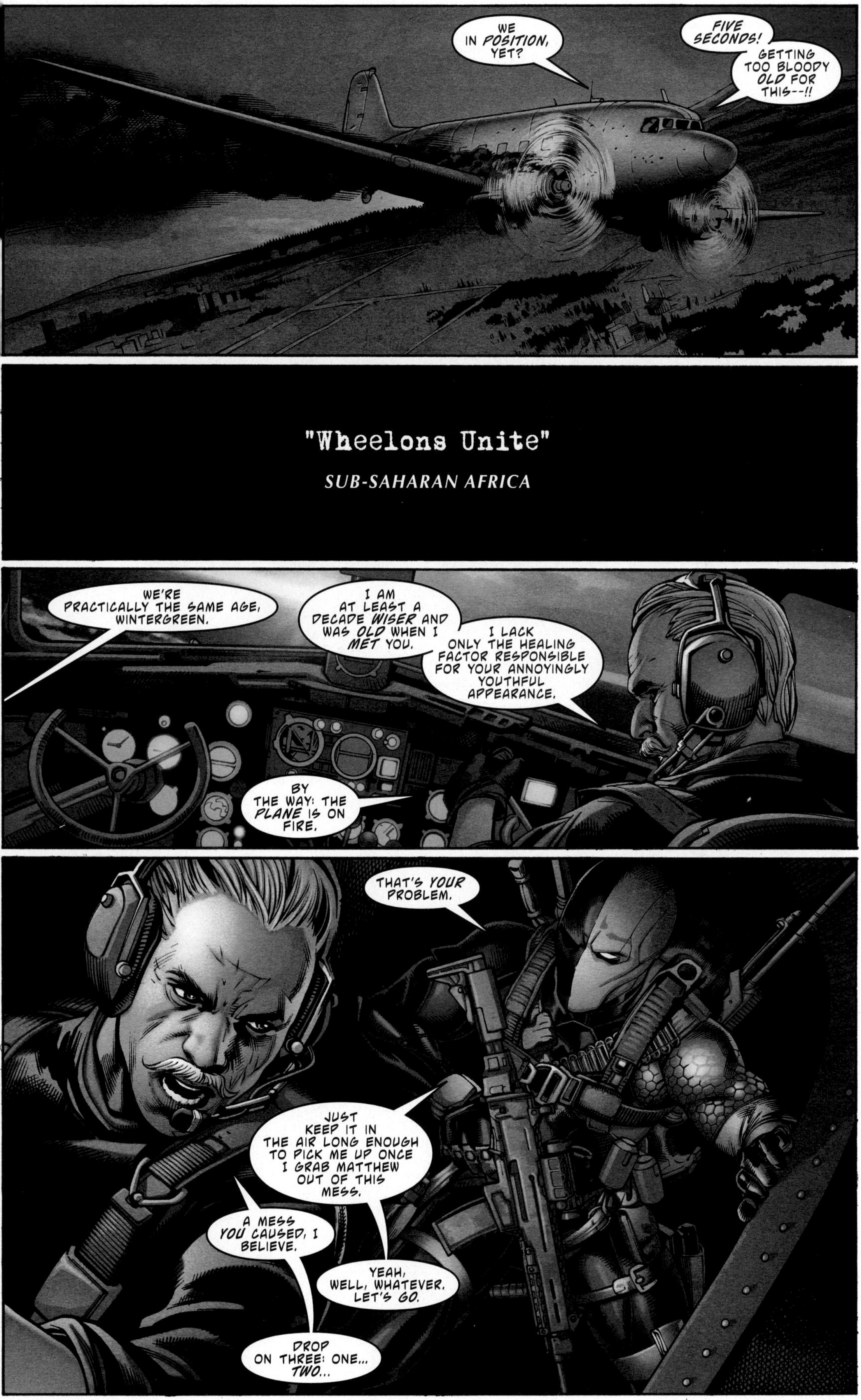
WE IN POSITION, YET?
FIVE SECONDS!
GETTING TOO BLOODY OLD FOR THIS--!!
"Wheelons Unite"
SUB-SAHARAN AFRICA
WE'RE PRACTICALLY THE SAME AGE, WINTERGREEN.
I AM AT LEAST A DECADE WISER AND WAS OLD WHEN I MET YOU.
I LACK ONLY THE HEALING FACTOR RESPONSIBLE FOR YOUR ANNOYINGLY YOUTHFUL APPEARANCE.
BY THE WAY: THE PLANE IS ON FIRE.
THAT'S YOUR PROBLEM.
JUST KEEP IT IN THE AIR LONG ENOUGH TO PICK ME UP ONCE I GRAB MATTHEW OUT OF THIS MESS.
A MESS YOU CAUSED, I BELIEVE.
YEAH, WELL, WHATEVER. LET'S GO.
DROP ON THREE: ONE... TWO...

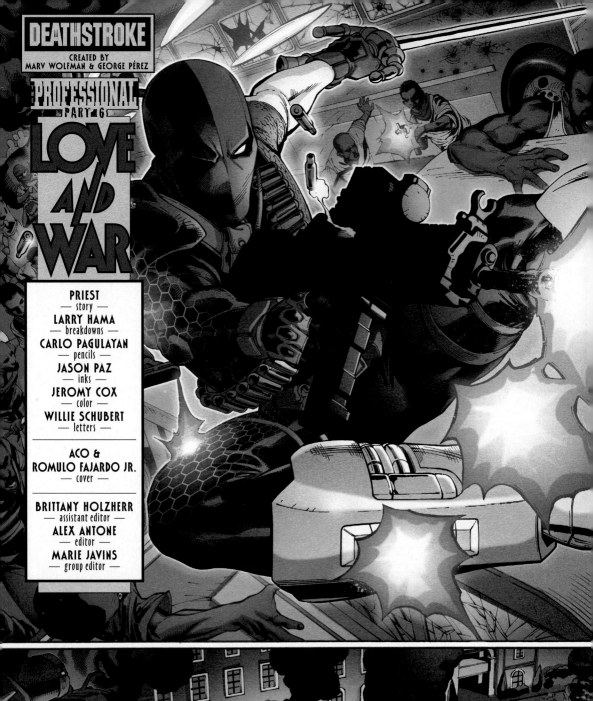

DEATHSTROKE

CREATED BY
MARV WOLFMAN & GEORGE PÉREZ

THE PROFESSIONAL
PART 6

LOVE
AND
WAR

PRIEST
— story —

LARRY HAMA
— breakdowns —

CARLO PAGULAYAN
— pencils —

JASON PAZ
— inks —

JEROMY COX
— color —

WILLIE SCHUBERT
— letters —

ACO &
ROMULO FAJARDO JR.
— cover —

BRITTANY HOLZHERR
— assistant editor —

ALEX ANTONE
— editor —

MARIE JAVINS
— group editor —

PRESIDENT-FOR-LIFE BLAND IS IN HIS MASTER SUITE.

ROGER THAT. FIVE MINUTES.

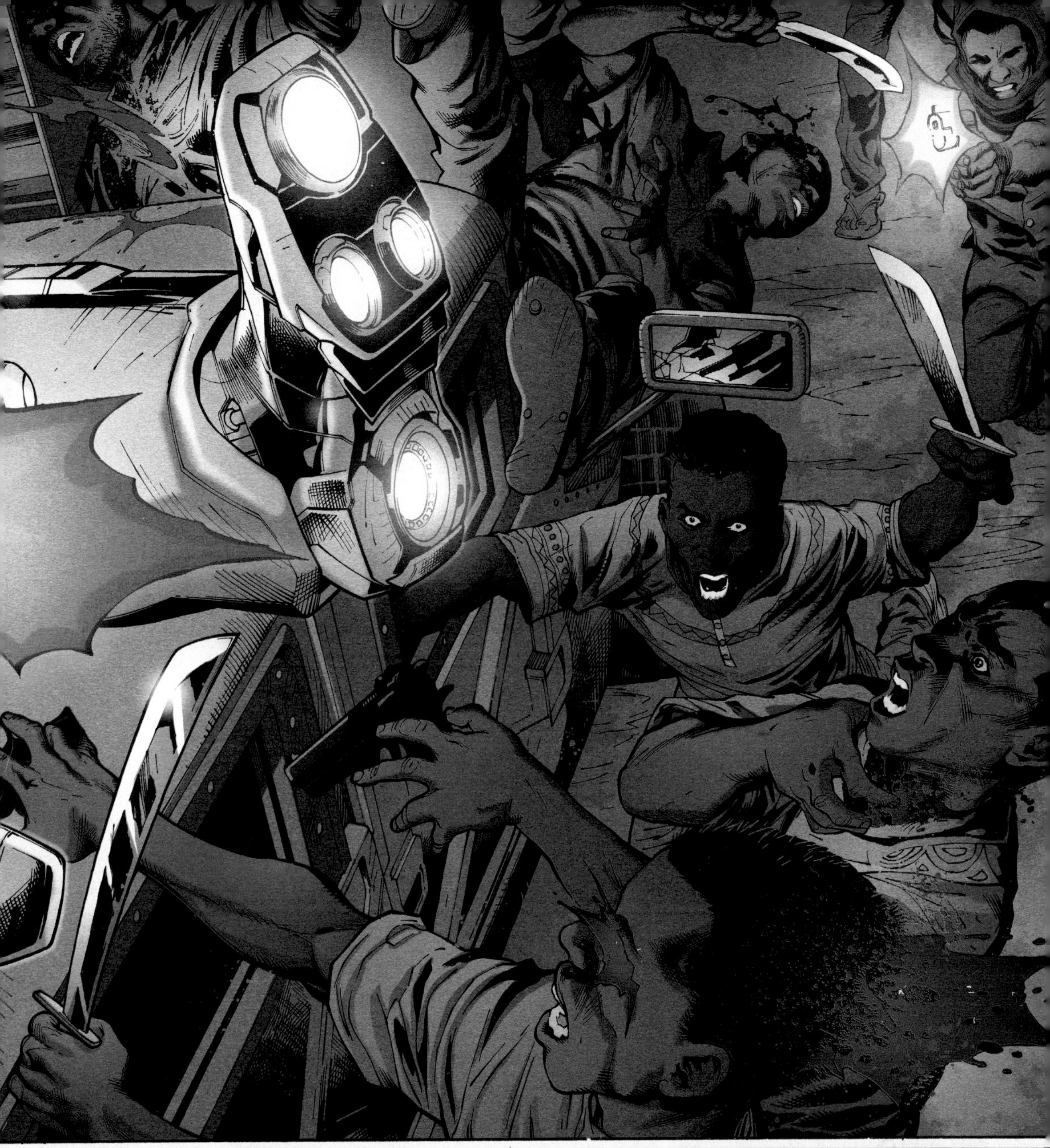

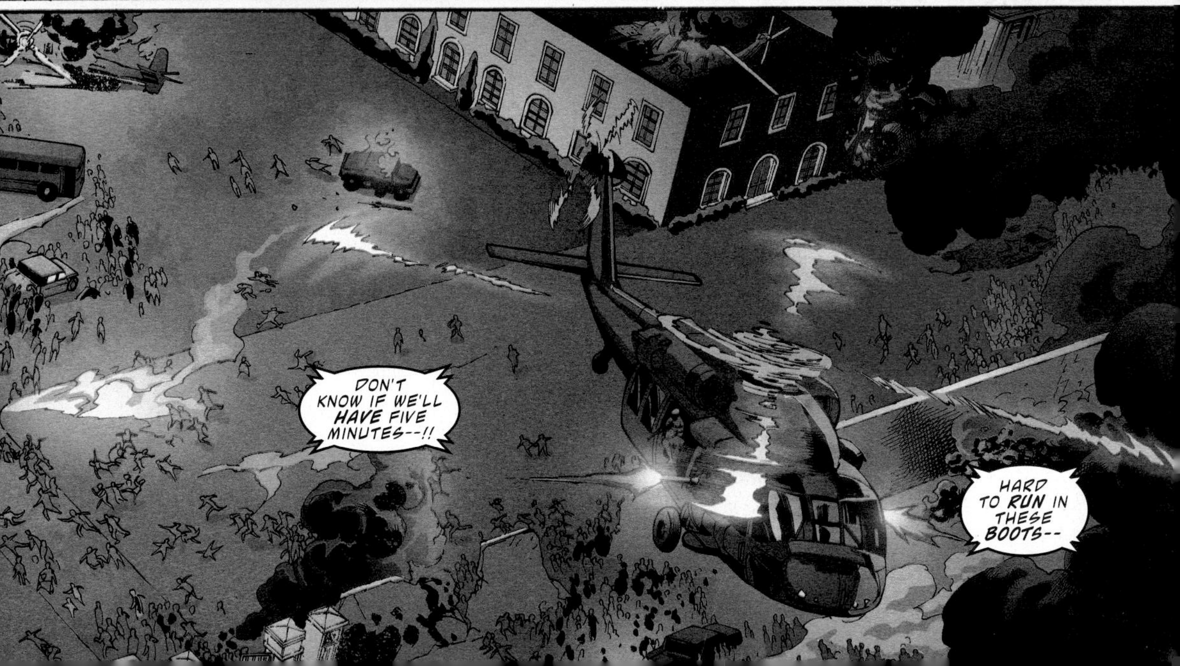
DON'T KNOW IF WE'LL HAVE FIVE MINUTES--!!
HARD TO RUN IN THESE BOOTS--

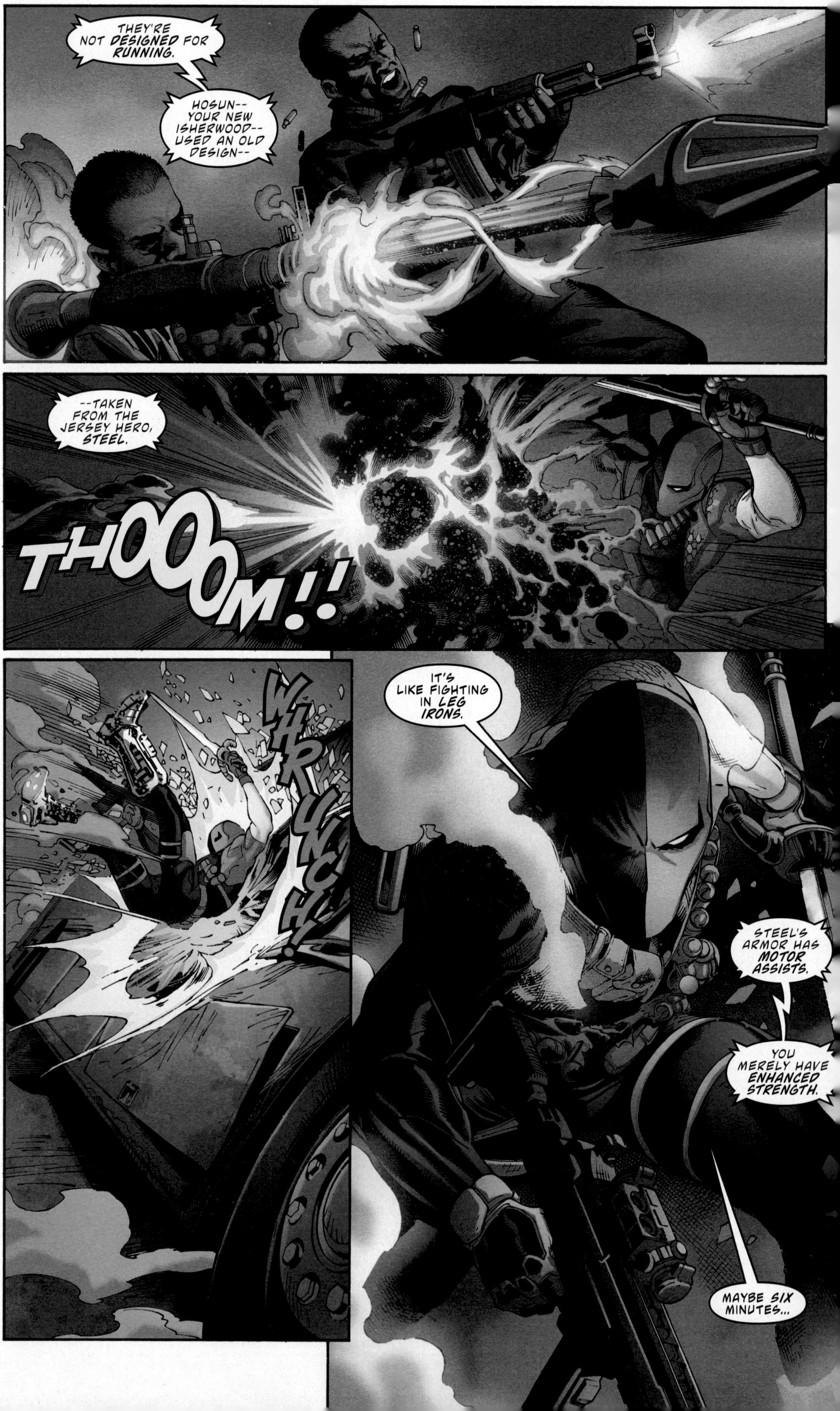
THEY'RE NOT DESIGNED FOR RUNNING.
HOSUN-- YOUR NEW ISHERWOOD-- USED AN OLD DESIGN--
--TAKEN FROM THE JERSEY HERO, STEEL.
THOOOM!!
WHRUNCH!
IT'S LIKE FIGHTING IN LEG IRONS.
STEEL'S ARMOR HAS MOTOR ASSISTS.
YOU MERELY HAVE ENHANCED STRENGTH.
MAYBE SIX MINUTES...

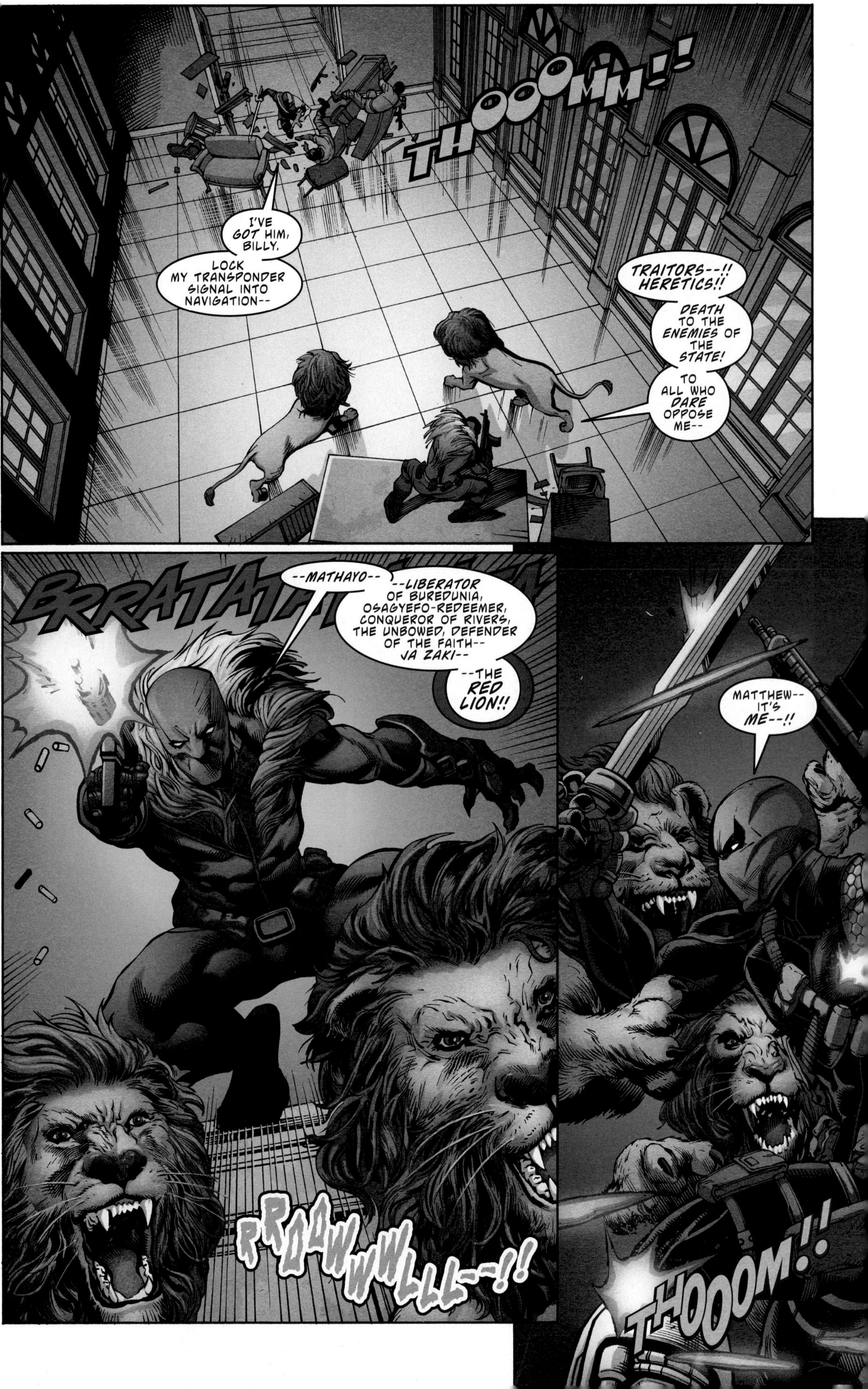
THOOOMM!!
I'VE GOT HIM, BILLY.
LOCK MY TRANSPONDER SIGNAL INTO NAVIGATION--
TRAITORS--!! HERETICS!!
DEATH TO THE ENEMIES OF THE STATE!
TO ALL WHO DARE OPPOSE ME--
BRRATATATATATA
--MATHAYO--
--LIBERATOR OF BUREDUNIA, OSAGYEFO-REDEEMER, CONQUEROR OF RIVERS, THE UNBOWED, DEFENDER OF THE FAITH-- JA ZAKI--
--THE RED LION!!
RRROWWWLLL--!!
MATTHEW-- IT'S ME--!!
THOOOM!!

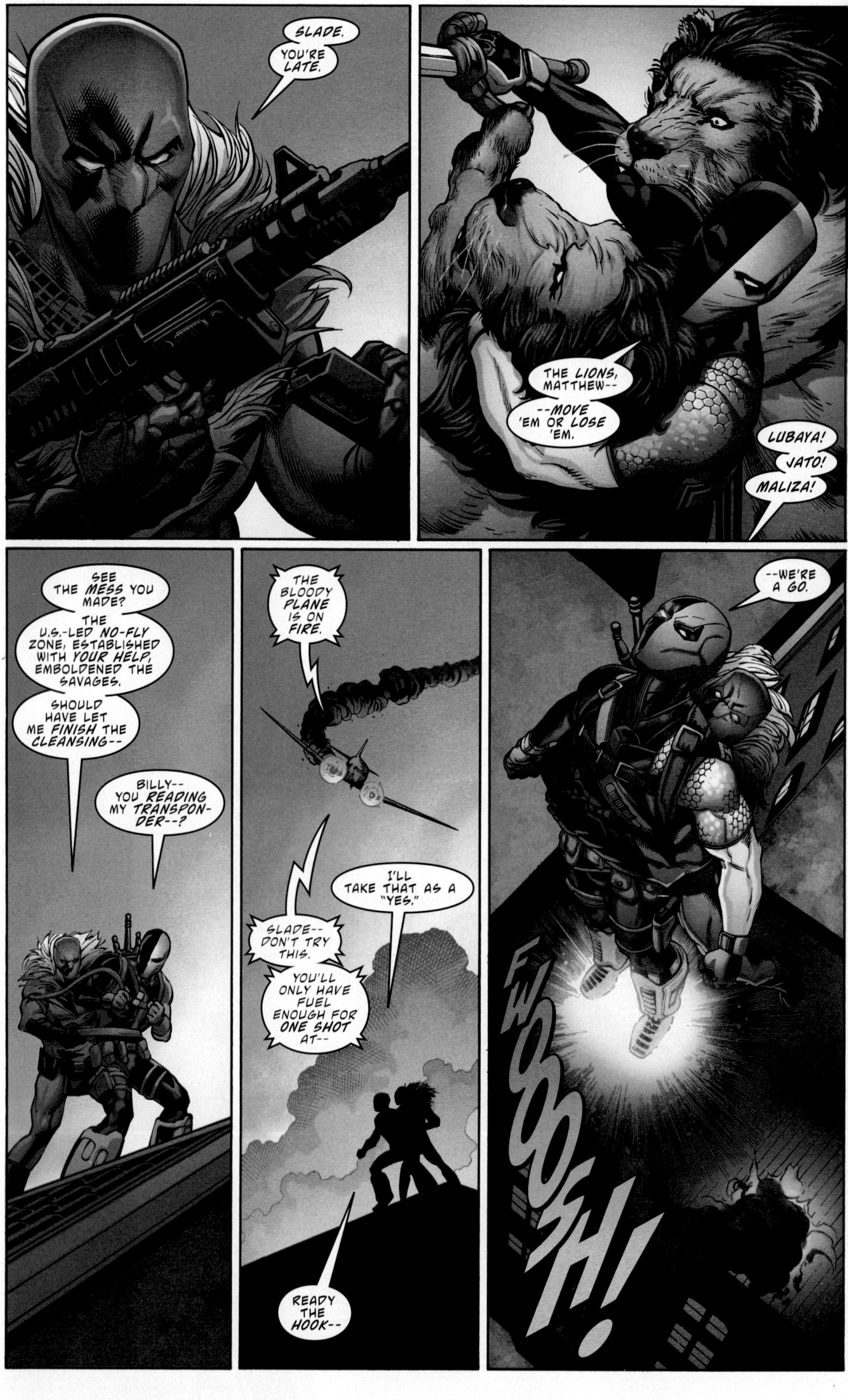

SLADE. YOU'RE LATE.
THE LIONS, MATTHEW--
--MOVE 'EM OR LOSE 'EM.
LUBAYA!
JATO!
MALIZA!
SEE THE MESS YOU MADE?
THE U.S.-LED NO-FLY ZONE, ESTABLISHED WITH YOUR HELP, EMBOLDENED THE SAVAGES.
SHOULD HAVE LET ME FINISH THE CLEANSING--
BILLY-- YOU READING MY TRANSPONDER--?
THE BLOODY PLANE IS ON FIRE.
I'LL TAKE THAT AS A "YES."
SLADE-- DON'T TRY THIS.
YOU'LL ONLY HAVE FUEL ENOUGH FOR ONE SHOT AT--
READY THE HOOK--
--WE'RE A GO.
FWOOOSH!

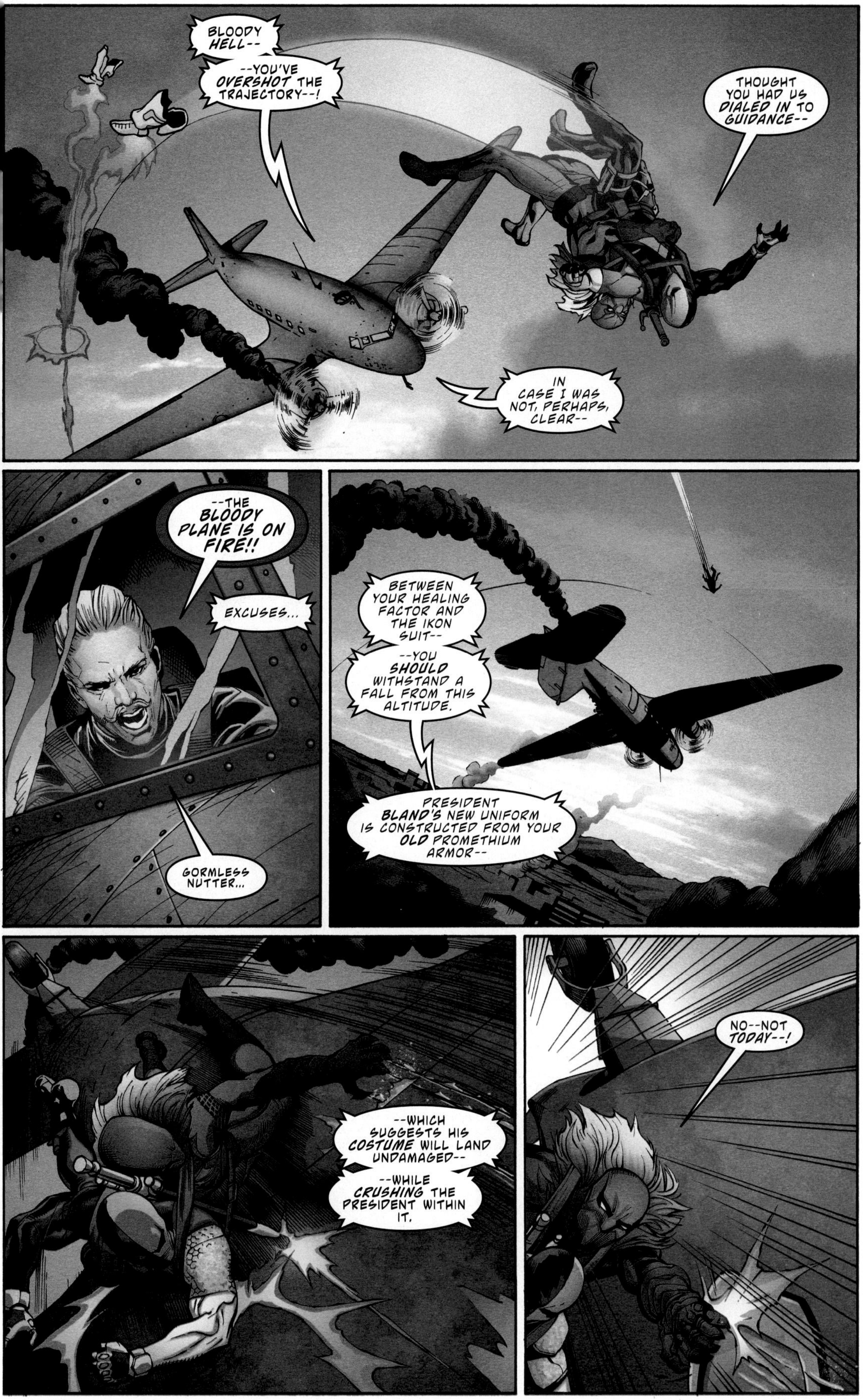
BLOODY HELL--
--YOU'VE OVERSHOT THE TRAJECTORY--!
THOUGHT YOU HAD US DIALED IN TO GUIDANCE--
IN CASE I WAS NOT, PERHAPS, CLEAR--
--THE BLOODY PLANE IS ON FIRE!!
EXCUSES...
GORMLESS NUTTER...
BETWEEN YOUR HEALING FACTOR AND THE IKON SUIT--
--YOU SHOULD WITHSTAND A FALL FROM THIS ALTITUDE.
PRESIDENT BLAND'S NEW UNIFORM IS CONSTRUCTED FROM YOUR OLD PROMETHIUM ARMOR--
--WHICH SUGGESTS HIS COSTUME WILL LAND UNDAMAGED--
--WHILE CRUSHING THE PRESIDENT WITHIN IT.
NO--NOT TODAY--!

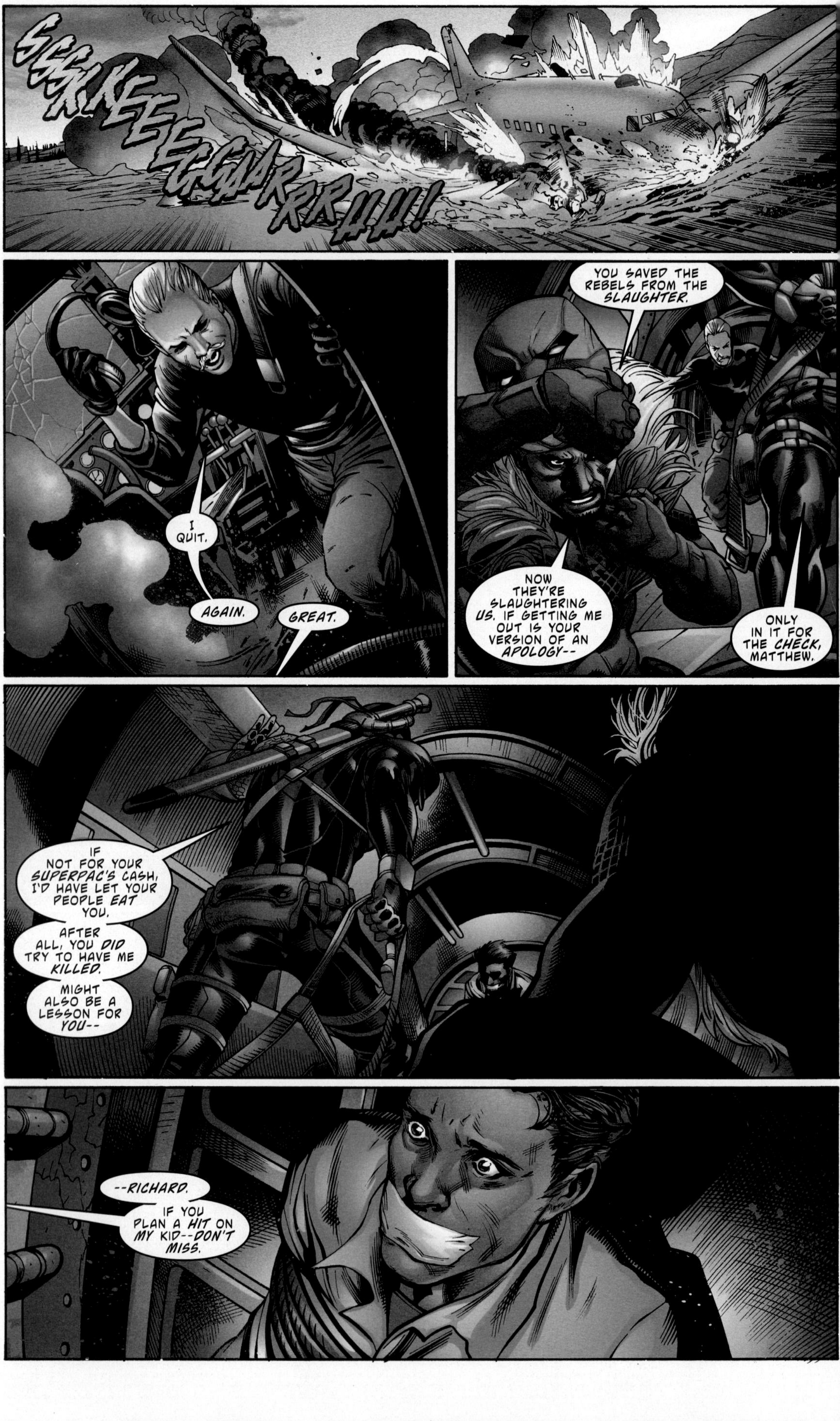
SSKKEEEGGAARRRRHHH!
I QUIT.
AGAIN.
GREAT.
YOU SAVED THE REBELS FROM THE *SLAUGHTER*.
NOW THEY'RE SLAUGHTERING US. IF GETTING ME OUT IS YOUR VERSION OF AN *APOLOGY*--
ONLY IN IT FOR THE *CHECK*, MATTHEW.
IF NOT FOR YOUR *SUPERPAC'S* CASH, I'D HAVE LET YOUR PEOPLE *EAT* YOU.
AFTER ALL, YOU *DID* TRY TO HAVE ME *KILLED*.
MIGHT ALSO BE A LESSON FOR *YOU*--
--*RICHARD*.
IF YOU PLAN A *HIT* ON *MY KID*--*DON'T MISS*.

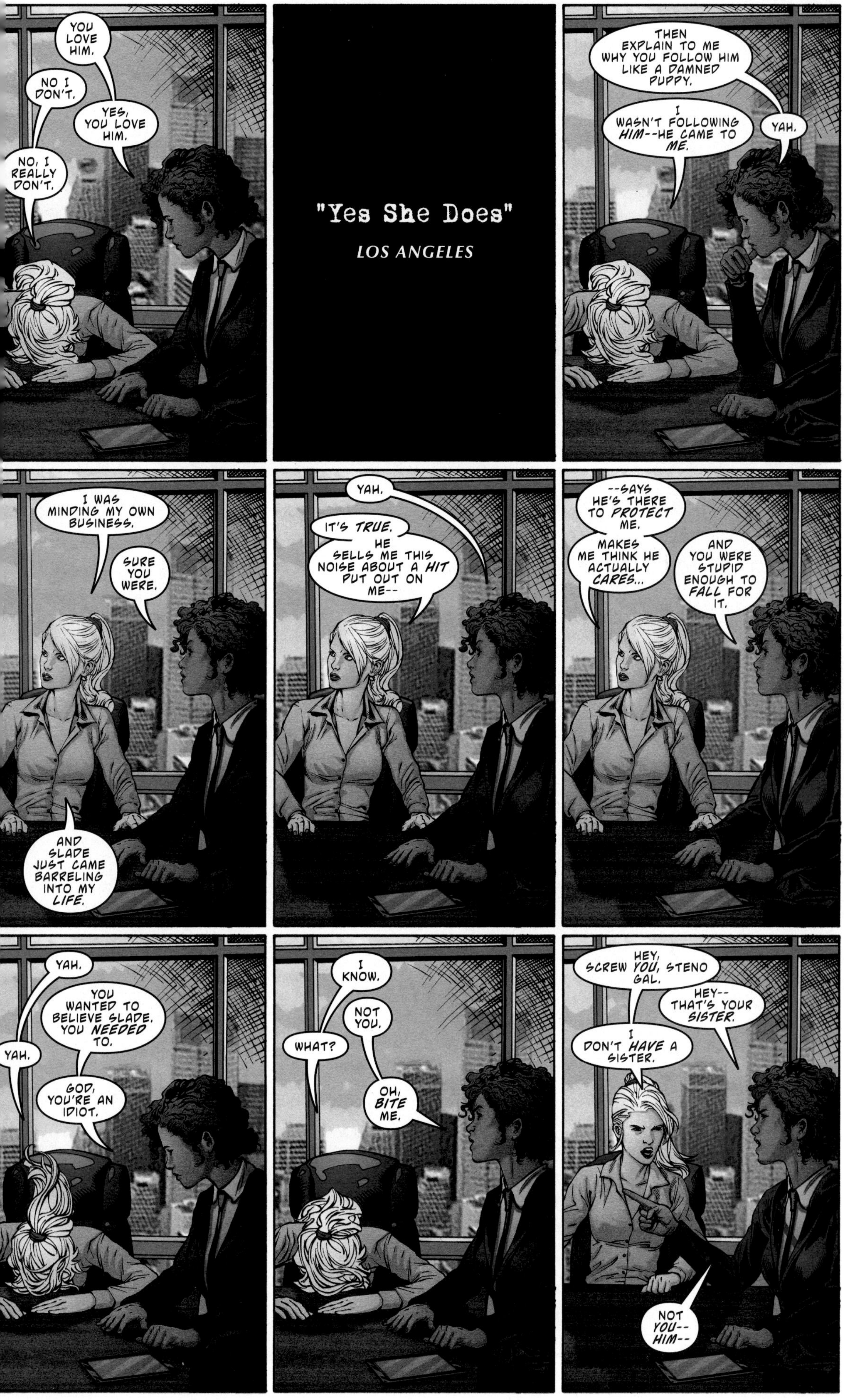

YOU LOVE HIM.
NO I DON'T.
YES, YOU LOVE HIM.
NO, I REALLY DON'T.
"Yes She Does"
LOS ANGELES
THEN EXPLAIN TO ME WHY YOU FOLLOW HIM LIKE A DAMNED PUPPY.
I WASN'T FOLLOWING *HIM*--HE CAME TO *ME*.
YAH.
I WAS MINDING MY OWN BUSINESS.
SURE YOU WERE.
AND SLADE JUST CAME BARRELING INTO MY *LIFE*.
YAH.
IT'S *TRUE*.
HE SELLS ME THIS NOISE ABOUT A *HIT* PUT OUT ON ME--
--SAYS HE'S THERE TO *PROTECT* ME.
MAKES ME THINK HE ACTUALLY *CARES*...
AND YOU WERE STUPID ENOUGH TO *FALL* FOR IT.
YAH.
YOU WANTED TO BELIEVE SLADE. YOU *NEEDED* TO.
YAH.
GOD, YOU'RE AN IDIOT.
I KNOW.
WHAT?
NOT YOU.
OH, *BITE* ME.
HEY, SCREW *YOU*, STENO GAL.
HEY-- THAT'S YOUR *SISTER*.
I DON'T *HAVE* A SISTER.
NOT *YOU*-- *HIM*--

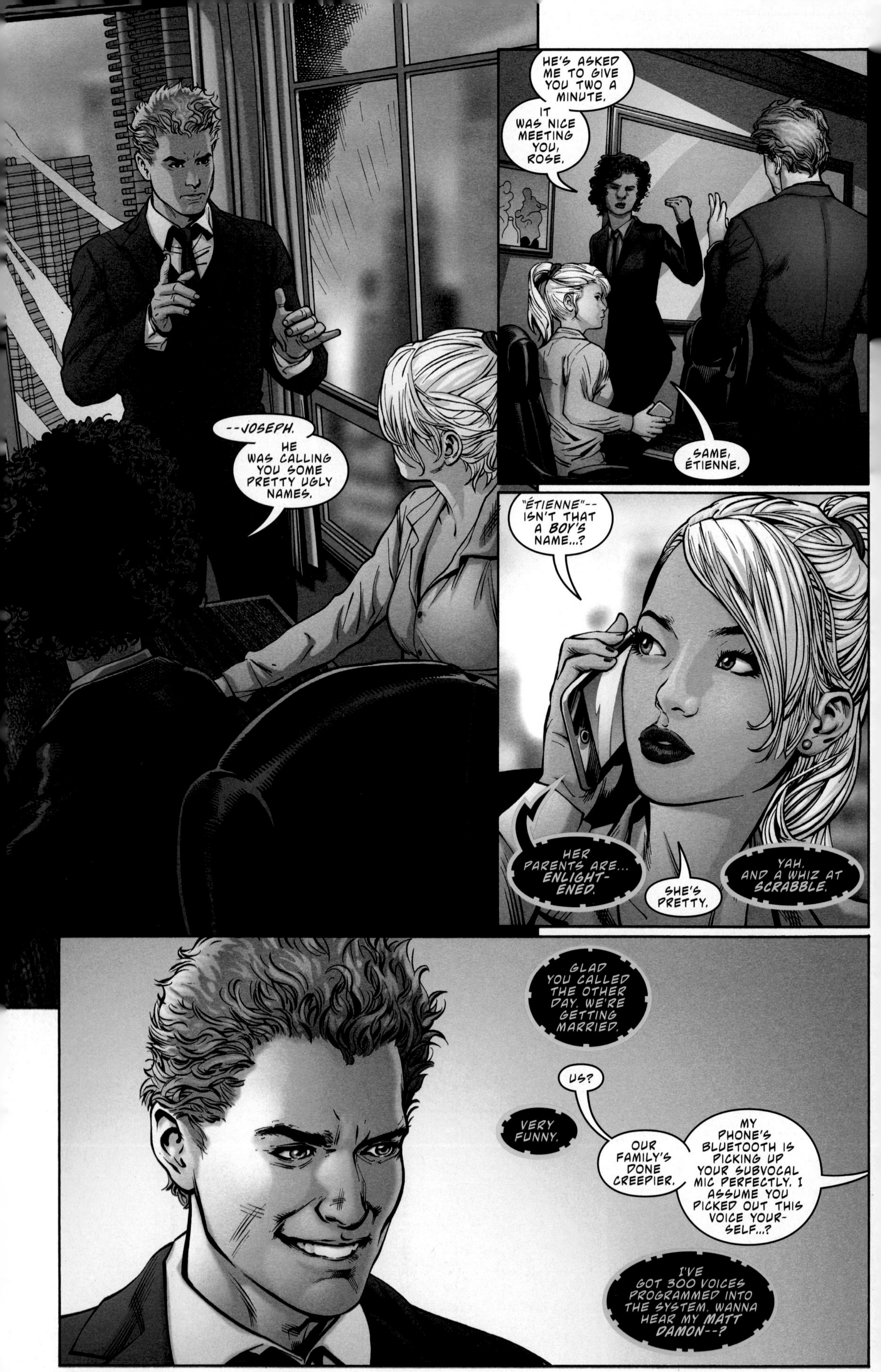
HE'S ASKED ME TO GIVE YOU TWO A MINUTE.
IT WAS NICE MEETING YOU, ROSE.
SAME, ÉTIENNE.
--JOSEPH.
HE WAS CALLING YOU SOME PRETTY UGLY NAMES.
"ÉTIENNE"-- ISN'T THAT A BOY'S NAME...?
HER PARENTS ARE... ENLIGHT-ENED.
SHE'S PRETTY.
YAH. AND A WHIZ AT SCRABBLE.
GLAD YOU CALLED THE OTHER DAY. WE'RE GETTING MARRIED.
US?
VERY FUNNY.
OUR FAMILY'S DONE CREEPIER.
MY PHONE'S BLUETOOTH IS PICKING UP YOUR SUBVOCAL MIC PERFECTLY. I ASSUME YOU PICKED OUT THIS VOICE YOUR-SELF...?
I'VE GOT 300 VOICES PROGRAMMED INTO THE SYSTEM. WANNA HEAR MY MATT DAMON--?

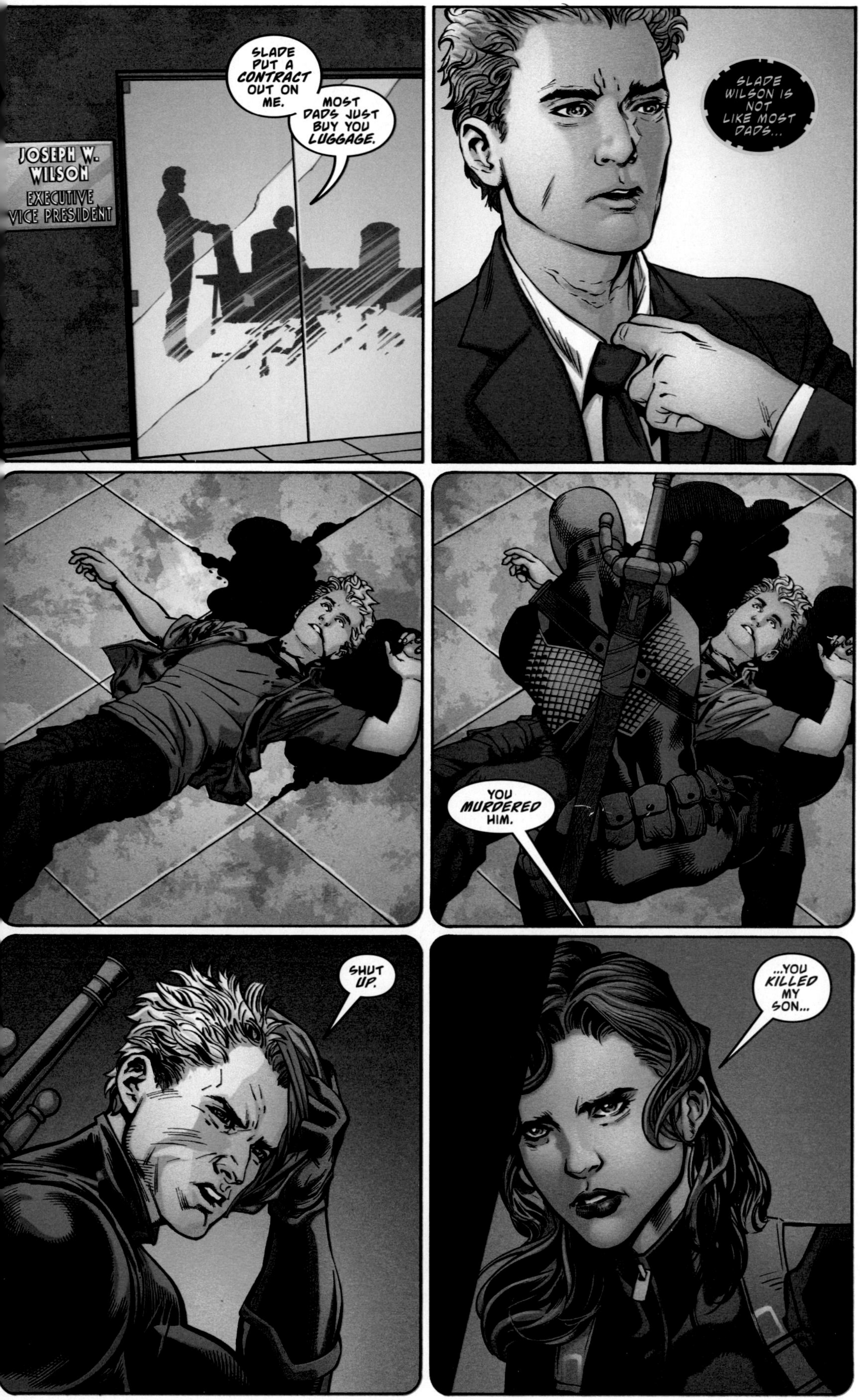
SLADE PUT A CONTRACT OUT ON ME.
MOST DADS JUST BUY YOU LUGGAGE.
JOSEPH W. WILSON
EXECUTIVE VICE PRESIDENT
SLADE WILSON IS NOT LIKE MOST DADS...
YOU MURDERED HIM.
SHUT UP.
...YOU KILLED MY SON...

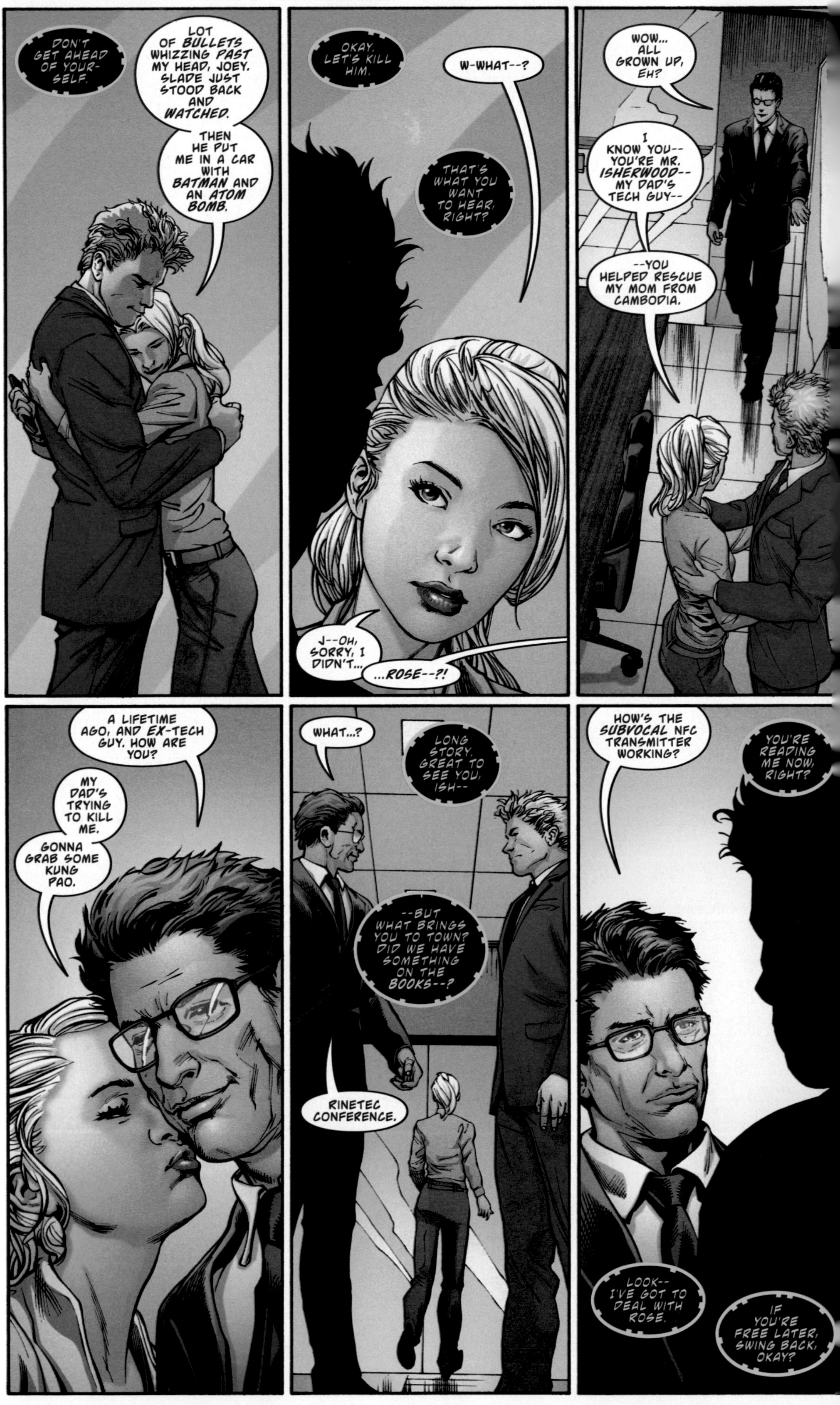
DON'T GET AHEAD OF YOURSELF.
LOT OF BULLETS WHIZZING PAST MY HEAD, JOEY. SLADE JUST STOOD BACK AND WATCHED.
THEN HE PUT ME IN A CAR WITH BATMAN AND AN ATOM BOMB.
OKAY. LET'S KILL HIM.
W-WHAT--?
THAT'S WHAT YOU WANT TO HEAR, RIGHT?
J--OH, SORRY, I DIDN'T...
...ROSE--?!
WOW... ALL GROWN UP, EH?
I KNOW YOU--YOU'RE MR. ISHERWOOD--MY DAD'S TECH GUY--
--YOU HELPED RESCUE MY MOM FROM CAMBODIA.
A LIFETIME AGO, AND EX-TECH GUY. HOW ARE YOU?
MY DAD'S TRYING TO KILL ME.
GONNA GRAB SOME KUNG PAO.
WHAT...?
LONG STORY. GREAT TO SEE YOU, ISH--
--BUT WHAT BRINGS YOU TO TOWN? DID WE HAVE SOMETHING ON THE BOOKS--?
RINETEC CONFERENCE.
HOW'S THE SUBVOCAL NFC TRANSMITTER WORKING?
YOU'RE READING ME NOW, RIGHT?
LOOK--I'VE GOT TO DEAL WITH ROSE.
IF YOU'RE FREE LATER, SWING BACK, OKAY?

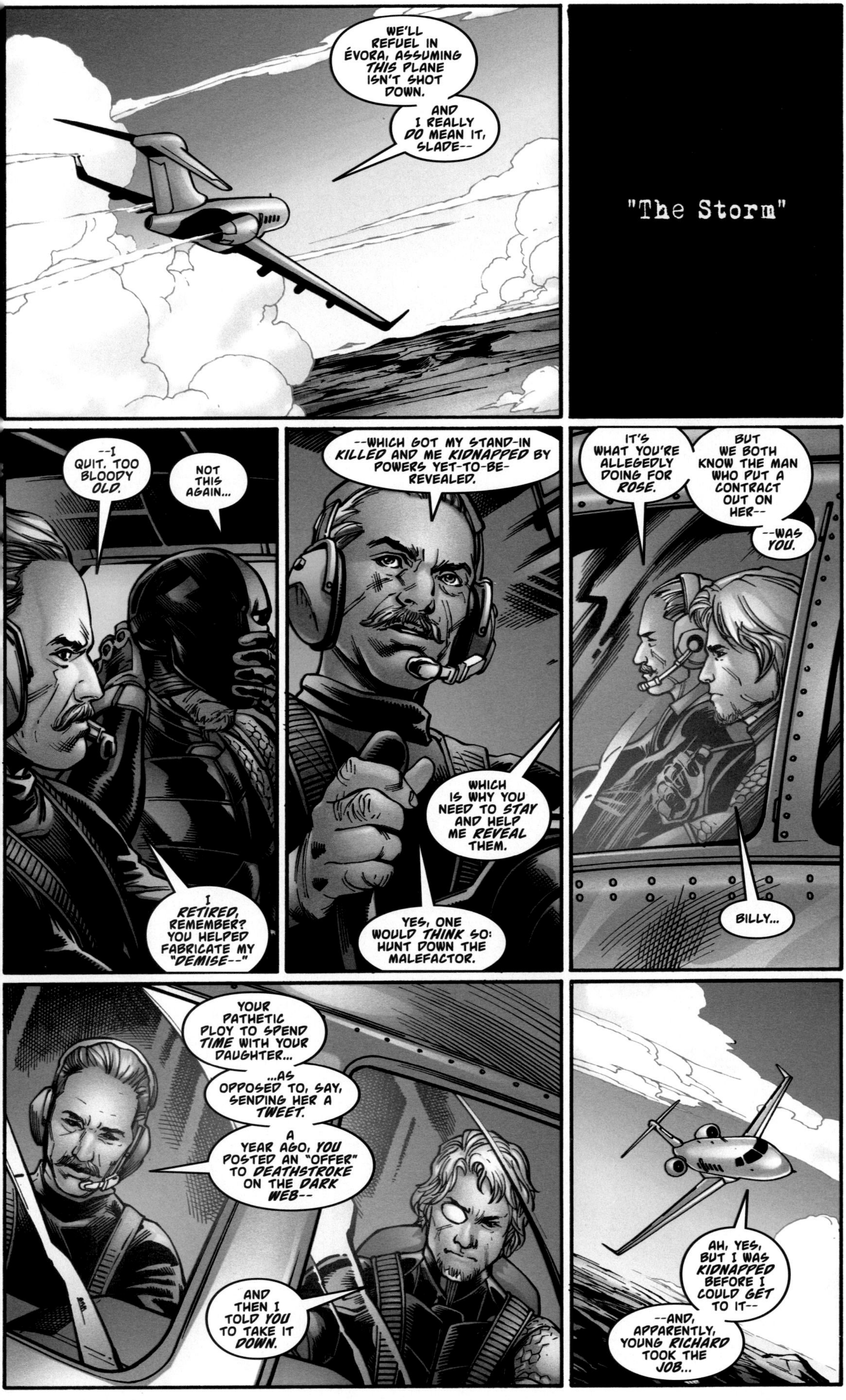
WE'LL REFUEL IN ÉVORA, ASSUMING *THIS* PLANE ISN'T SHOT DOWN.
AND I REALLY *DO* MEAN IT, SLADE--
"The Storm"
--I QUIT. TOO BLOODY *OLD*.
NOT THIS AGAIN...
I *RETIRED*, REMEMBER? YOU HELPED FABRICATE MY *"DEMISE--"*
--WHICH GOT MY STAND-IN *KILLED* AND ME *KIDNAPPED* BY POWERS YET-TO-BE-REVEALED.
WHICH IS WHY YOU NEED TO *STAY* AND HELP ME *REVEAL* THEM.
YES, ONE WOULD *THINK* SO: HUNT DOWN THE MALEFACTOR.
IT'S WHAT YOU'RE ALLEGEDLY DOING FOR *ROSE*.
BUT WE BOTH KNOW THE MAN WHO PUT A CONTRACT OUT ON HER--
--WAS *YOU*.
BILLY...
YOUR PATHETIC PLOY TO SPEND *TIME* WITH YOUR DAUGHTER...
...AS OPPOSED TO, SAY, SENDING HER A *TWEET*.
A YEAR AGO, *YOU* POSTED AN "OFFER" TO *DEATHSTROKE* ON THE *DARK WEB*--
AND THEN I TOLD *YOU* TO TAKE IT *DOWN*.
AH, YES, BUT I WAS *KIDNAPPED* BEFORE I COULD *GET* TO IT--
--AND, APPARENTLY, YOUNG *RICHARD* TOOK THE *JOB*...

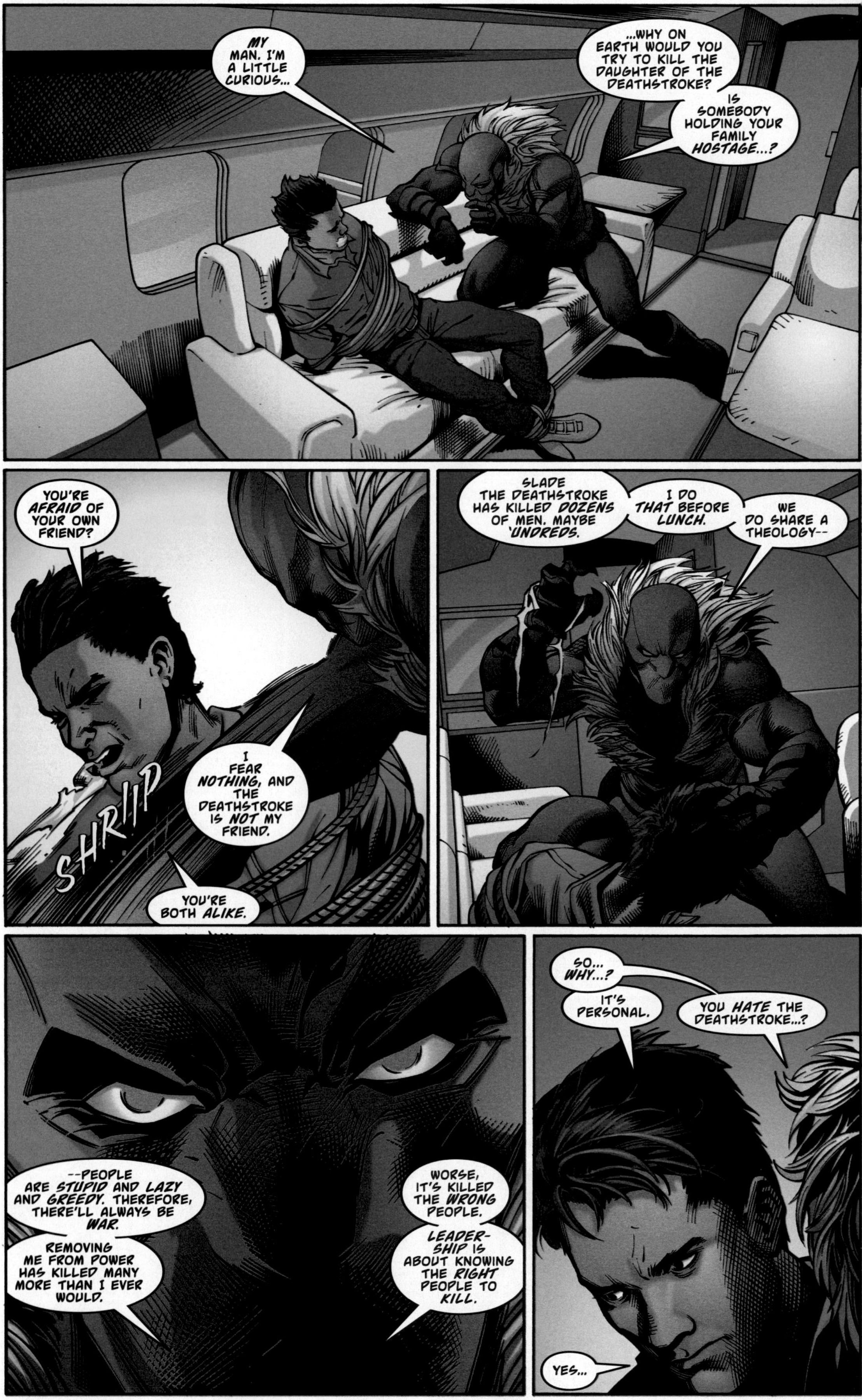
MY MAN. I'M A LITTLE CURIOUS...
...WHY ON EARTH WOULD YOU TRY TO KILL THE DAUGHTER OF THE DEATHSTROKE?
IS SOMEBODY HOLDING YOUR FAMILY HOSTAGE...?
YOU'RE AFRAID OF YOUR OWN FRIEND?
SHRIIP
I FEAR NOTHING, AND THE DEATHSTROKE IS NOT MY FRIEND.
YOU'RE BOTH ALIKE.
SLADE THE DEATHSTROKE HAS KILLED DOZENS OF MEN. MAYBE 'UNDREDS.
I DO THAT BEFORE LUNCH.
WE DO SHARE A THEOLOGY--
--PEOPLE ARE STUPID AND LAZY AND GREEDY. THEREFORE, THERE'LL ALWAYS BE WAR.
REMOVING ME FROM POWER HAS KILLED MANY MORE THAN I EVER WOULD.
WORSE, IT'S KILLED THE WRONG PEOPLE.
LEADER-SHIP IS ABOUT KNOWING THE RIGHT PEOPLE TO KILL.
SO... WHY...?
IT'S PERSONAL.
YOU HATE THE DEATHSTROKE...?
YES...

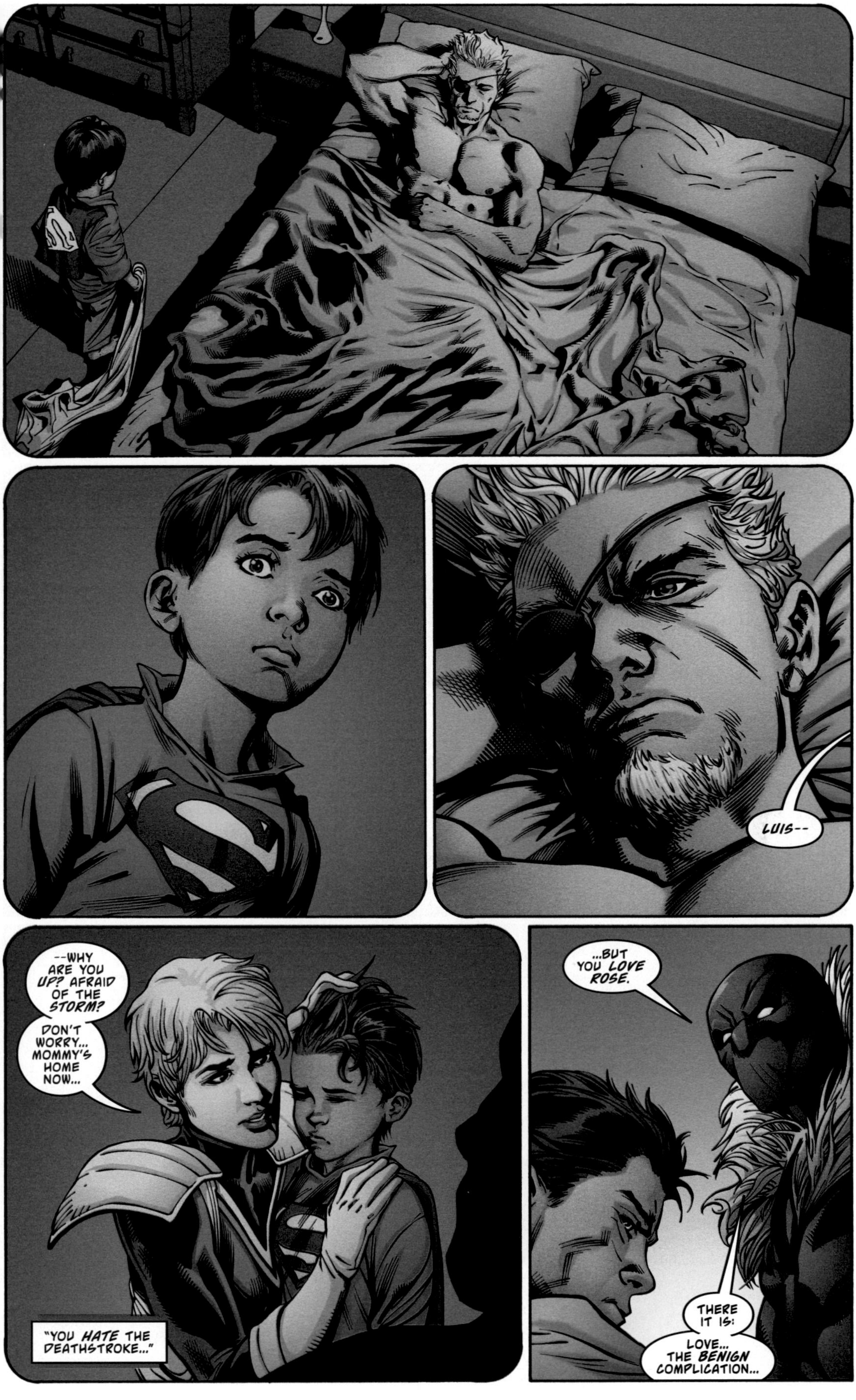
LUIS--
--WHY ARE YOU UP? AFRAID OF THE STORM?
DON'T WORRY... MOMMY'S HOME NOW...
"YOU HATE THE DEATHSTROKE..."
...BUT YOU LOVE ROSE.
THERE IT IS:
LOVE... THE BENIGN COMPLICATION...

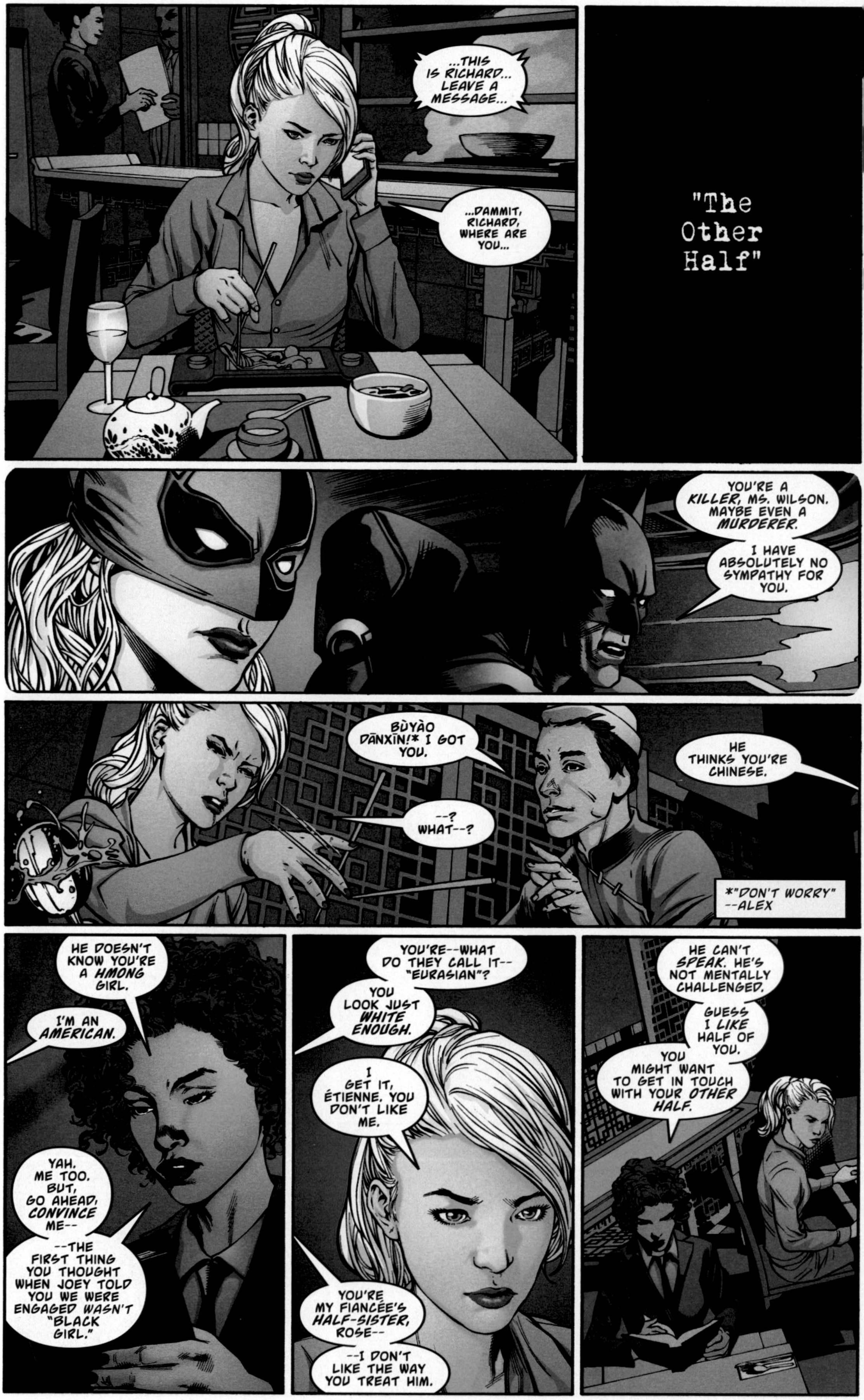
...THIS IS RICHARD... LEAVE A MESSAGE...
...DAMMIT, RICHARD, WHERE ARE YOU...
"The Other Half"
YOU'RE A KILLER, MS. WILSON. MAYBE EVEN A MURDERER.
I HAVE ABSOLUTELY NO SYMPATHY FOR YOU.
BÙYÀO DĀNXĪN!* I GOT YOU.
--? WHAT--?
HE THINKS YOU'RE CHINESE.
*"DON'T WORRY" --ALEX
HE DOESN'T KNOW YOU'RE A HMONG GIRL.
I'M AN AMERICAN.
YAH. ME TOO. BUT, GO AHEAD, CONVINCE ME--
--THE FIRST THING YOU THOUGHT WHEN JOEY TOLD YOU WE WERE ENGAGED WASN'T "BLACK GIRL."
YOU'RE--WHAT DO THEY CALL IT-- "EURASIAN"?
YOU LOOK JUST WHITE ENOUGH.
I GET IT, ÉTIENNE. YOU DON'T LIKE ME.
YOU'RE MY FIANCÉE'S HALF-SISTER, ROSE--
--I DON'T LIKE THE WAY YOU TREAT HIM.
HE CAN'T SPEAK. HE'S NOT MENTALLY CHALLENGED.
GUESS I LIKE HALF OF YOU.
YOU MIGHT WANT TO GET IN TOUCH WITH YOUR OTHER HALF.

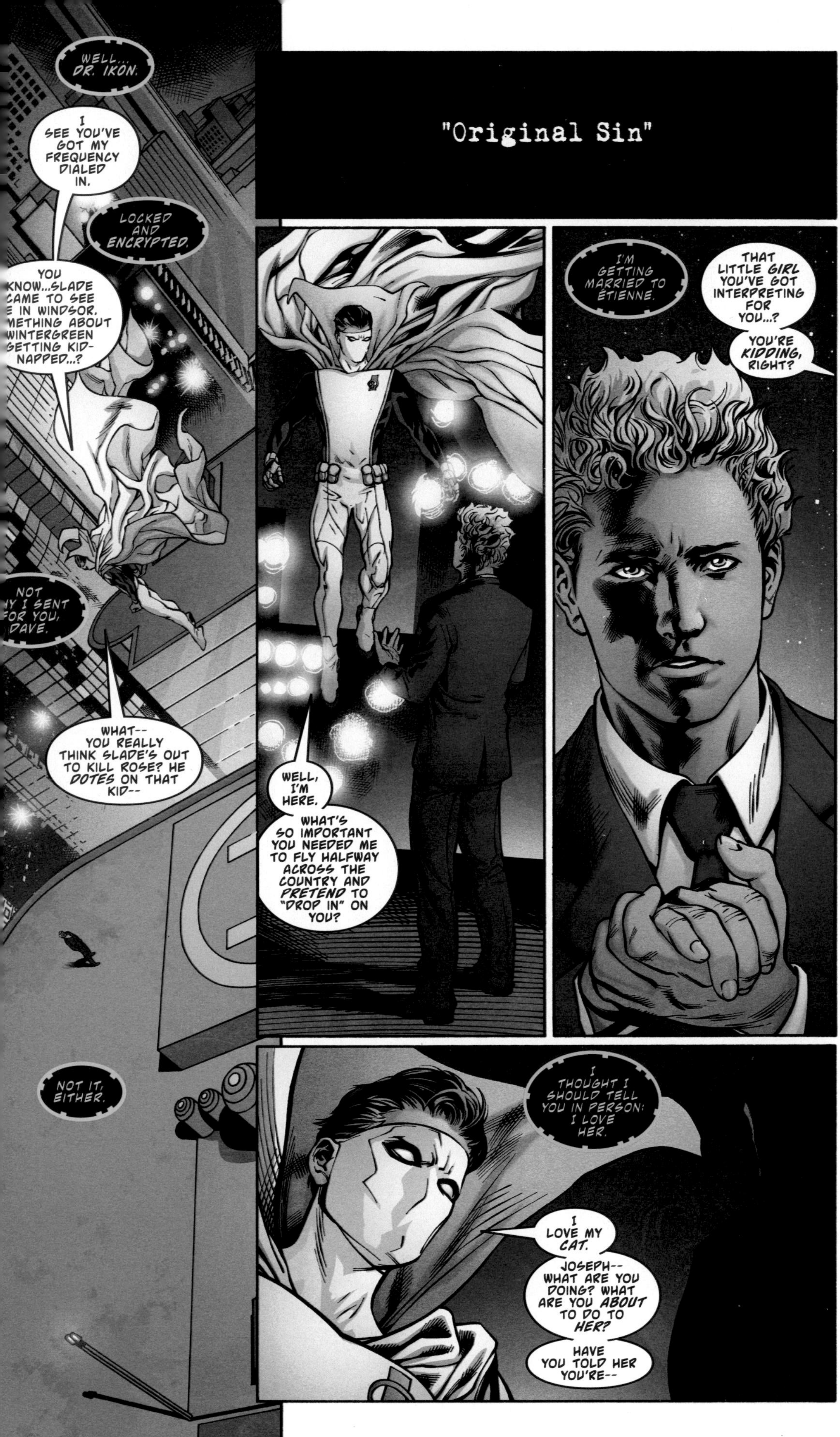

WELL... DR. IKON.
I SEE YOU'VE GOT MY FREQUENCY DIALED IN.
LOCKED AND ENCRYPTED.
YOU KNOW...SLADE CAME TO SEE E IN WINDSOR. METHING ABOUT WINTERGREEN GETTING KID-NAPPED...?
NOT Y I SENT FOR YOU, DAVE.
WHAT-- YOU REALLY THINK SLADE'S OUT TO KILL ROSE? HE DOTES ON THAT KID--
NOT IT, EITHER.
"Original Sin"
WELL, I'M HERE.
WHAT'S SO IMPORTANT YOU NEEDED ME TO FLY HALFWAY ACROSS THE COUNTRY AND PRETEND TO "DROP IN" ON YOU?
I'M GETTING MARRIED TO ÉTIENNE.
THAT LITTLE GIRL YOU'VE GOT INTERPRETING FOR YOU...?
YOU'RE KIDDING, RIGHT?
I THOUGHT I SHOULD TELL YOU IN PERSON: I LOVE HER.
I LOVE MY CAT.
JOSEPH-- WHAT ARE YOU DOING? WHAT ARE YOU ABOUT TO DO TO HER?
HAVE YOU TOLD HER YOU'RE--

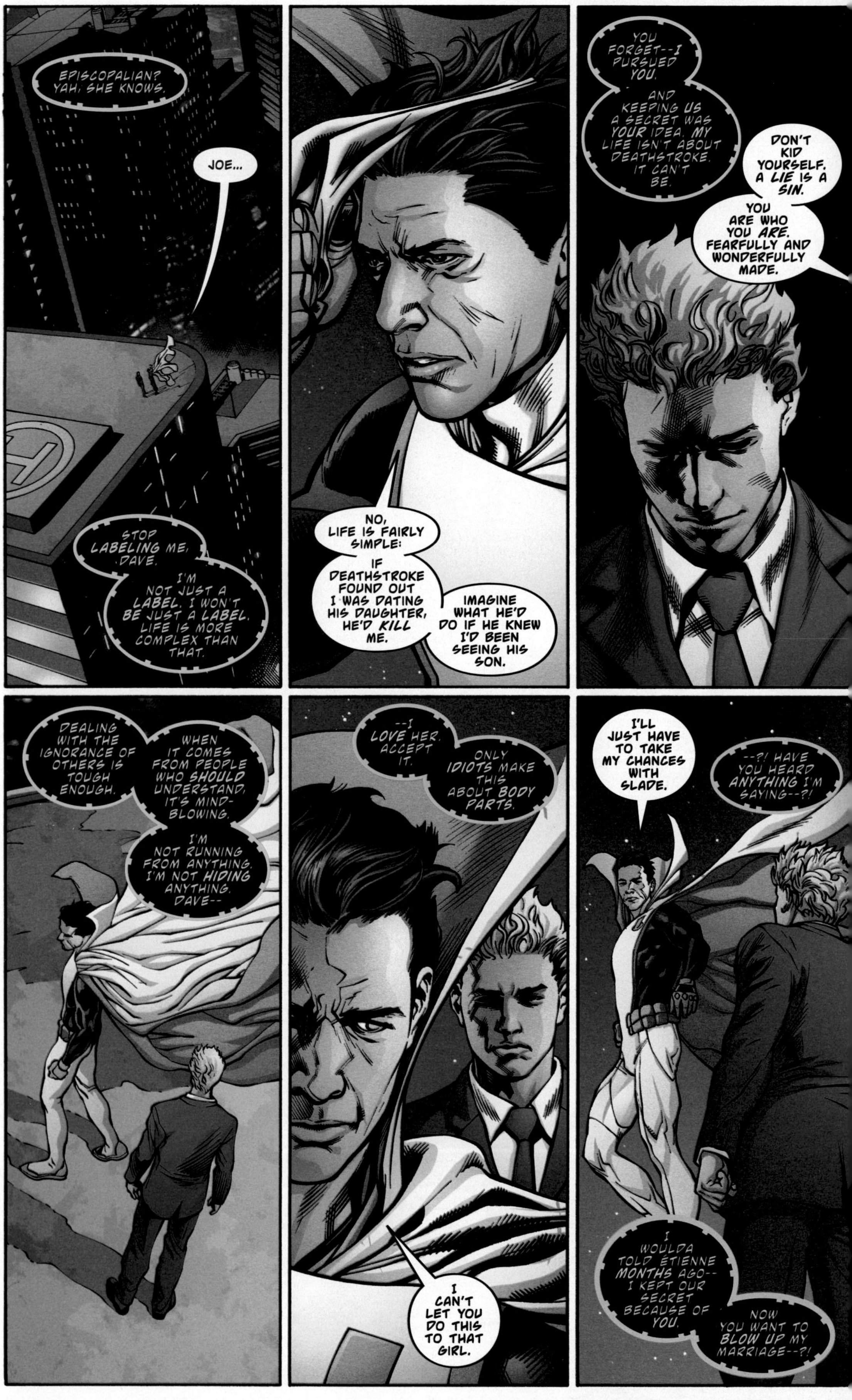
EPISCOPALIAN? YAH, SHE KNOWS.
JOE...
STOP LABELING ME, DAVE.
I'M NOT JUST A LABEL. I WON'T BE JUST A LABEL. LIFE IS MORE COMPLEX THAN THAT.
NO, LIFE IS FAIRLY SIMPLE:
IF DEATHSTROKE FOUND OUT I WAS DATING HIS DAUGHTER, HE'D KILL ME.
IMAGINE WHAT HE'D DO IF HE KNEW I'D BEEN SEEING HIS SON.
YOU FORGET--I PURSUED YOU.
AND KEEPING US A SECRET WAS YOUR IDEA. MY LIFE ISN'T ABOUT DEATHSTROKE. IT CAN'T BE.
DON'T KID YOURSELF. A LIE IS A SIN.
YOU ARE WHO YOU ARE. FEARFULLY AND WONDERFULLY MADE.
DEALING WITH THE IGNORANCE OF OTHERS IS TOUGH ENOUGH.
WHEN IT COMES FROM PEOPLE WHO SHOULD UNDERSTAND, IT'S MIND-BLOWING.
I'M NOT RUNNING FROM ANYTHING. I'M NOT HIDING ANYTHING. DAVE--
--I LOVE HER. ACCEPT IT.
ONLY IDIOTS MAKE THIS ABOUT BODY PARTS.
I CAN'T LET YOU DO THIS TO THAT GIRL.
I'LL JUST HAVE TO TAKE MY CHANCES WITH SLADE.
--?! HAVE YOU HEARD ANYTHING I'M SAYING--?!
I WOULDA TOLD ÉTIENNE MONTHS AGO--I KEPT OUR SECRET BECAUSE OF YOU.
NOW YOU WANT TO BLOW UP MY MARRIAGE--?!

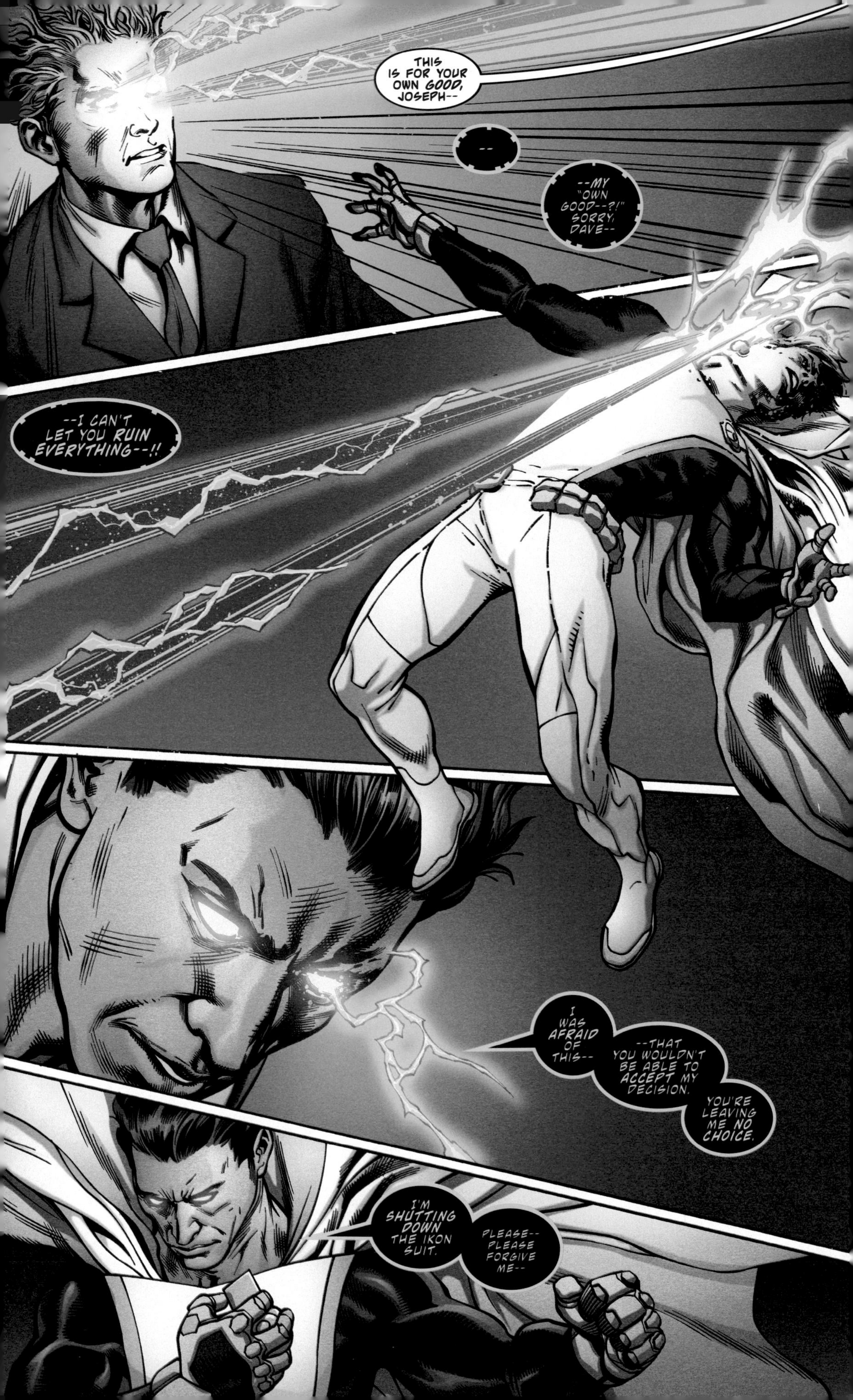
THIS IS FOR YOUR OWN GOOD, JOSEPH--
--
--MY "OWN GOOD--?!" SORRY, DAVE--
--I CAN'T LET YOU RUIN EVERYTHING--!!
I WAS AFRAID OF THIS--
--THAT YOU WOULDN'T BE ABLE TO ACCEPT MY DECISION.
YOU'RE LEAVING ME NO CHOICE.
I'M SHUTTING DOWN THE IKON SUIT.
PLEASE-- PLEASE FORGIVE ME--

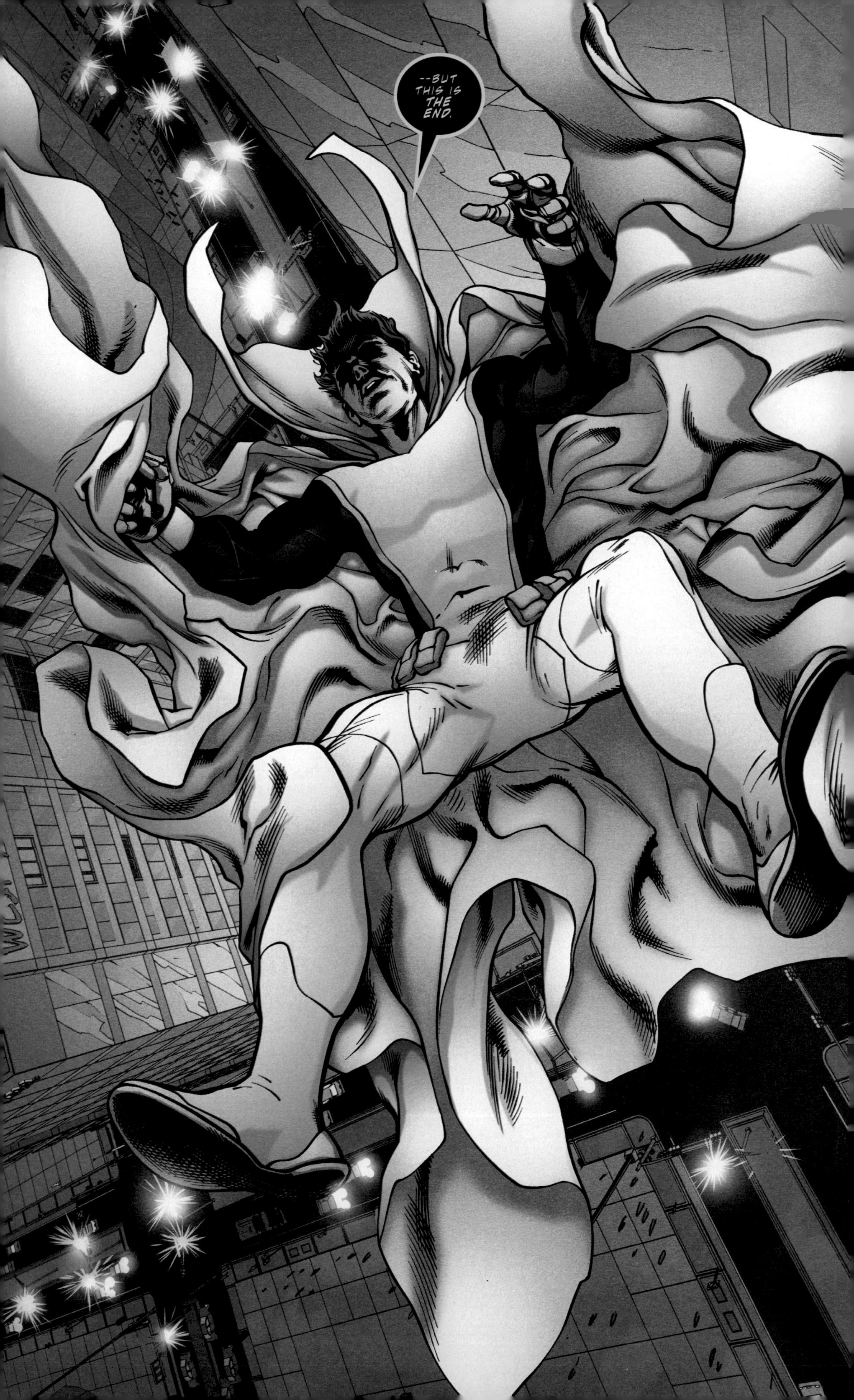
--BUT THIS IS THE END.

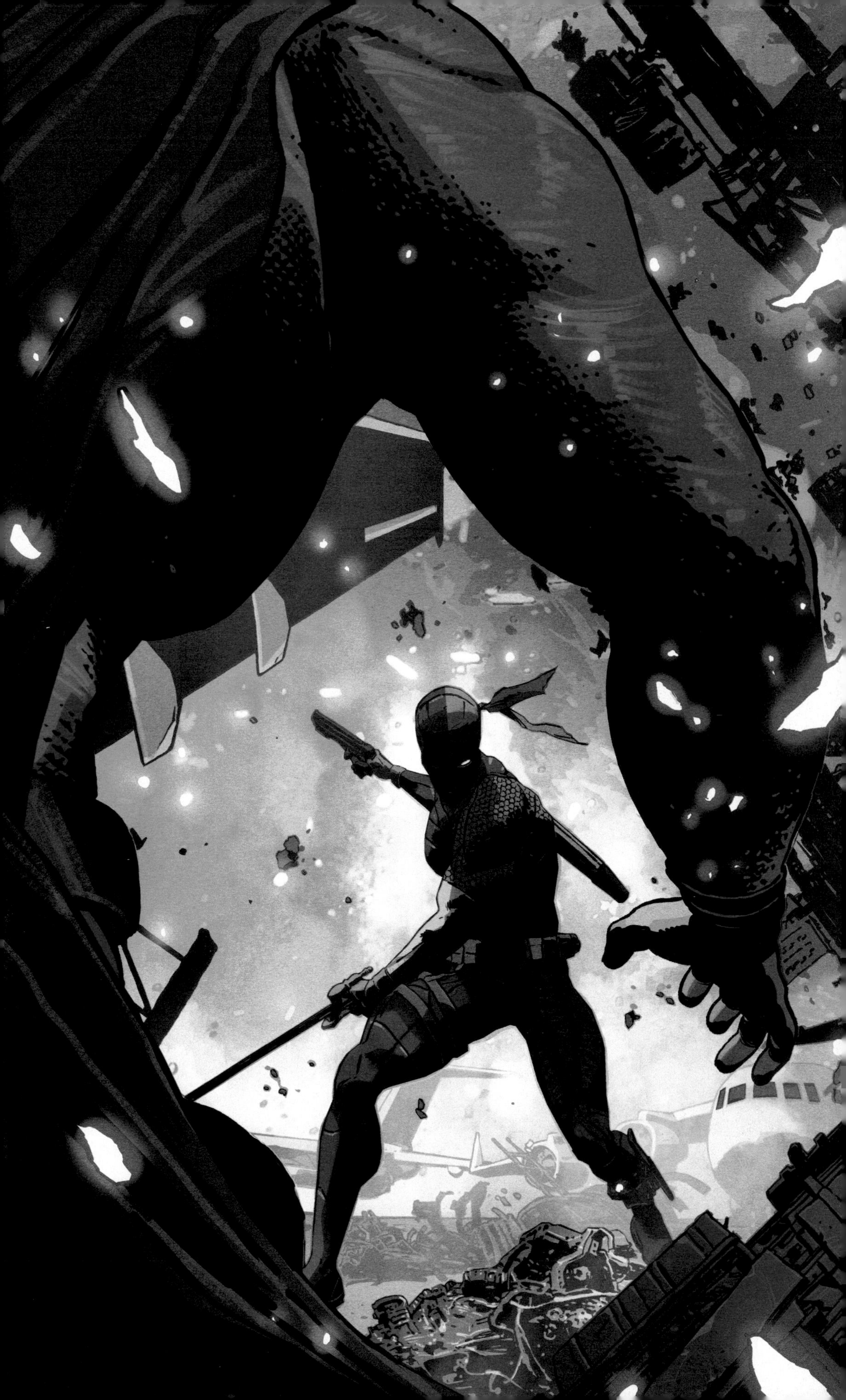

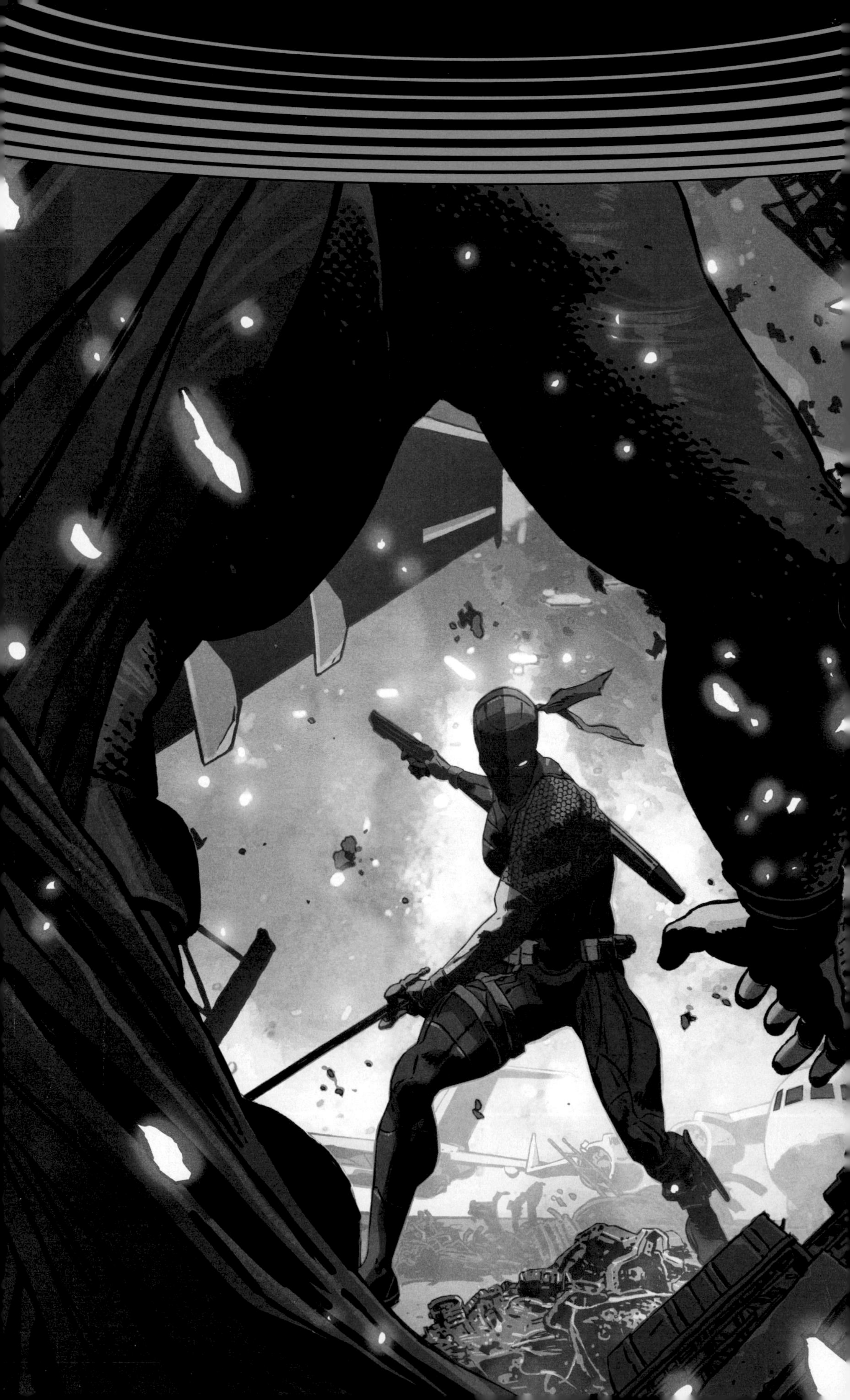

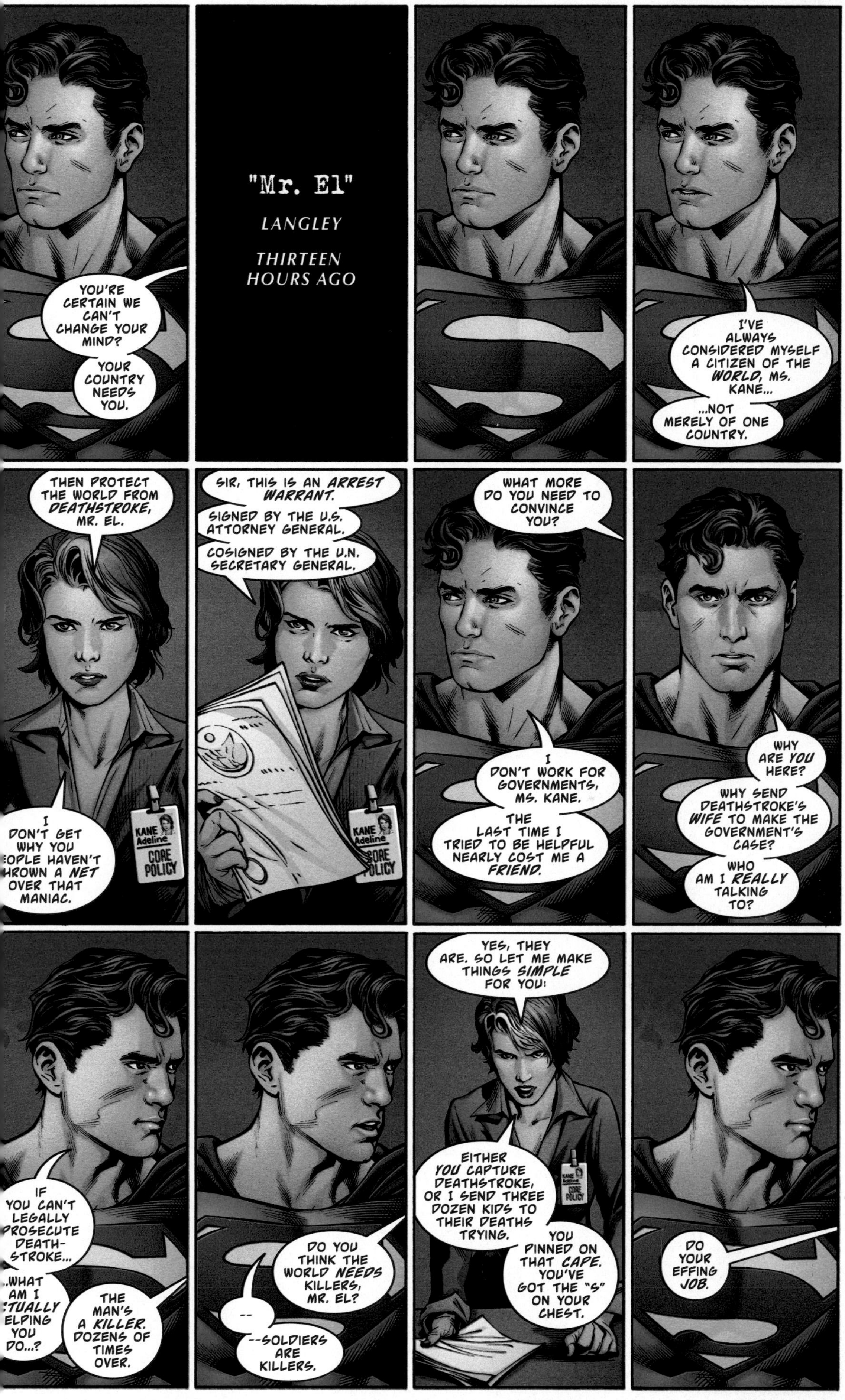
YOU'RE CERTAIN WE CAN'T CHANGE YOUR MIND?
YOUR COUNTRY NEEDS YOU.
"Mr. El"
LANGLEY
THIRTEEN HOURS AGO
I'VE ALWAYS CONSIDERED MYSELF A CITIZEN OF THE WORLD, MS. KANE...
...NOT MERELY OF ONE COUNTRY.
THEN PROTECT THE WORLD FROM DEATHSTROKE, MR. EL.
I DON'T GET WHY YOU PEOPLE HAVEN'T THROWN A NET OVER THAT MANIAC.
KANE Adeline CORE POLICY
SIR, THIS IS AN ARREST WARRANT.
SIGNED BY THE U.S. ATTORNEY GENERAL.
COSIGNED BY THE U.N. SECRETARY GENERAL.
WHAT MORE DO YOU NEED TO CONVINCE YOU?
I DON'T WORK FOR GOVERNMENTS, MS. KANE.
THE LAST TIME I TRIED TO BE HELPFUL NEARLY COST ME A FRIEND.
WHY ARE YOU HERE?
WHY SEND DEATHSTROKE'S WIFE TO MAKE THE GOVERNMENT'S CASE?
WHO AM I REALLY TALKING TO?
IF YOU CAN'T LEGALLY PROSECUTE DEATH-STROKE...
...WHAT AM I ACTUALLY HELPING YOU DO...?
THE MAN'S A KILLER. DOZENS OF TIMES OVER.
DO YOU THINK THE WORLD NEEDS KILLERS, MR. EL?
--
--SOLDIERS ARE KILLERS.
YES, THEY ARE. SO LET ME MAKE THINGS SIMPLE FOR YOU:
EITHER YOU CAPTURE DEATHSTROKE, OR I SEND THREE DOZEN KIDS TO THEIR DEATHS TRYING.
YOU PINNED ON THAT CAPE. YOU'VE GOT THE "S" ON YOUR CHEST.
DO YOUR EFFING JOB.

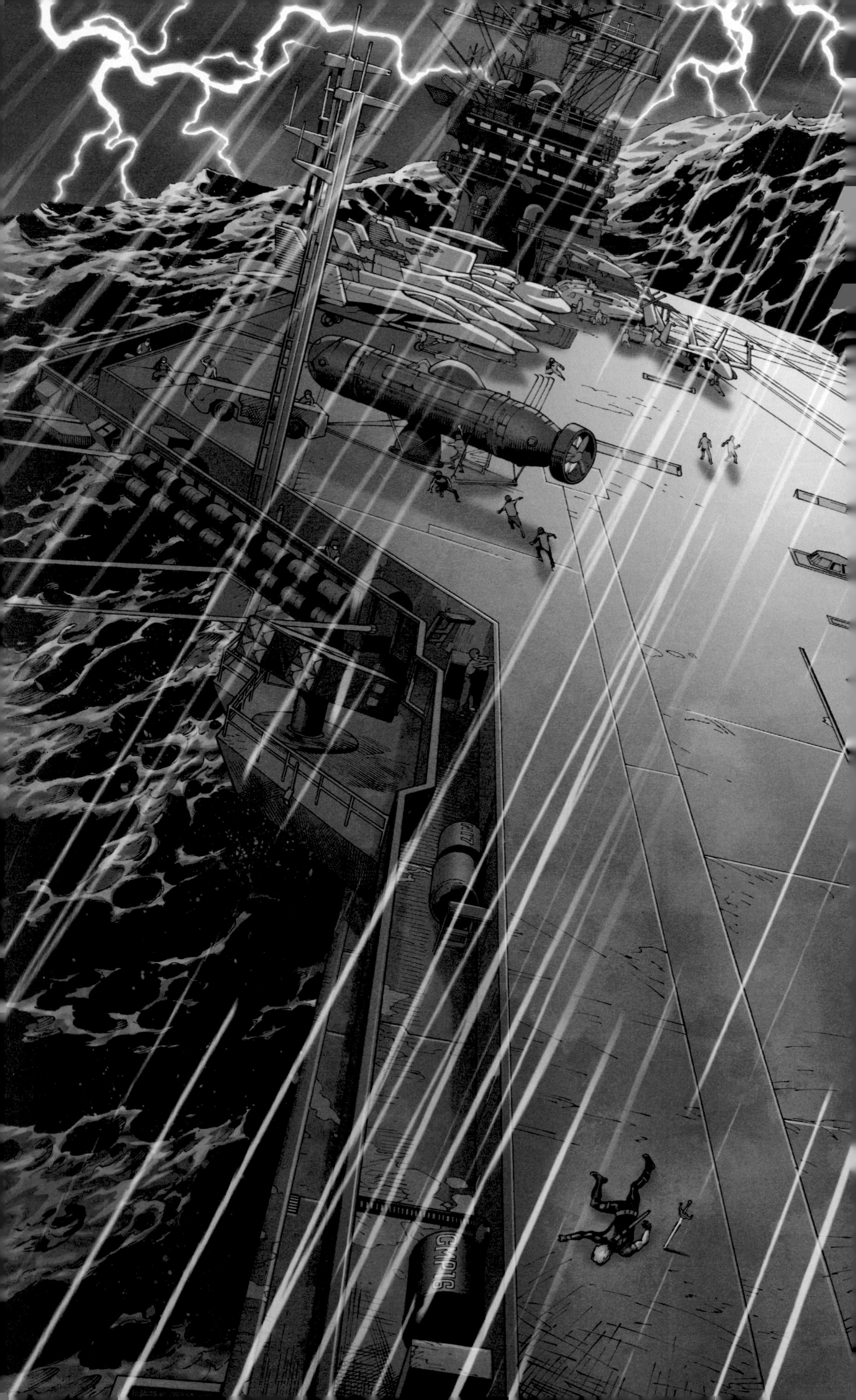

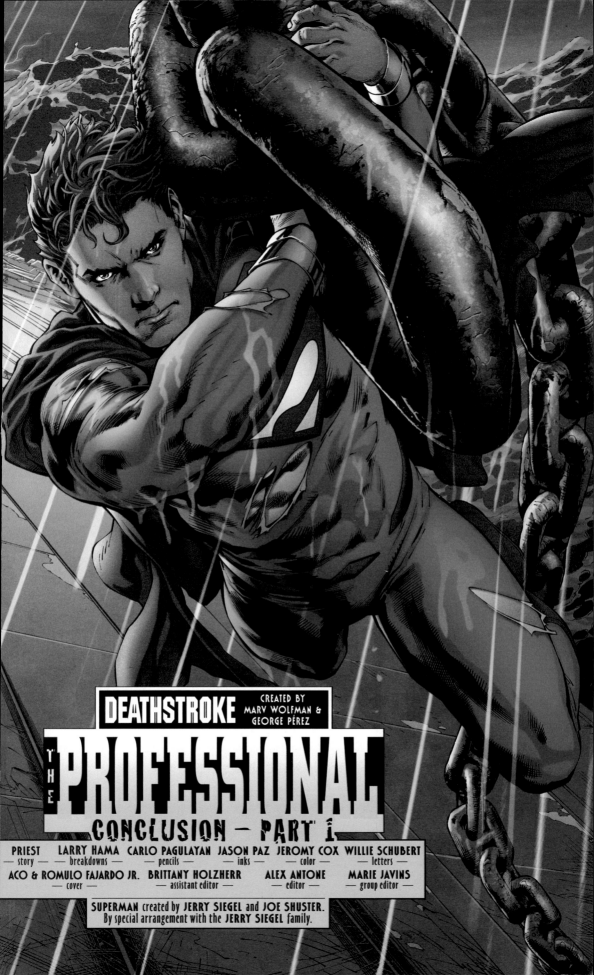

DEATHSTROKE

CREATED BY
MARV WOLFMAN &
GEORGE PÉREZ

THE PROFESSIONAL
CONCLUSION — PART 1

PRIEST — story —
LARRY HAMA — breakdowns —
CARLO PAGULAYAN — pencils —
JASON PAZ — inks —
JEROMY COX — color —
WILLIE SCHUBERT — letters —

ACO & ROMULO FAJARDO JR. — cover —
BRITTANY HOLZHERR — assistant editor —
ALEX ANTONE — editor —
MARIE JAVINS — group editor —

SUPERMAN created by JERRY SIEGEL and JOE SHUSTER.
By special arrangement with the JERRY SIEGEL family.

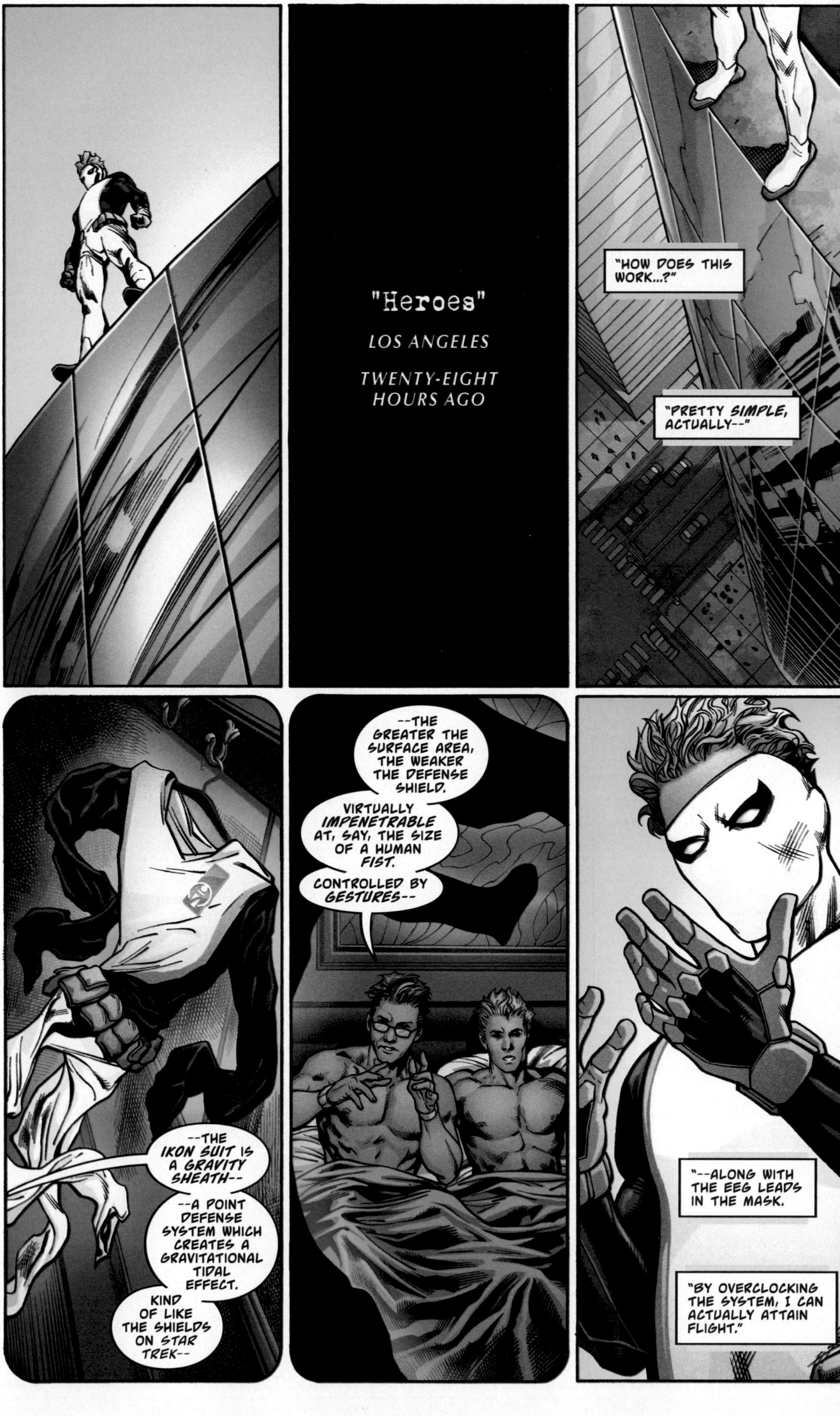
"Heroes"
LOS ANGELES
TWENTY-EIGHT HOURS AGO
"HOW DOES THIS WORK...?"
"PRETTY SIMPLE, ACTUALLY--"
--THE IKON SUIT IS A GRAVITY SHEATH--
--A POINT DEFENSE SYSTEM WHICH CREATES A GRAVITATIONAL TIDAL EFFECT.
KIND OF LIKE THE SHIELDS ON STAR TREK--
--THE GREATER THE SURFACE AREA, THE WEAKER THE DEFENSE SHIELD.
VIRTUALLY IMPENETRABLE AT, SAY, THE SIZE OF A HUMAN FIST.
CONTROLLED BY GESTURES--
"--ALONG WITH THE EEG LEADS IN THE MASK.
"BY OVERCLOCKING THE SYSTEM, I CAN ACTUALLY ATTAIN FLIGHT."

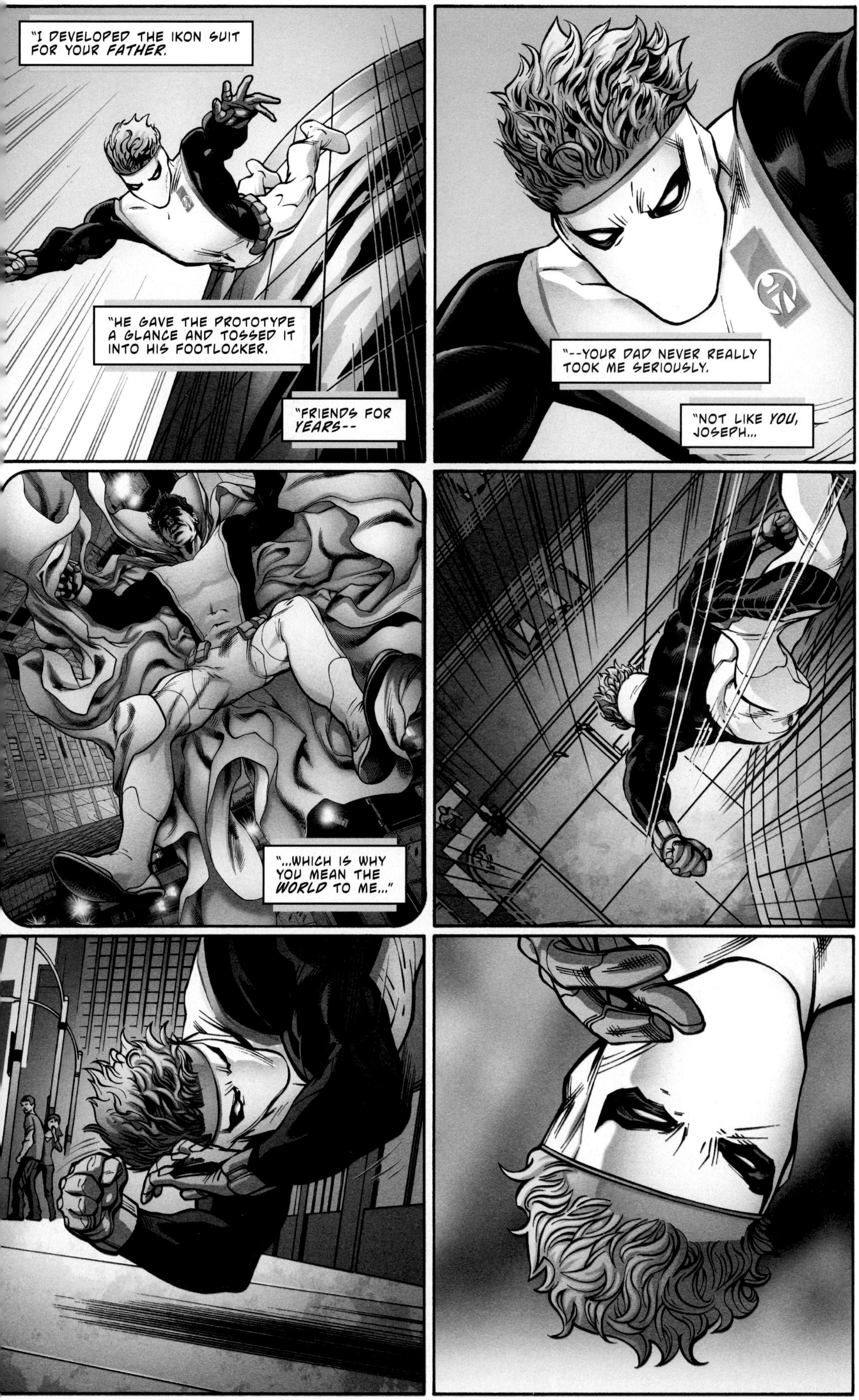
"I DEVELOPED THE IKON SUIT FOR YOUR FATHER.
"HE GAVE THE PROTOTYPE A GLANCE AND TOSSED IT INTO HIS FOOTLOCKER.
"FRIENDS FOR YEARS--
"--YOUR DAD NEVER REALLY TOOK ME SERIOUSLY.
"NOT LIKE YOU, JOSEPH...
"...WHICH IS WHY YOU MEAN THE WORLD TO ME..."

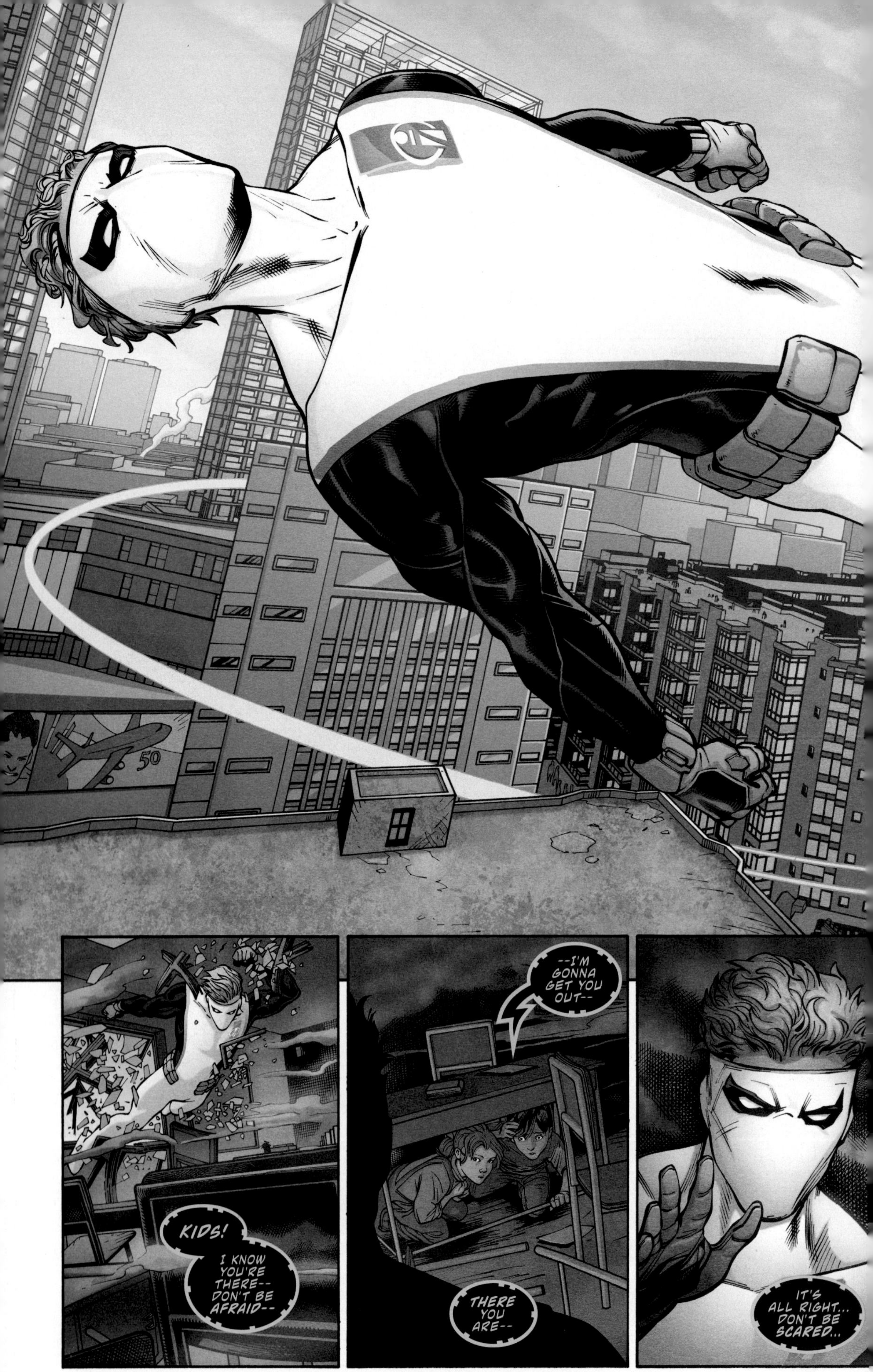
KIDS!
I KNOW YOU'RE THERE-- DON'T BE AFRAID--
--I'M GONNA GET YOU OUT--
THERE YOU ARE--
IT'S ALL RIGHT... DON'T BE SCARED...

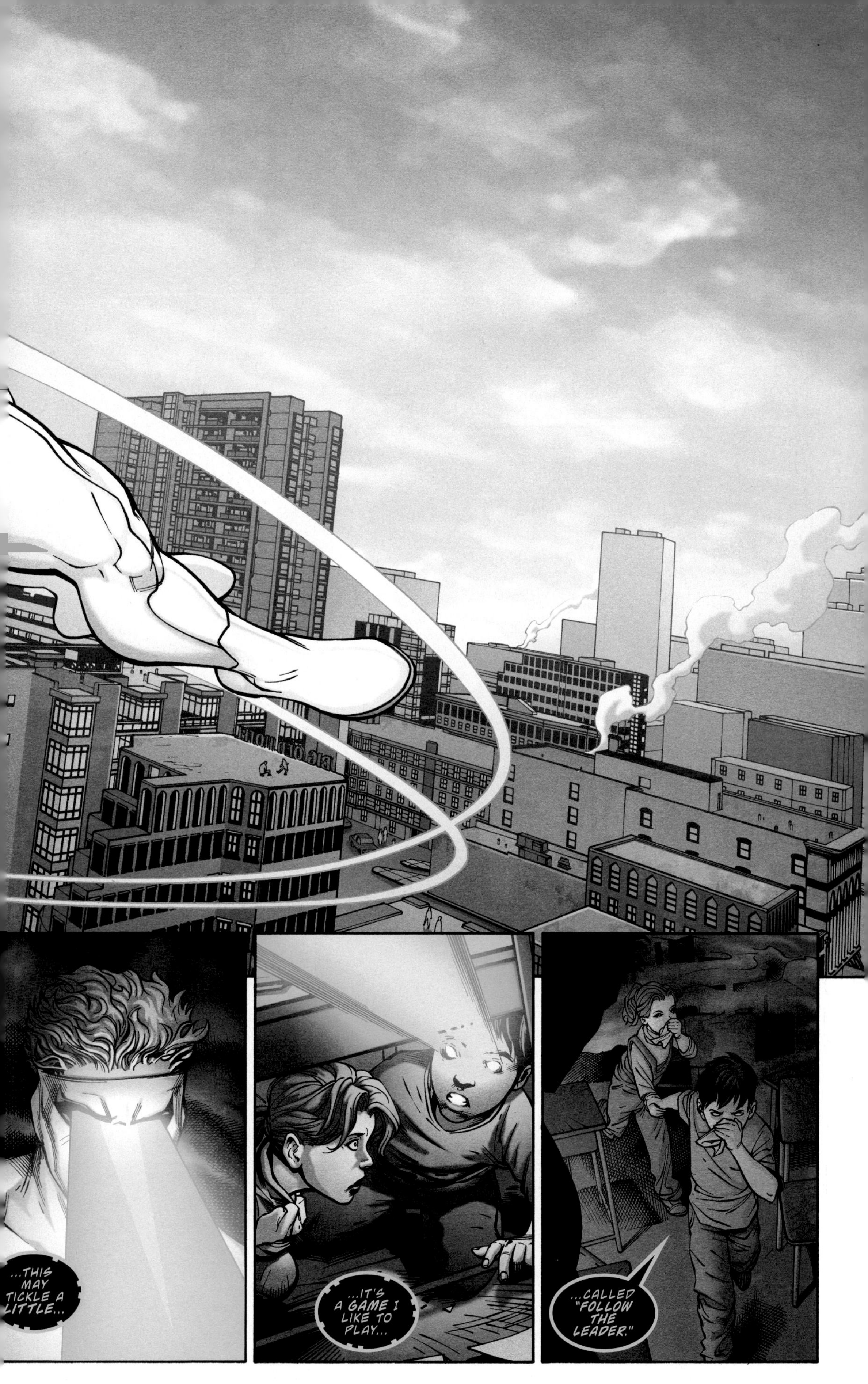
...THIS MAY TICKLE A LITTLE...
...IT'S A GAME I LIKE TO PLAY...
...CALLED "FOLLOW THE LEADER."

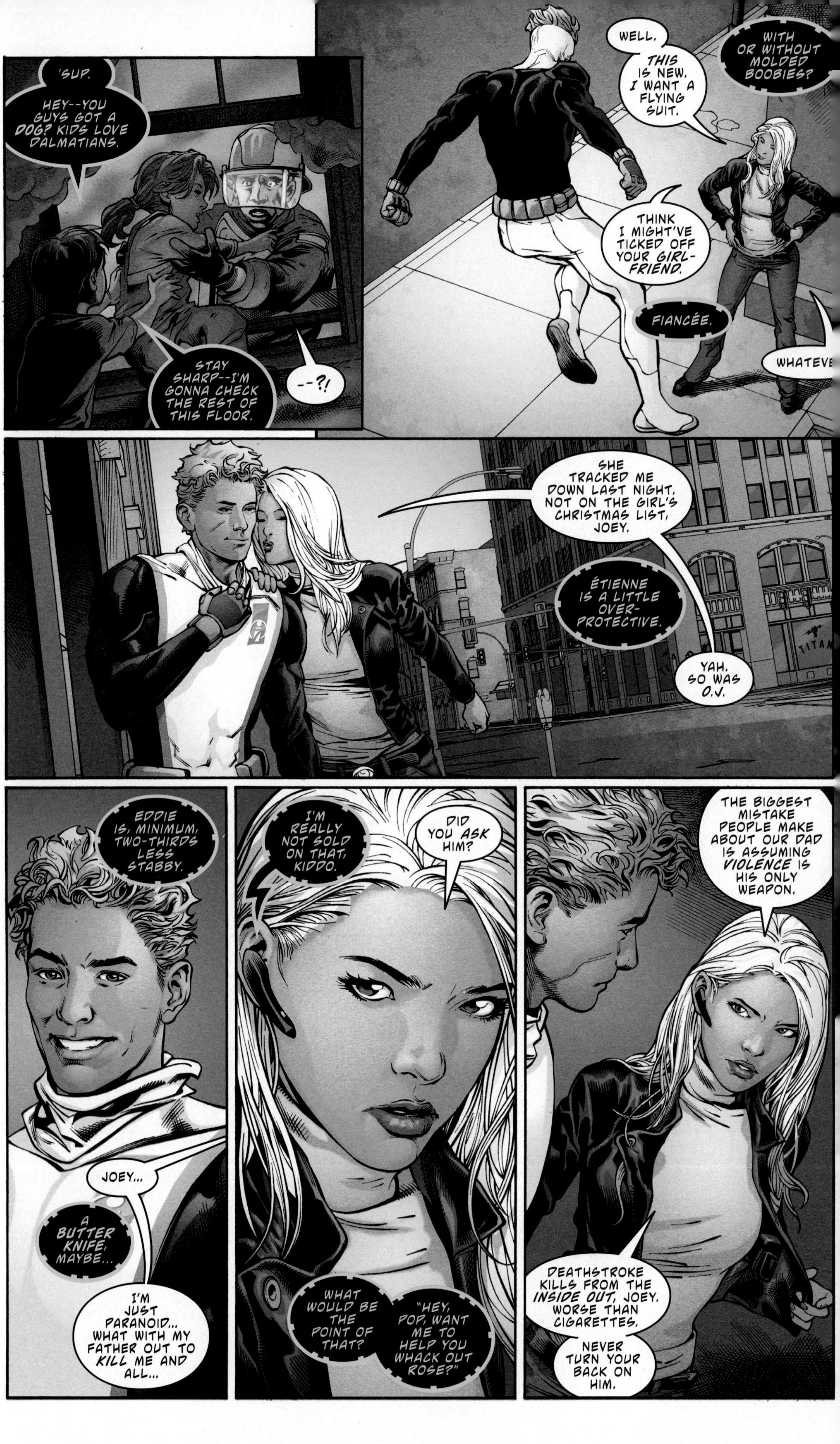
'SUP.
HEY--YOU GUYS GOT A DOG? KIDS LOVE DALMATIANS.
STAY SHARP--I'M GONNA CHECK THE REST OF THIS FLOOR.
--?!
WELL.
THIS IS NEW. I WANT A FLYING SUIT.
WITH OR WITHOUT MOLDED BOOBIES?
THINK I MIGHT'VE TICKED OFF YOUR GIRLFRIEND.
FIANCÉE.
WHATEVE
SHE TRACKED ME DOWN LAST NIGHT. NOT ON THE GIRL'S CHRISTMAS LIST, JOEY.
ÉTIENNE IS A LITTLE OVER-PROTECTIVE.
YAH. SO WAS O.J.
TITAN
EDDIE IS, MINIMUM, TWO-THIRDS LESS STABBY.
JOEY...
A BUTTER KNIFE, MAYBE...
I'M JUST PARANOID... WHAT WITH MY FATHER OUT TO KILL ME AND ALL...
I'M REALLY NOT SOLD ON THAT, KIDDO.
DID YOU ASK HIM?
WHAT WOULD BE THE POINT OF THAT?
"HEY, POP, WANT ME TO HELP YOU WHACK OUT ROSE?"
THE BIGGEST MISTAKE PEOPLE MAKE ABOUT OUR DAD IS ASSUMING VIOLENCE IS HIS ONLY WEAPON.
DEATHSTROKE KILLS FROM THE INSIDE OUT, JOEY. WORSE THAN CIGARETTES.
NEVER TURN YOUR BACK ON HIM.

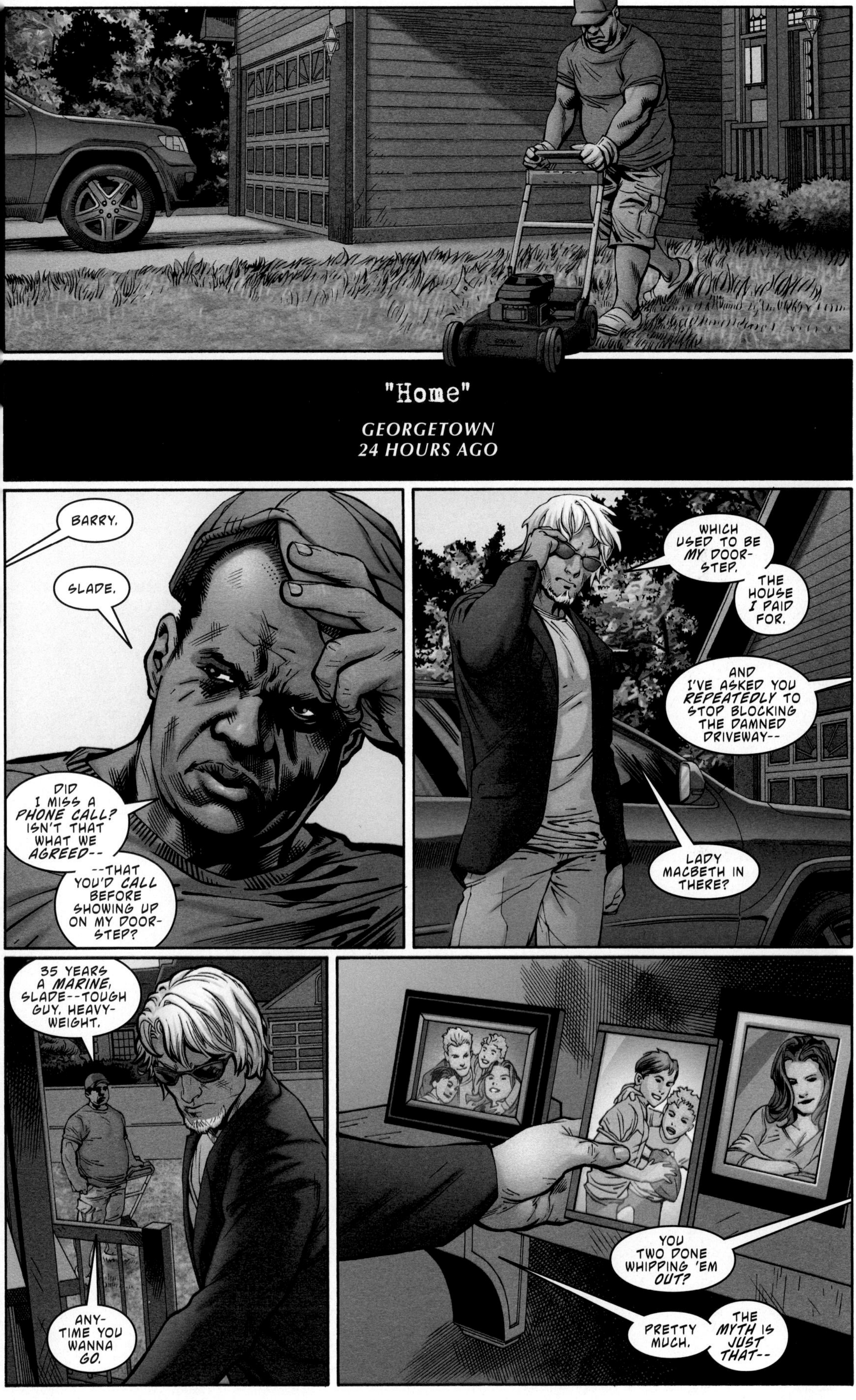
"Home"
GEORGETOWN
24 HOURS AGO
BARRY.
SLADE.
DID I MISS A PHONE CALL? ISN'T THAT WHAT WE AGREED--
--THAT YOU'D CALL BEFORE SHOWING UP ON MY DOOR-STEP?
WHICH USED TO BE MY DOOR-STEP.
THE HOUSE I PAID FOR.
AND I'VE ASKED YOU REPEATEDLY TO STOP BLOCKING THE DAMNED DRIVEWAY--
LADY MACBETH IN THERE?
35 YEARS A MARINE, SLADE--TOUGH GUY. HEAVY-WEIGHT.
ANY-TIME YOU WANNA GO.
YOU TWO DONE WHIPPING 'EM OUT?
PRETTY MUCH.
THE MYTH IS JUST THAT--

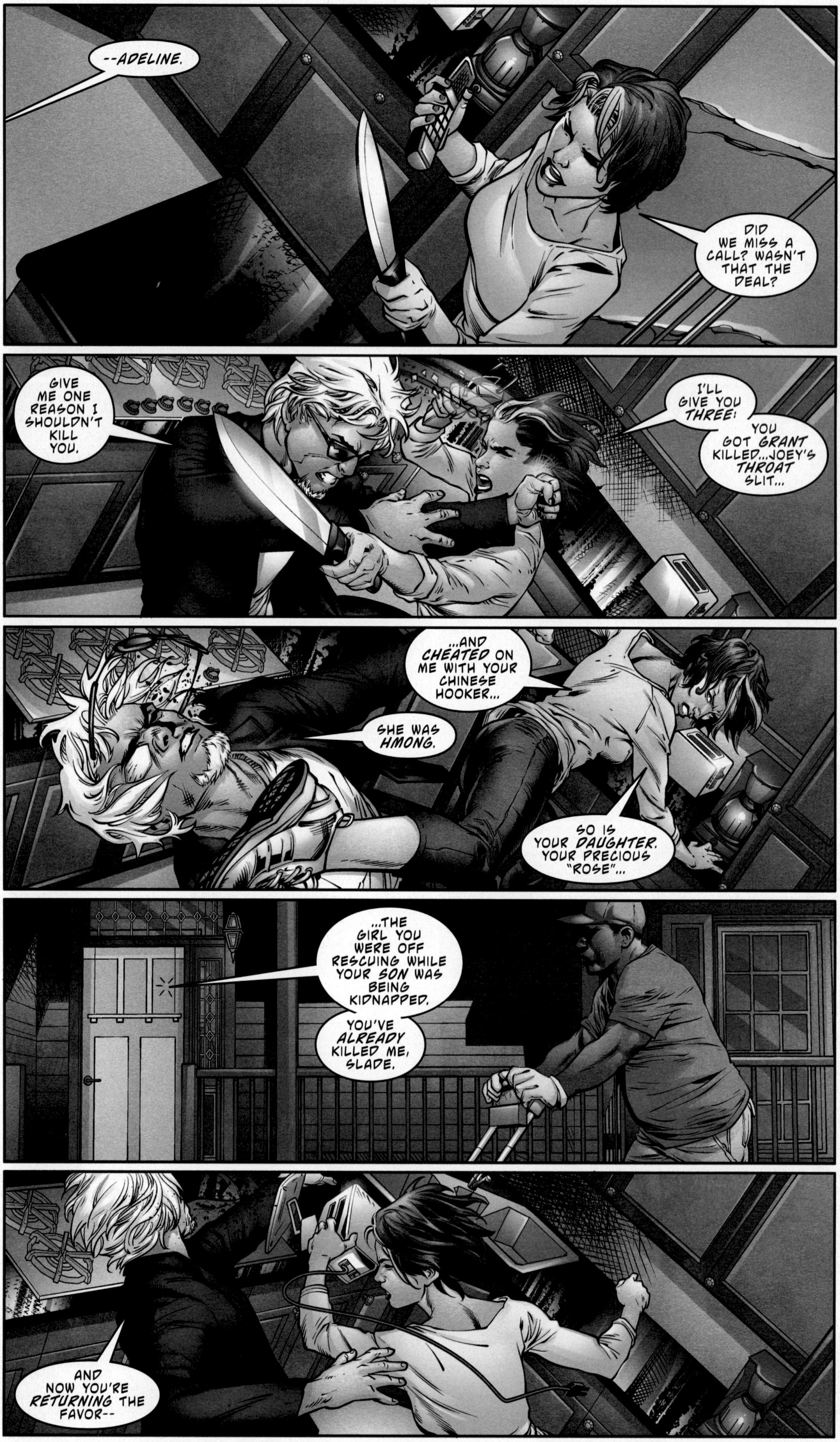
--ADELINE.
DID WE MISS A CALL? WASN'T THAT THE DEAL?
GIVE ME ONE REASON I SHOULDN'T KILL YOU.
I'LL GIVE YOU THREE:
YOU GOT GRANT KILLED...JOEY'S THROAT SLIT...
...AND CHEATED ON ME WITH YOUR CHINESE HOOKER...
SHE WAS HMONG.
SO IS YOUR DAUGHTER. YOUR PRECIOUS "ROSE"...
...THE GIRL YOU WERE OFF RESCUING WHILE YOUR SON WAS BEING KIDNAPPED.
YOU'VE ALREADY KILLED ME, SLADE.
AND NOW YOU'RE RETURNING THE FAVOR--

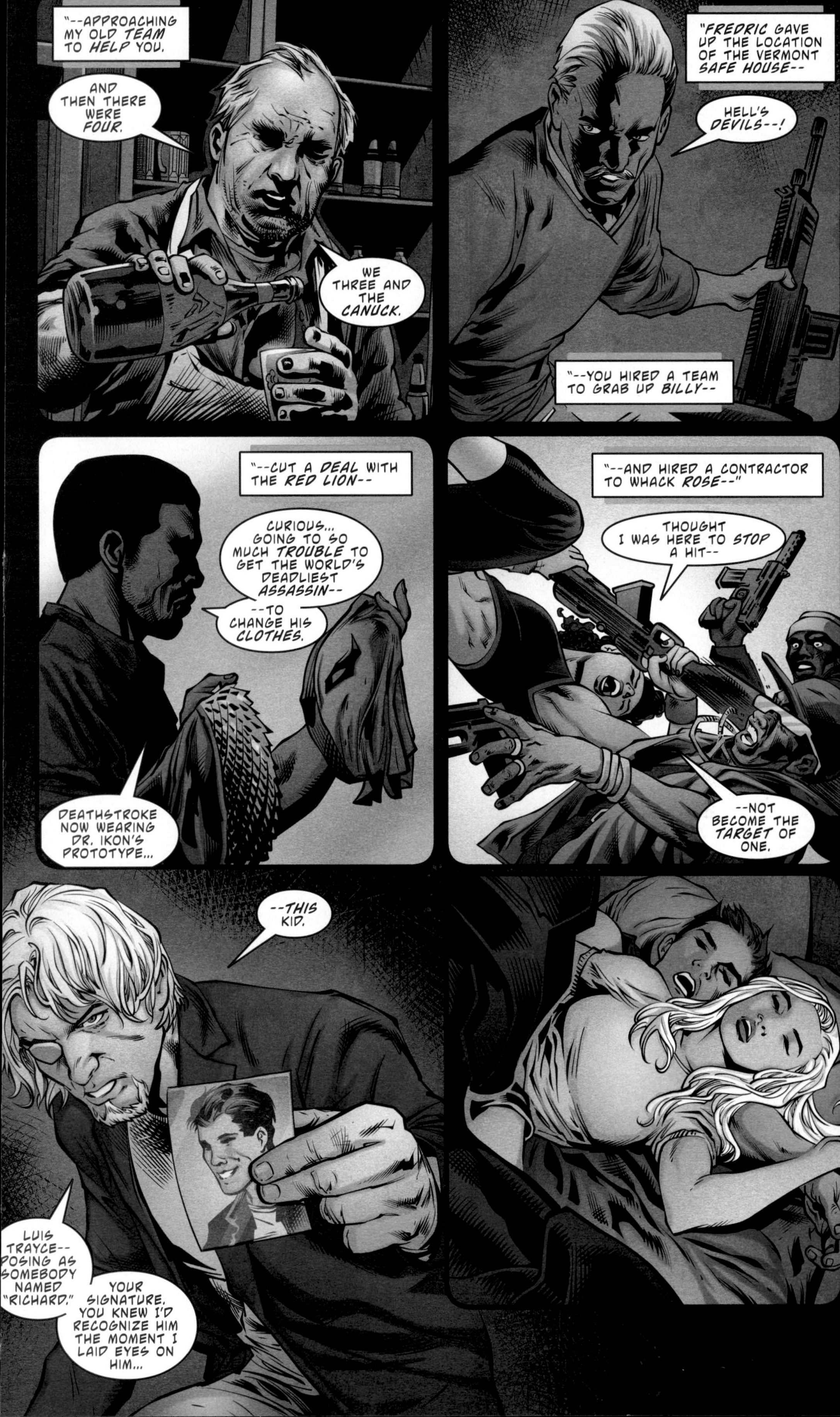
"--APPROACHING MY OLD TEAM TO HELP YOU.
AND THEN THERE WERE FOUR.
WE THREE AND THE CANUCK.
"FREDRIC GAVE UP THE LOCATION OF THE VERMONT SAFE HOUSE--
HELL'S DEVILS--!
"--YOU HIRED A TEAM TO GRAB UP BILLY--
"--CUT A DEAL WITH THE RED LION--
CURIOUS... GOING TO SO MUCH TROUBLE TO GET THE WORLD'S DEADLIEST ASSASSIN--
--TO CHANGE HIS CLOTHES.
DEATHSTROKE NOW WEARING DR. IKON'S PROTOTYPE...
"--AND HIRED A CONTRACTOR TO WHACK ROSE--"
THOUGHT I WAS HERE TO STOP A HIT--
--NOT BECOME THE TARGET OF ONE.
--THIS KID.
LUIS TRAYCE--POSING AS SOMEBODY NAMED "RICHARD."
YOUR SIGNATURE. YOU KNEW I'D RECOGNIZE HIM THE MOMENT I LAID EYES ON HIM...

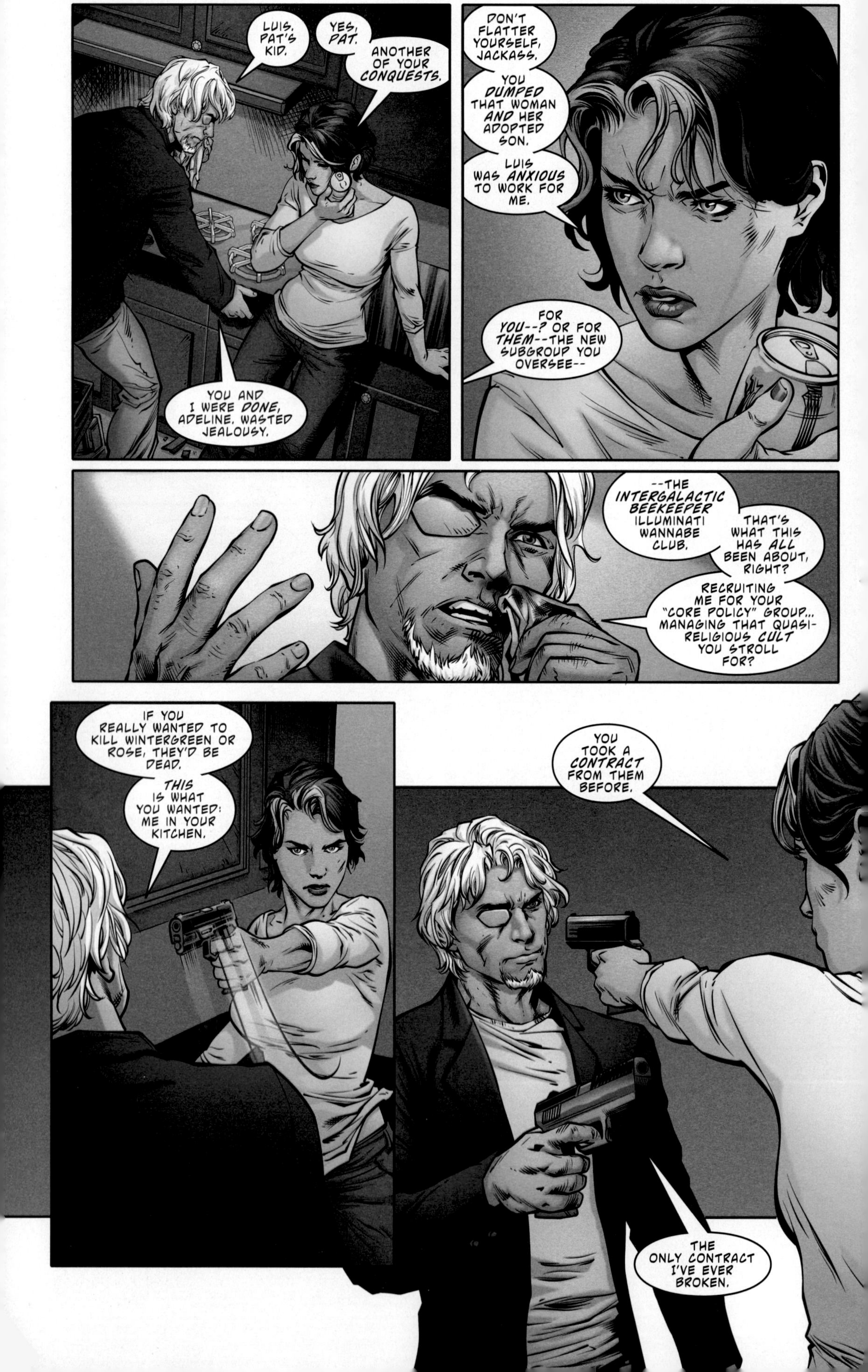
LUIS. PAT'S KID.
YES, PAT.
ANOTHER OF YOUR CONQUESTS.
YOU AND I WERE DONE, ADELINE. WASTED JEALOUSY.
DON'T FLATTER YOURSELF, JACKASS.
YOU DUMPED THAT WOMAN AND HER ADOPTED SON.
LUIS WAS ANXIOUS TO WORK FOR ME.
FOR YOU--? OR FOR THEM--THE NEW SUBGROUP YOU OVERSEE--
--THE INTERGALACTIC BEEKEEPER ILLUMINATI WANNABE CLUB.
THAT'S WHAT THIS HAS ALL BEEN ABOUT, RIGHT?
RECRUITING ME FOR YOUR "CORE POLICY" GROUP... MANAGING THAT QUASI-RELIGIOUS CULT YOU STROLL FOR?
IF YOU REALLY WANTED TO KILL WINTERGREEN OR ROSE, THEY'D BE DEAD.
THIS IS WHAT YOU WANTED: ME IN YOUR KITCHEN.
YOU TOOK A CONTRACT FROM THEM BEFORE.
THE ONLY CONTRACT I'VE EVER BROKEN.

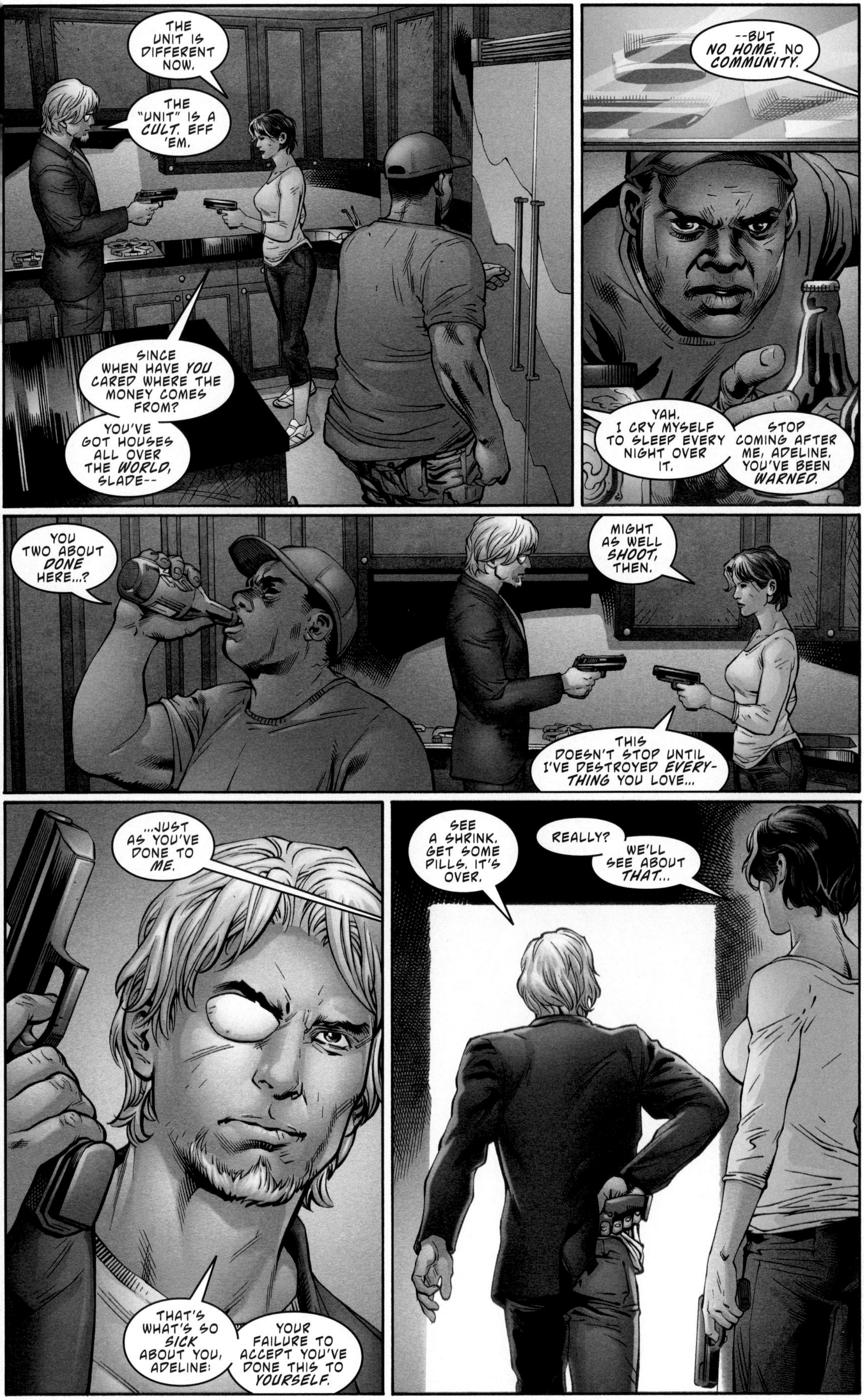
THE UNIT IS DIFFERENT NOW.
THE "UNIT" IS A CULT. EFF 'EM.
SINCE WHEN HAVE YOU CARED WHERE THE MONEY COMES FROM?
YOU'VE GOT HOUSES ALL OVER THE WORLD, SLADE--
--BUT NO HOME. NO COMMUNITY.
YAH. I CRY MYSELF TO SLEEP EVERY NIGHT OVER IT.
STOP COMING AFTER ME, ADELINE. YOU'VE BEEN WARNED.
YOU TWO ABOUT DONE HERE...?
MIGHT AS WELL SHOOT, THEN.
THIS DOESN'T STOP UNTIL I'VE DESTROYED EVERY-THING YOU LOVE...
...JUST AS YOU'VE DONE TO ME.
THAT'S WHAT'S SO SICK ABOUT YOU, ADELINE:
YOUR FAILURE TO ACCEPT YOU'VE DONE THIS TO YOURSELF.
SEE A SHRINK. GET SOME PILLS. IT'S OVER.
REALLY?
WE'LL SEE ABOUT THAT...

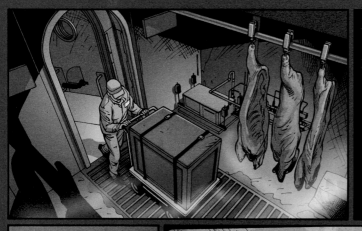

CLEAR.

NINE O'CLOCK.

...THE REAR OF THE MEAT LOCKER IS JUST STEEL--

--THERE'S NO BULKHEAD BEHIND IT.

BUNKER

THE PLASMA TORCH WE ADDED TO YOUR TITANIUM STAFF SHOULD SLICE IT LIKE CHEESE.

SPEAKING OF CHEESE--

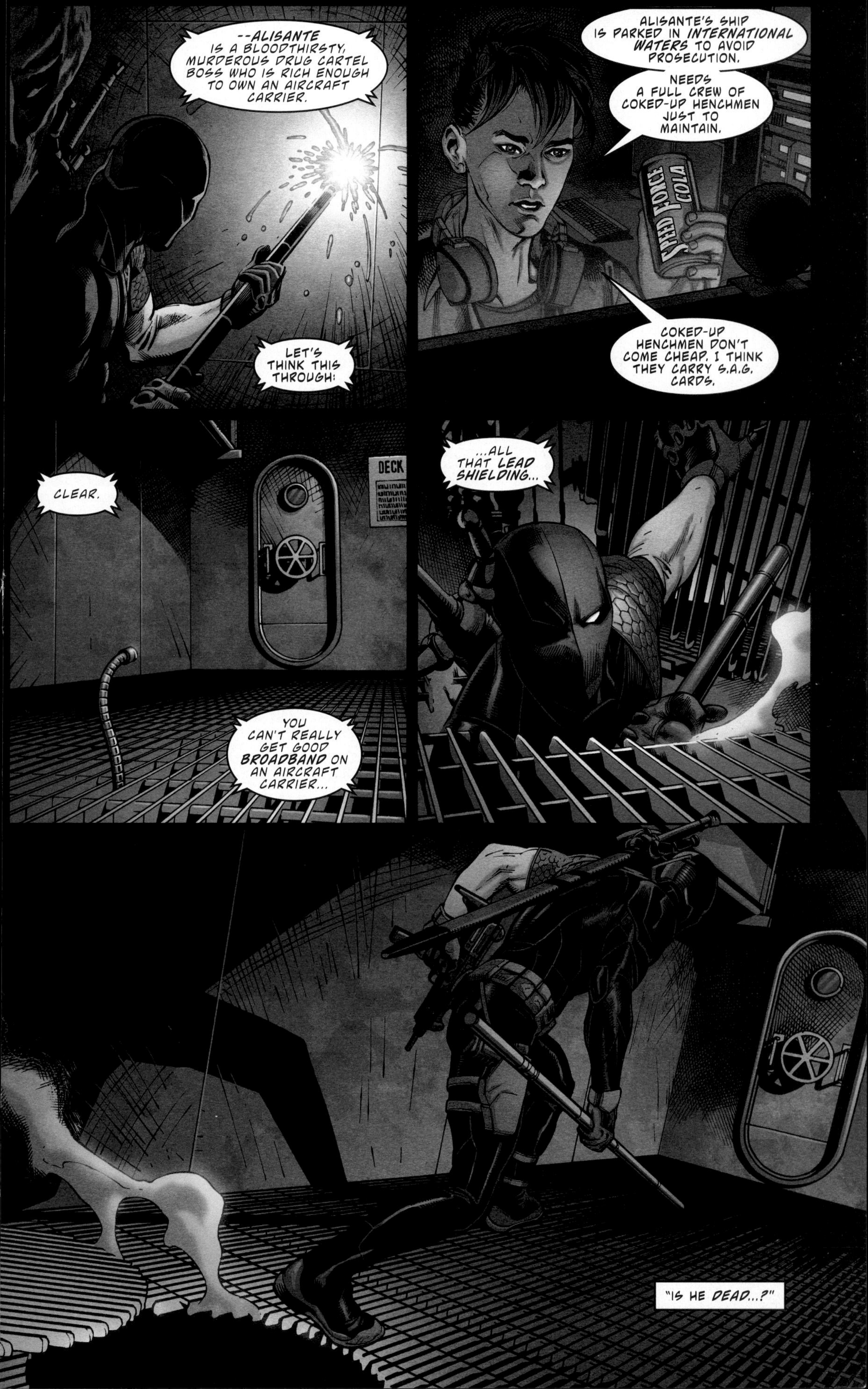
--ALISANTE IS A BLOODTHIRSTY, MURDEROUS DRUG CARTEL BOSS WHO IS RICH ENOUGH TO OWN AN AIRCRAFT CARRIER.
LET'S THINK THIS THROUGH:
ALISANTE'S SHIP IS PARKED IN INTERNATIONAL WATERS TO AVOID PROSECUTION.
NEEDS A FULL CREW OF COKED-UP HENCHMEN JUST TO MAINTAIN.
SPEED FORCE COLA
COKED-UP HENCHMEN DON'T COME CHEAP. I THINK THEY CARRY S.A.G. CARDS.
CLEAR.
DECK
YOU CAN'T REALLY GET GOOD BROADBAND ON AN AIRCRAFT CARRIER...
...ALL THAT LEAD SHIELDING...
"IS HE DEAD...?"

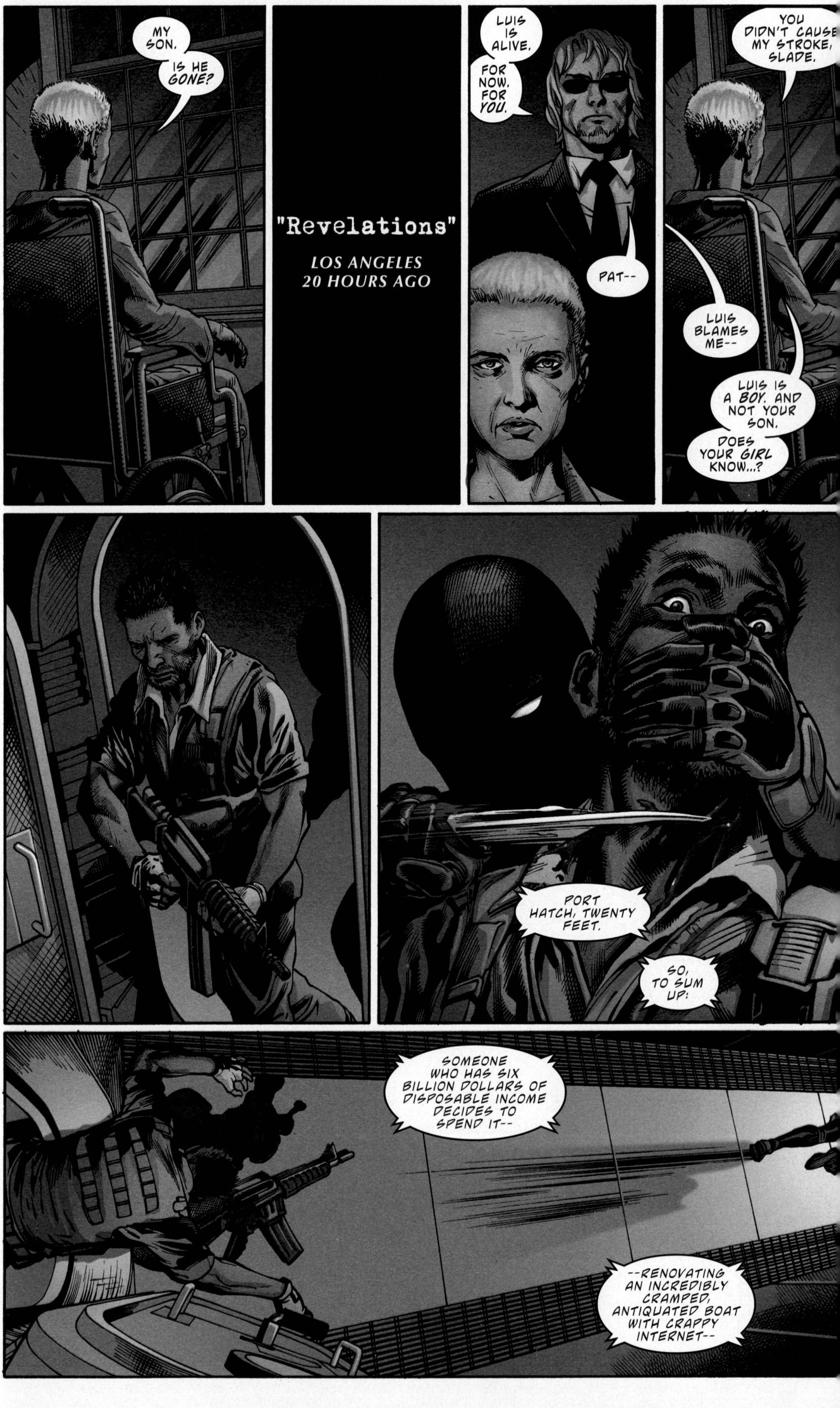
MY SON.
IS HE GONE?
"Revelations"
LOS ANGELES
20 HOURS AGO
LUIS IS ALIVE.
FOR NOW. FOR YOU.
PAT--
YOU DIDN'T CAUSE MY STROKE, SLADE.
LUIS BLAMES ME--
LUIS IS A BOY. AND NOT YOUR SON.
DOES YOUR GIRL KNOW...?
PORT HATCH, TWENTY FEET.
SO, TO SUM UP:
SOMEONE WHO HAS SIX BILLION DOLLARS OF DISPOSABLE INCOME DECIDES TO SPEND IT--
--RENOVATING AN INCREDIBLY CRAMPED, ANTIQUATED BOAT WITH CRAPPY INTERNET--

--AND THEN DECIDES "HEY, THAT'S NOT ENOUGH--

"--I'M GOING TO INSTALL MOVEABLE DECKS I CAN RECONFIGURE WITH THE CLICK OF A BUTTON...

"...JUST IN CASE SOME GUY COMES TO KILL ME--

BLEEP!

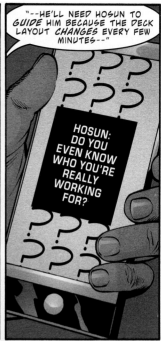

"--HE'LL NEED HOSUN TO GUIDE HIM BECAUSE THE DECK LAYOUT CHANGES EVERY FEW MINUTES--"

HOSUN: DO YOU EVEN KNOW WHO YOU'RE REALLY WORKING FOR?

WAIT-- ONE,

--MOMMY...

HOSUN.

HOSUN. THEY'VE CHANGED THE *DECK* CONFIG--

--

--BLIND, LOST.

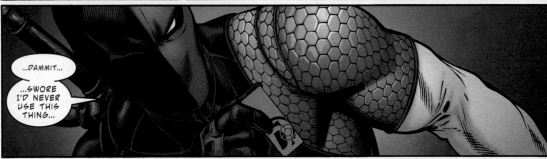

...DAMMIT...

...SWORE I'D NEVER USE THIS THING...

VW ACTIVE-- AUDIO ONLY.

Well now, Slade--

--it's about bloody time.

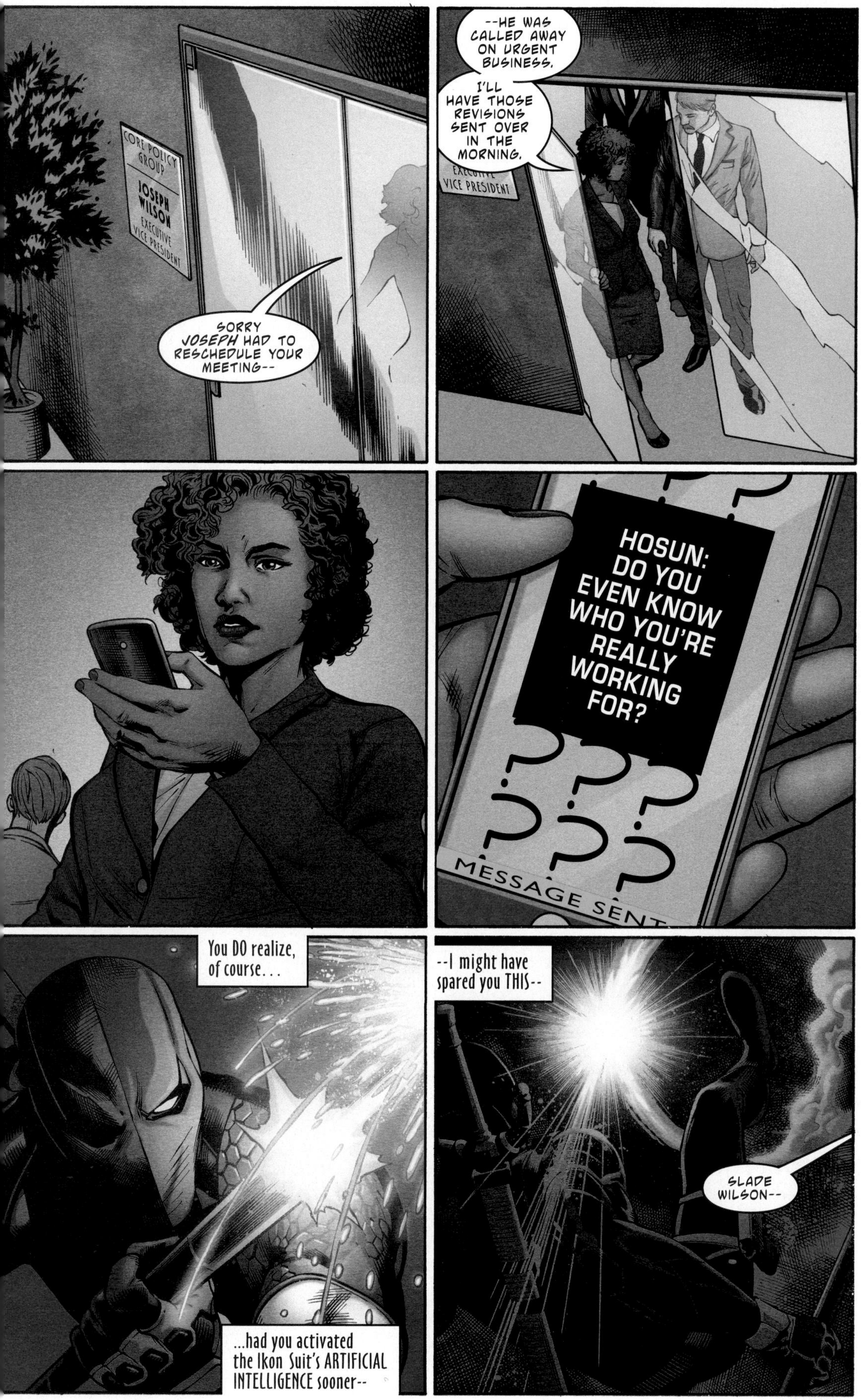
CORE POLICY GROUP
JOSEPH WILSON
EXECUTIVE VICE PRESIDENT
SORRY JOSEPH HAD TO RESCHEDULE YOUR MEETING--
--HE WAS CALLED AWAY ON URGENT BUSINESS.
I'LL HAVE THOSE REVISIONS SENT OVER IN THE MORNING.
EXECUTIVE VICE PRESIDENT
HOSUN: DO YOU EVEN KNOW WHO YOU'RE REALLY WORKING FOR?
MESSAGE SENT
You DO realize, of course...
...had you activated the Ikon Suit's ARTIFICIAL INTELLIGENCE sooner--
--I might have spared you THIS--
SLADE WILSON--

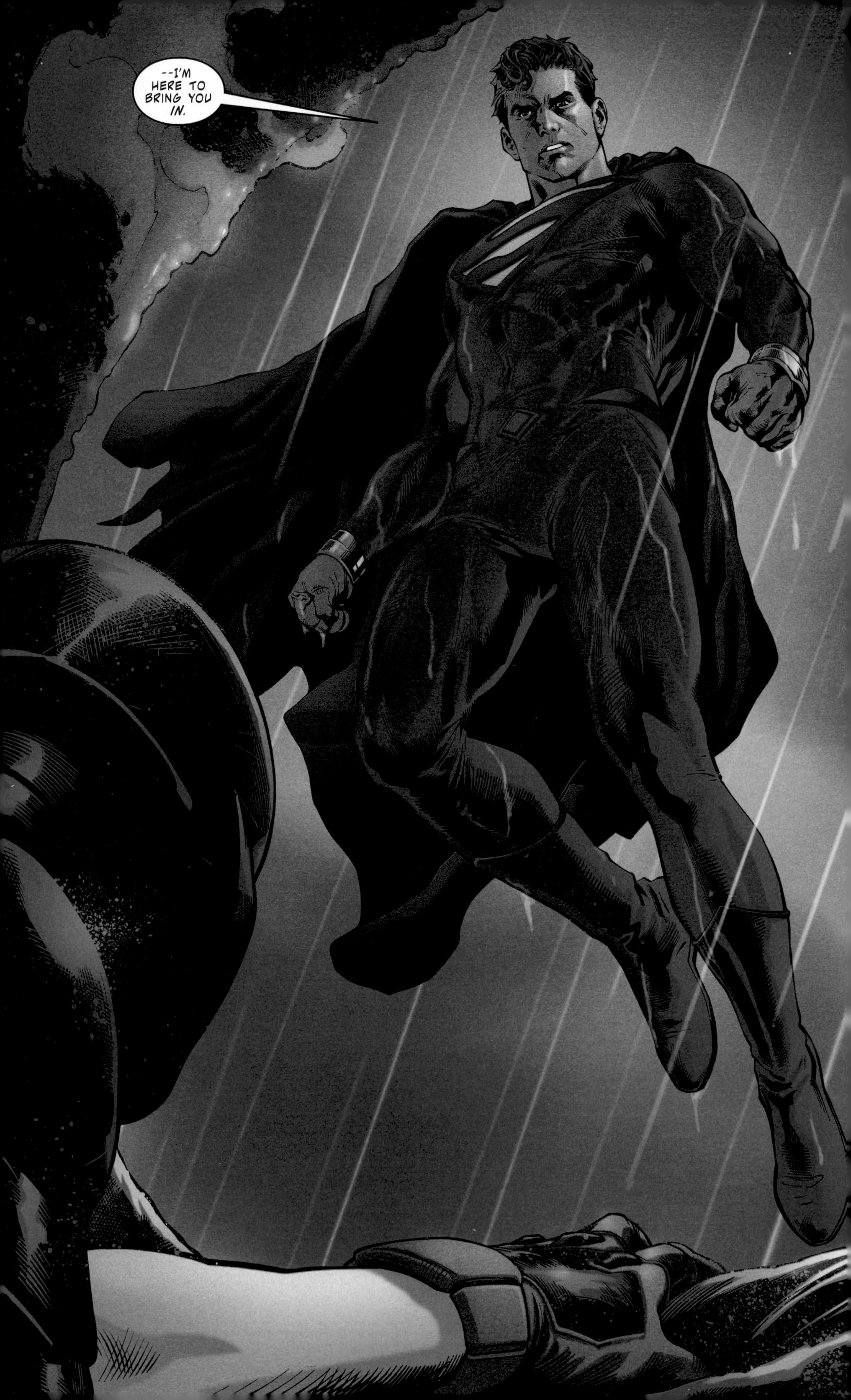
--I'M HERE TO BRING YOU IN.

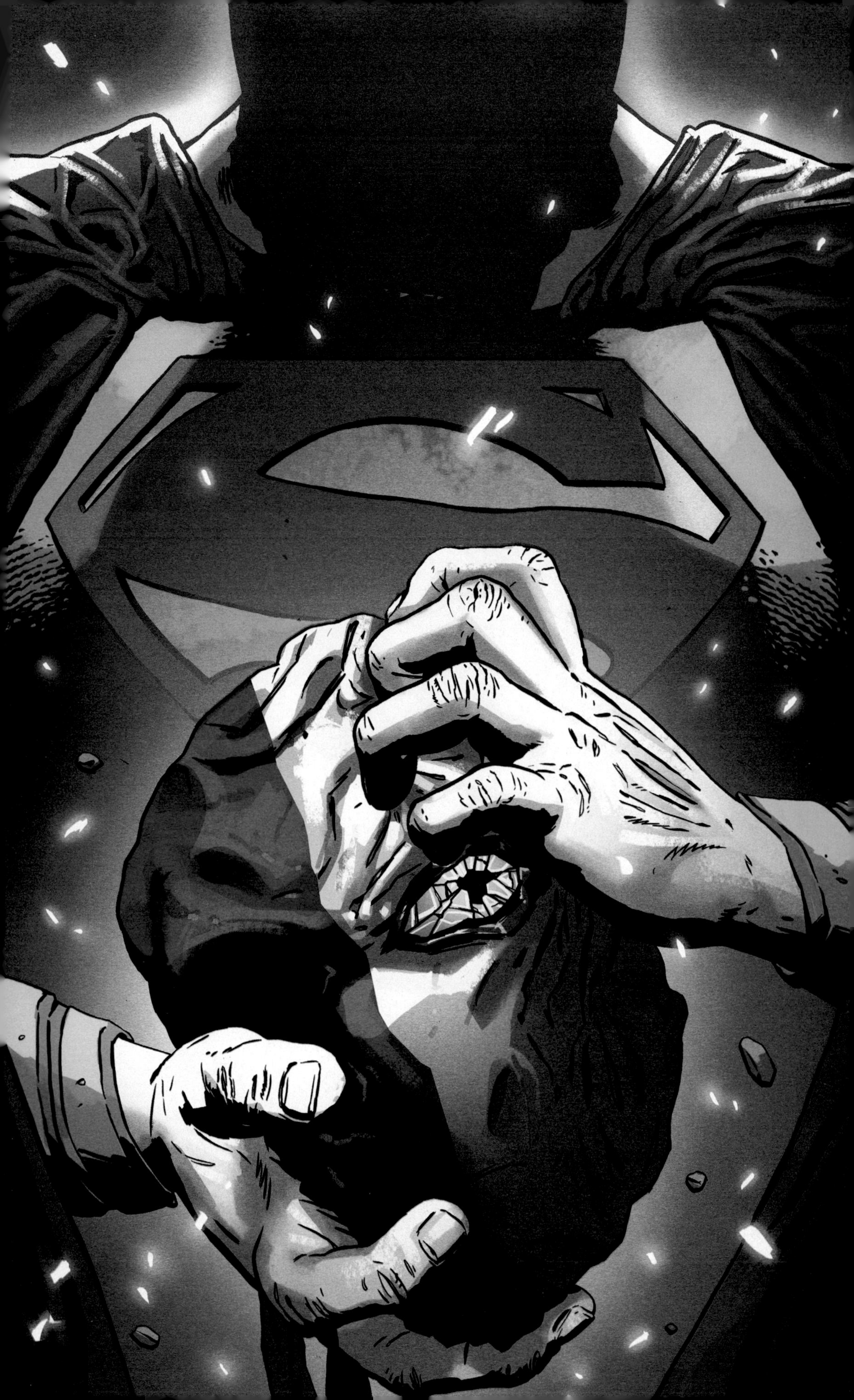

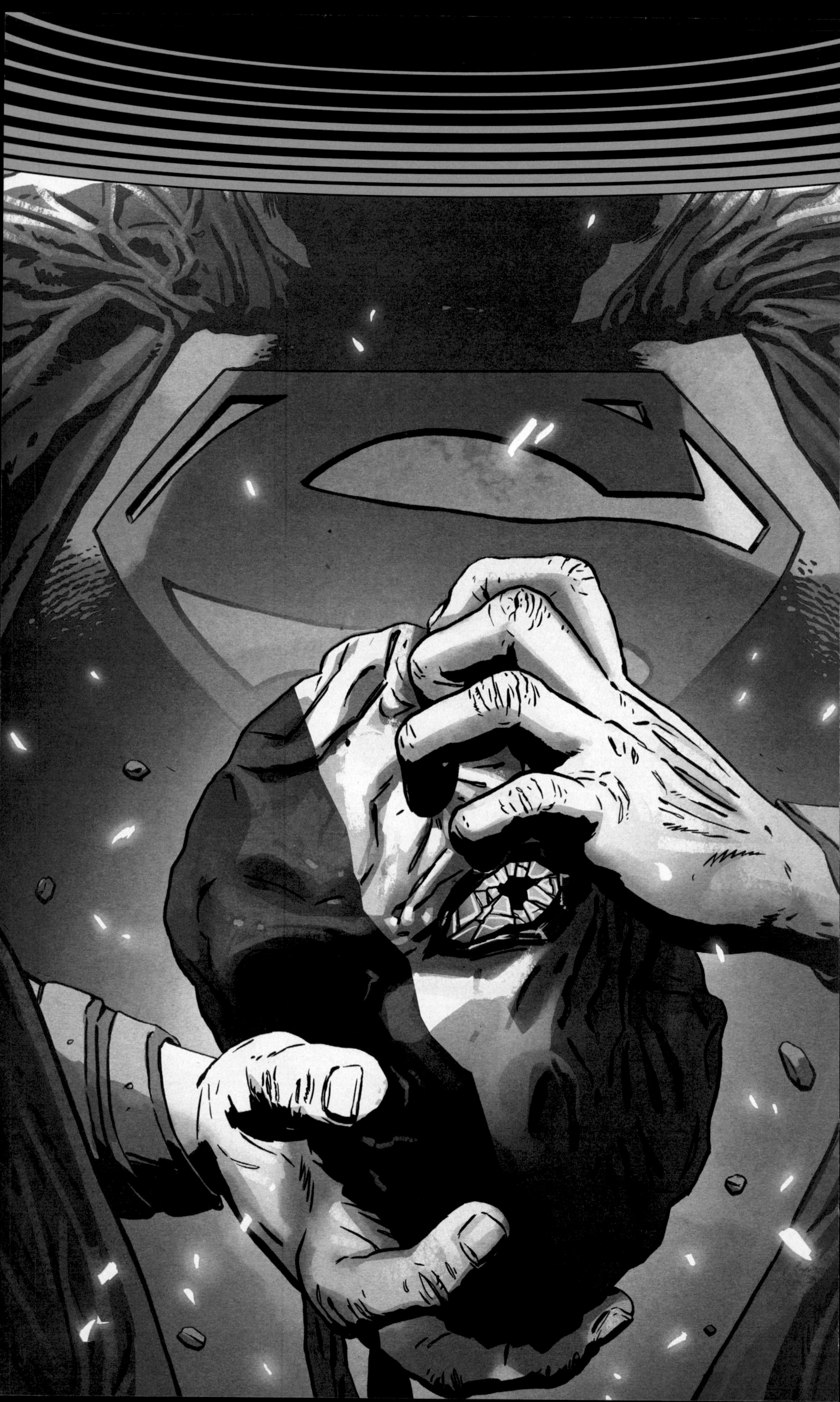

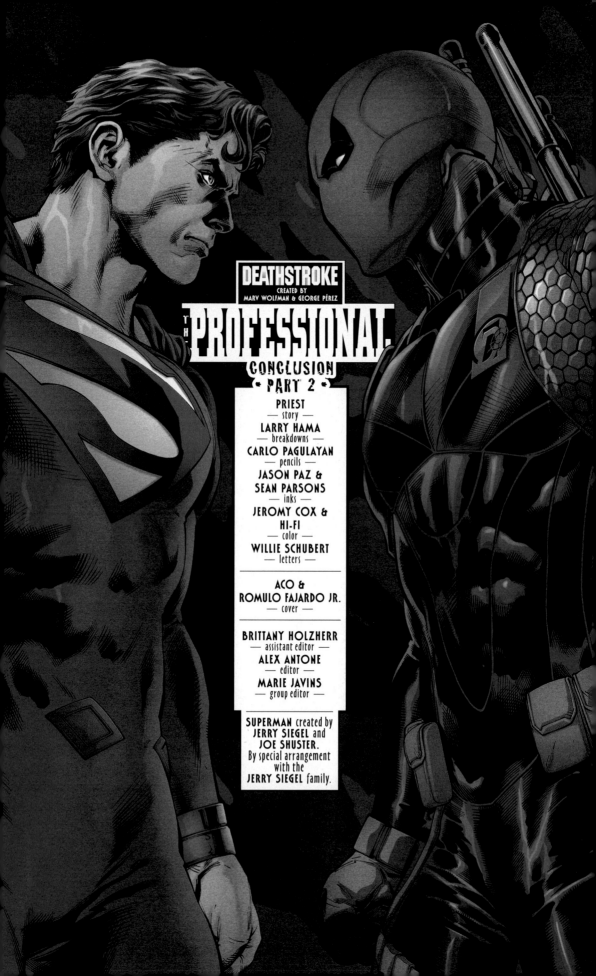

DEATHSTROKE
CREATED BY
MARV WOLFMAN & George Pérez

THE PROFESSIONAL
CONCLUSION
· PART 2 ·

PRIEST
— story —

LARRY HAMA
— breakdowns —

CARLO PAGULAYAN
— pencils —

**JASON PAZ &
SEAN PARSONS**
— inks —

**JEROMY COX &
HI-FI**
— color —

WILLIE SCHUBERT
— letters —

**ACO &
ROMULO FAJARDO JR.**
— cover —

BRITTANY HOLZHERR
— assistant editor —

ALEX ANTONE
— editor —

MARIE JAVINS
— group editor —

SUPERMAN created by
JERRY SIEGEL and
JOE SHUSTER.
By special arrangement
with the
JERRY SIEGEL family.

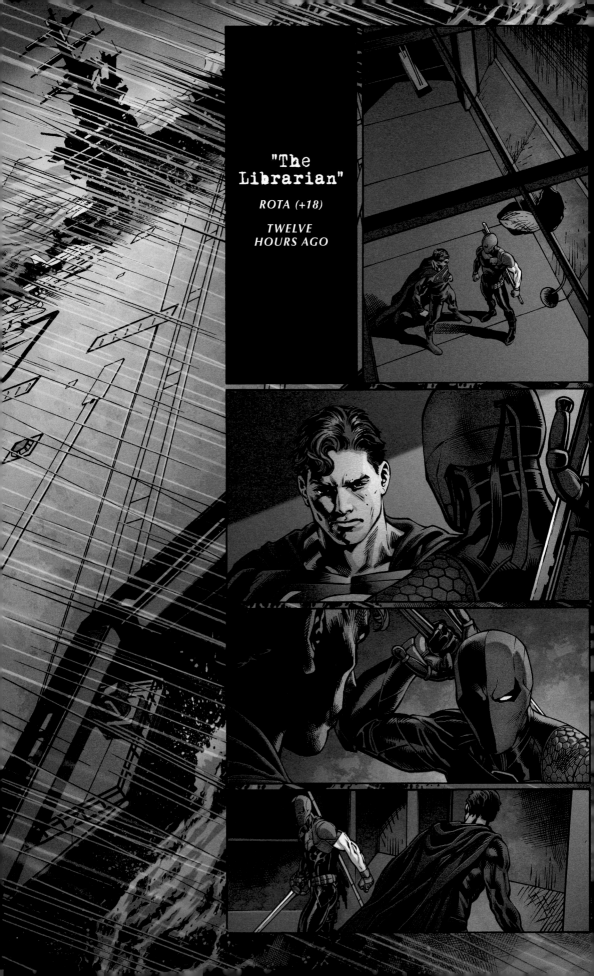

"The Librarian"

ROTA (+18)

TWELVE HOURS AGO

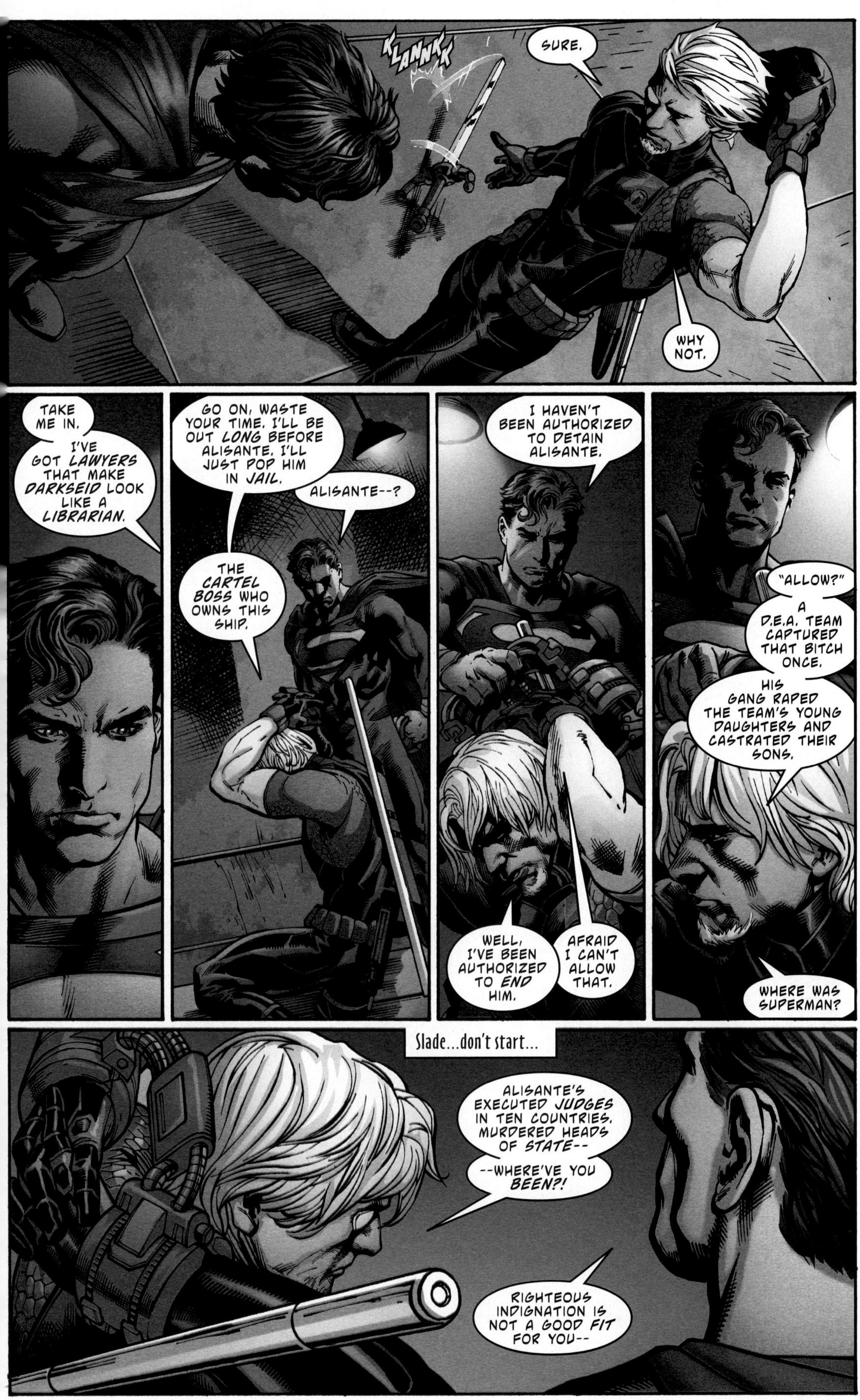
KLANNKK
SURE.
WHY NOT.
TAKE ME IN.
I'VE GOT LAWYERS THAT MAKE DARKSEID LOOK LIKE A LIBRARIAN.
GO ON, WASTE YOUR TIME. I'LL BE OUT LONG BEFORE ALISANTE. I'LL JUST POP HIM IN JAIL.
ALISANTE--?
THE CARTEL BOSS WHO OWNS THIS SHIP.
I HAVEN'T BEEN AUTHORIZED TO DETAIN ALISANTE.
WELL, I'VE BEEN AUTHORIZED TO END HIM.
AFRAID I CAN'T ALLOW THAT.
"ALLOW?"
A D.E.A. TEAM CAPTURED THAT BITCH ONCE.
HIS GANG RAPED THE TEAM'S YOUNG DAUGHTERS AND CASTRATED THEIR SONS.
WHERE WAS SUPERMAN?
Slade...don't start...
ALISANTE'S EXECUTED JUDGES IN TEN COUNTRIES. MURDERED HEADS OF STATE--
--WHERE'VE YOU BEEN?!
RIGHTEOUS INDIGNATION IS NOT A GOOD FIT FOR YOU--

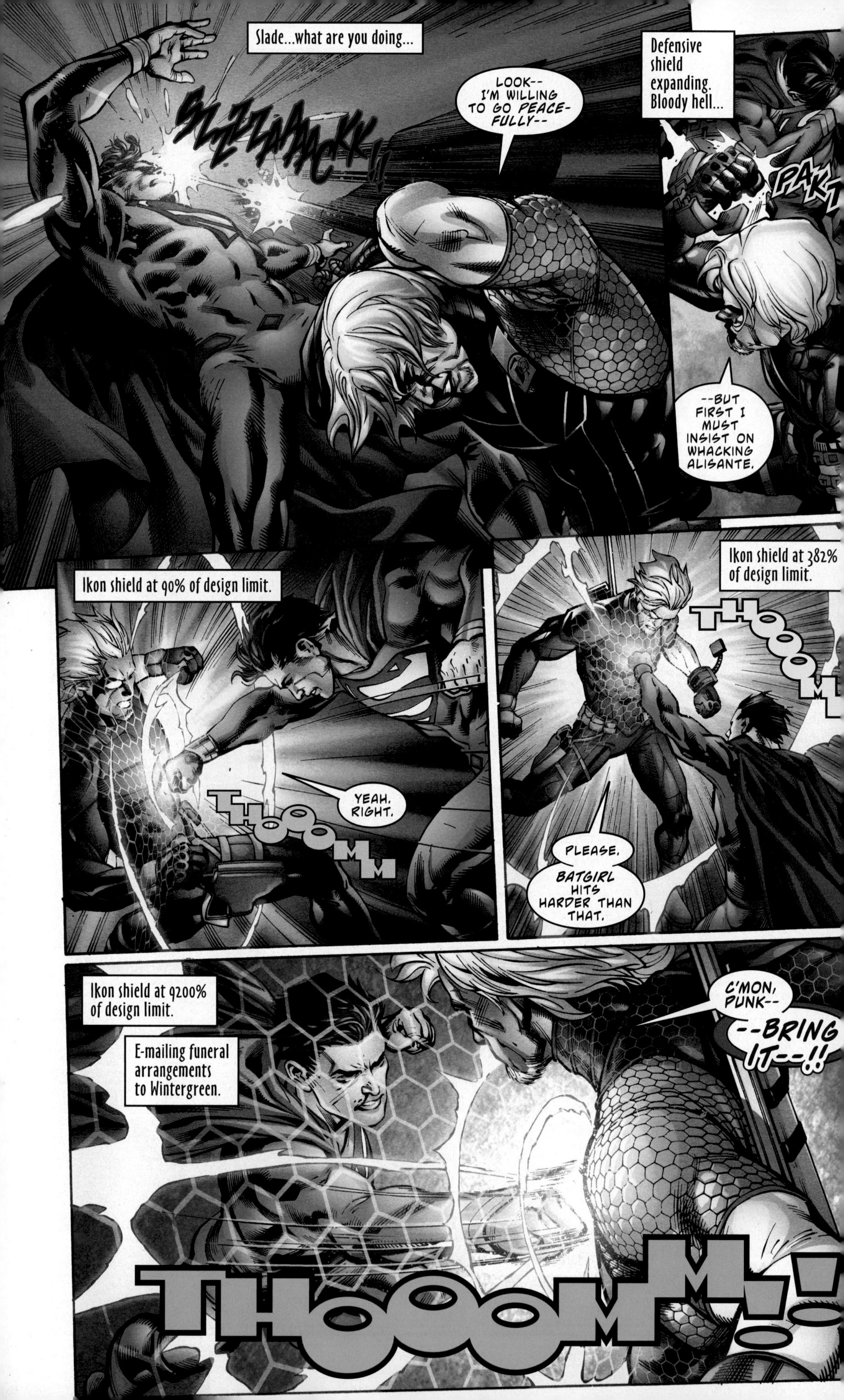

Slade...what are you doing...
SSZZZZAAACKK!!
LOOK-- I'M WILLING TO GO PEACE-FULLY--
Defensive shield expanding. Bloody hell...
PAK
--BUT FIRST I MUST INSIST ON WHACKING ALISANTE.
Ikon shield at 90% of design limit.
THOOOMM
YEAH, RIGHT.
Ikon shield at 382% of design limit.
THOOOM
PLEASE. BATGIRL HITS HARDER THAN THAT.
Ikon shield at 9200% of design limit.
E-mailing funeral arrangements to Wintergreen.
C'MON, PUNK--
--BRING IT--!!
THOOOMM!!

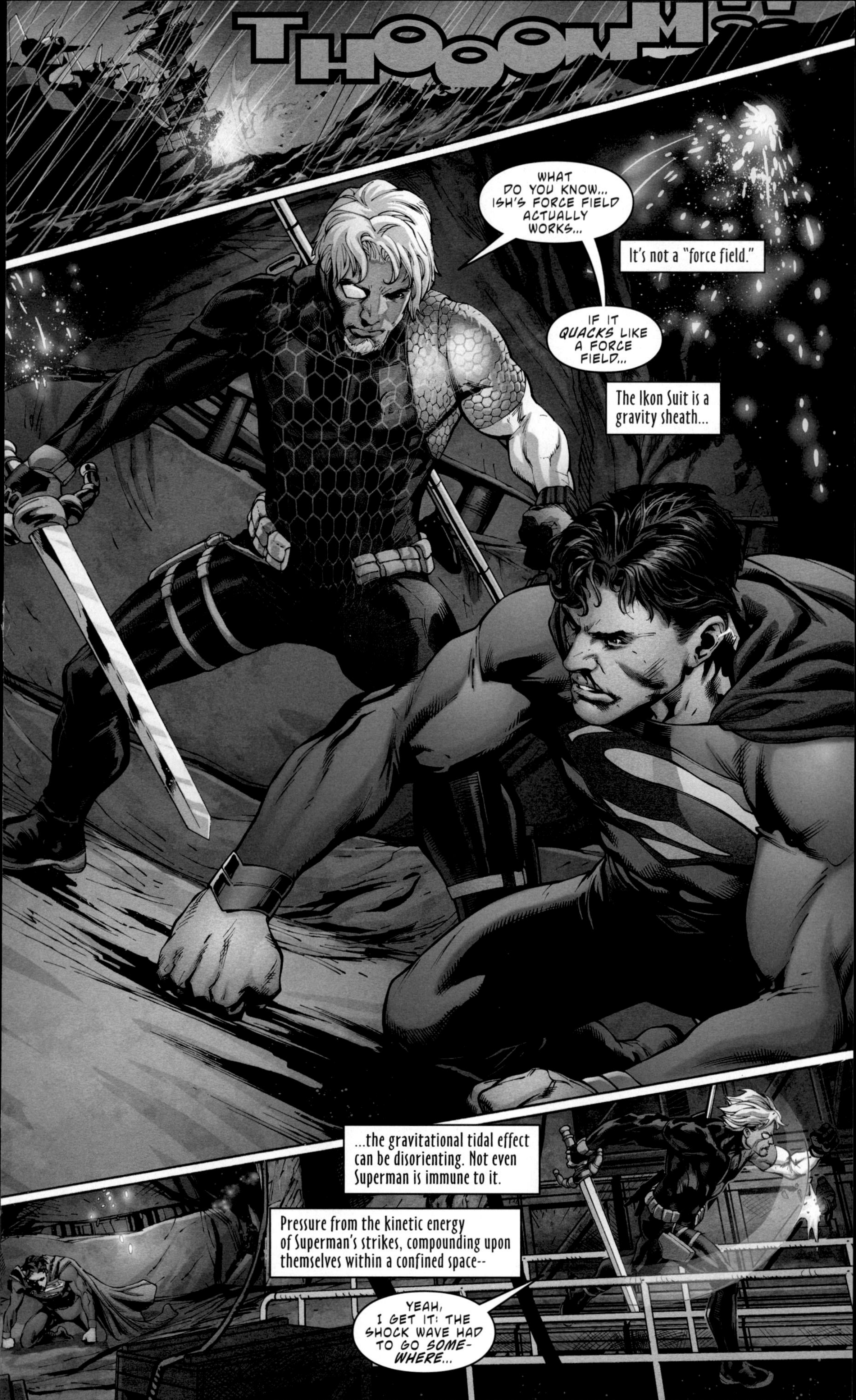
THOOOMM!!
WHAT DO YOU KNOW... ISH'S FORCE FIELD ACTUALLY WORKS...
It's not a "force field."
IF IT QUACKS LIKE A FORCE FIELD...
The Ikon Suit is a gravity sheath...
...the gravitational tidal effect can be disorienting. Not even Superman is immune to it.
Pressure from the kinetic energy of Superman's strikes, compounding upon themselves within a confined space--
YEAH, I GET IT: THE SHOCK WAVE HAD TO GO SOME-WHERE...

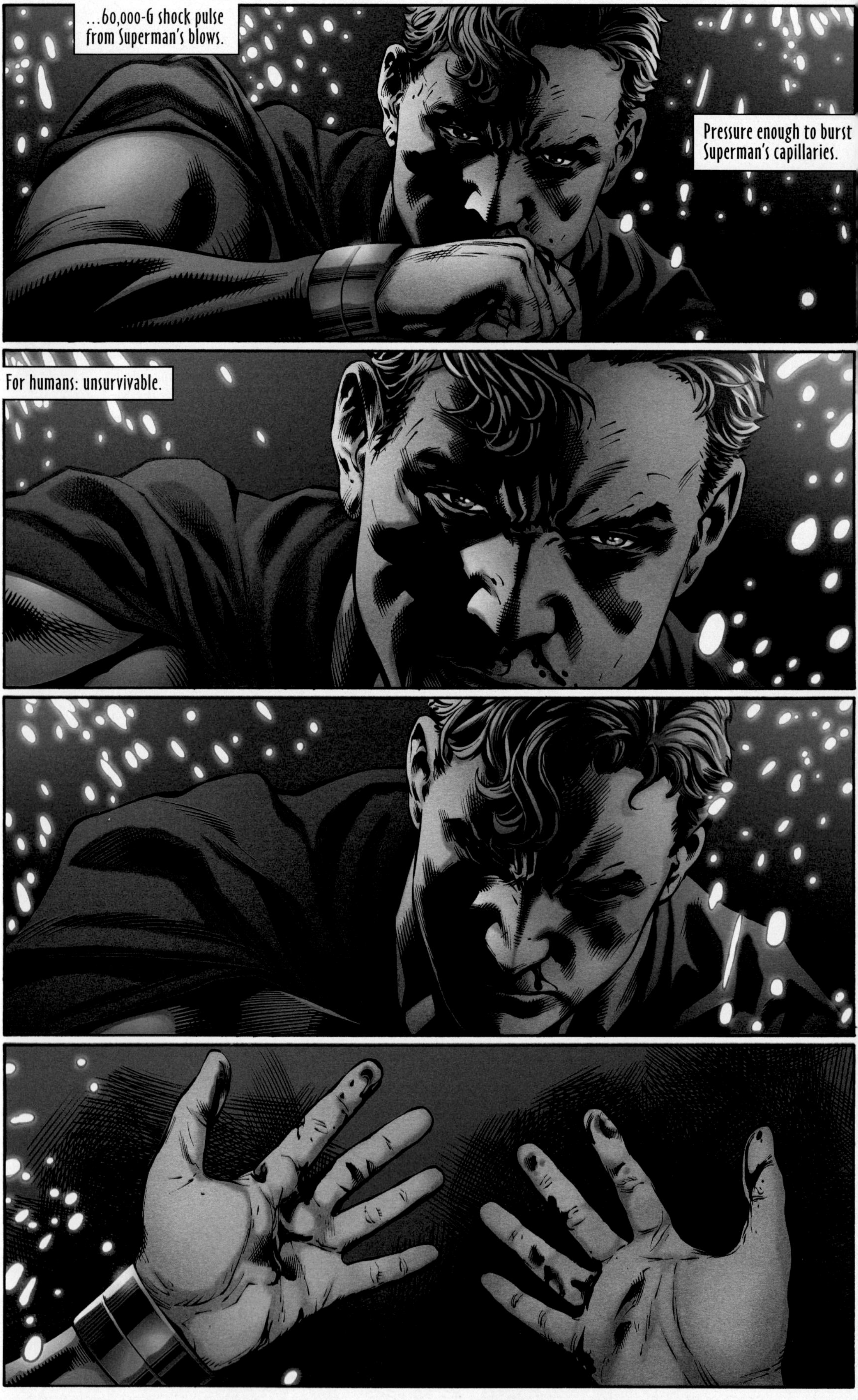
...60,000-G shock pulse from Superman's blows.
Pressure enough to burst Superman's capillaries.
For humans: unsurvivable.

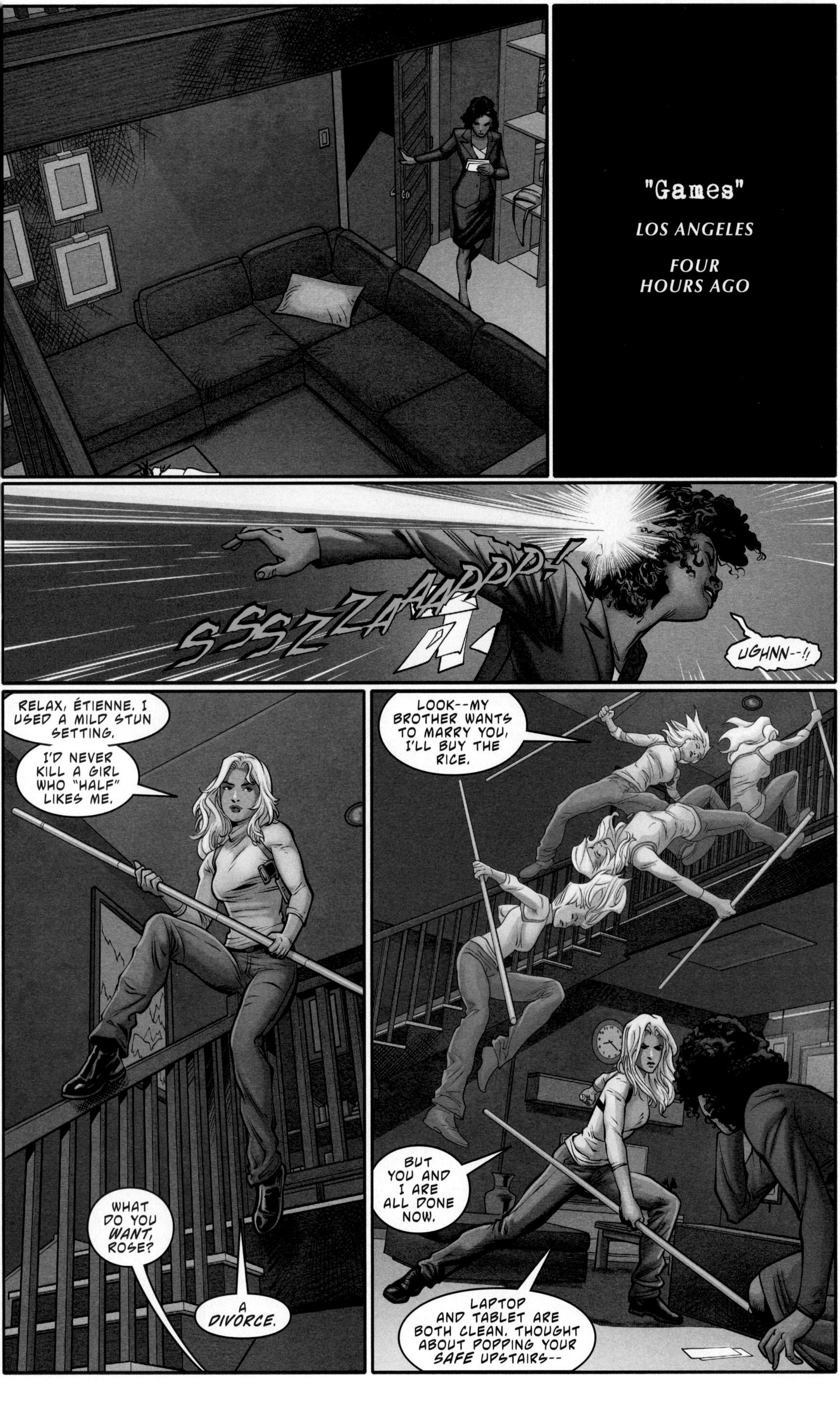
"Games"
LOS ANGELES
FOUR HOURS AGO
SSSZZAAARDDD!
UGHNN--!!
RELAX, ÉTIENNE. I USED A MILD STUN SETTING.
I'D NEVER KILL A GIRL WHO "HALF" LIKES ME.
WHAT DO YOU WANT, ROSE?
A DIVORCE.
LOOK--MY BROTHER WANTS TO MARRY YOU, I'LL BUY THE RICE.
BUT YOU AND I ARE ALL DONE NOW.
LAPTOP AND TABLET ARE BOTH CLEAN. THOUGHT ABOUT POPPING YOUR SAFE UPSTAIRS--

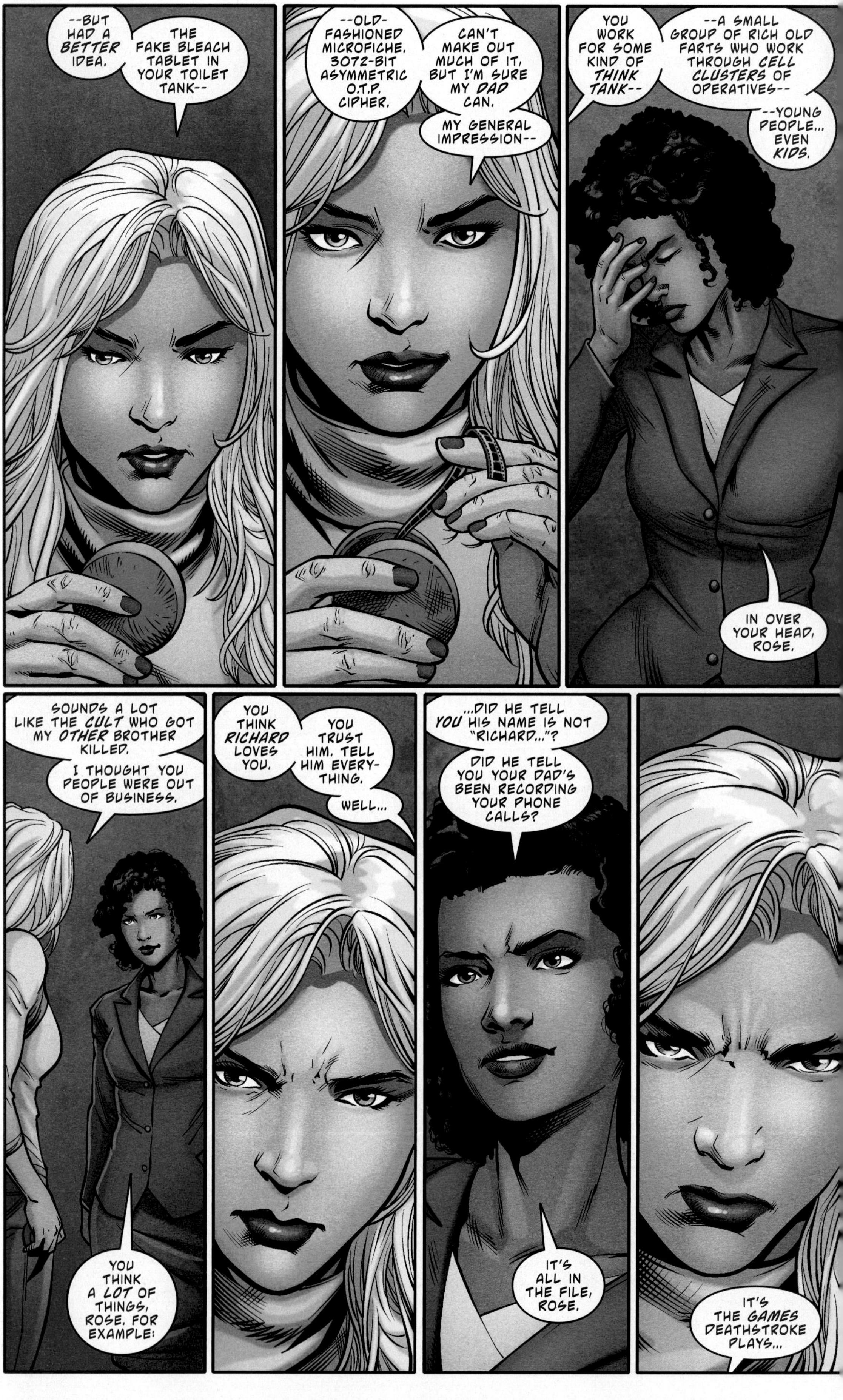
--BUT HAD A BETTER IDEA.
THE FAKE BLEACH TABLET IN YOUR TOILET TANK--
--OLD-FASHIONED MICROFICHE. 3072-BIT ASYMMETRIC O.T.P. CIPHER.
CAN'T MAKE OUT MUCH OF IT, BUT I'M SURE MY DAD CAN.
MY GENERAL IMPRESSION--
YOU WORK FOR SOME KIND OF THINK TANK--
--A SMALL GROUP OF RICH OLD FARTS WHO WORK THROUGH CELL CLUSTERS OF OPERATIVES--
--YOUNG PEOPLE... EVEN KIDS.
IN OVER YOUR HEAD, ROSE.
SOUNDS A LOT LIKE THE CULT WHO GOT MY OTHER BROTHER KILLED.
I THOUGHT YOU PEOPLE WERE OUT OF BUSINESS.
YOU THINK A LOT OF THINGS, ROSE. FOR EXAMPLE:
YOU THINK RICHARD LOVES YOU.
YOU TRUST HIM. TELL HIM EVERY-THING.
WELL...
...DID HE TELL YOU HIS NAME IS NOT "RICHARD..."?
DID HE TELL YOU YOUR DAD'S BEEN RECORDING YOUR PHONE CALLS?
IT'S ALL IN THE FILE, ROSE.
IT'S THE GAMES DEATHSTROKE PLAYS...

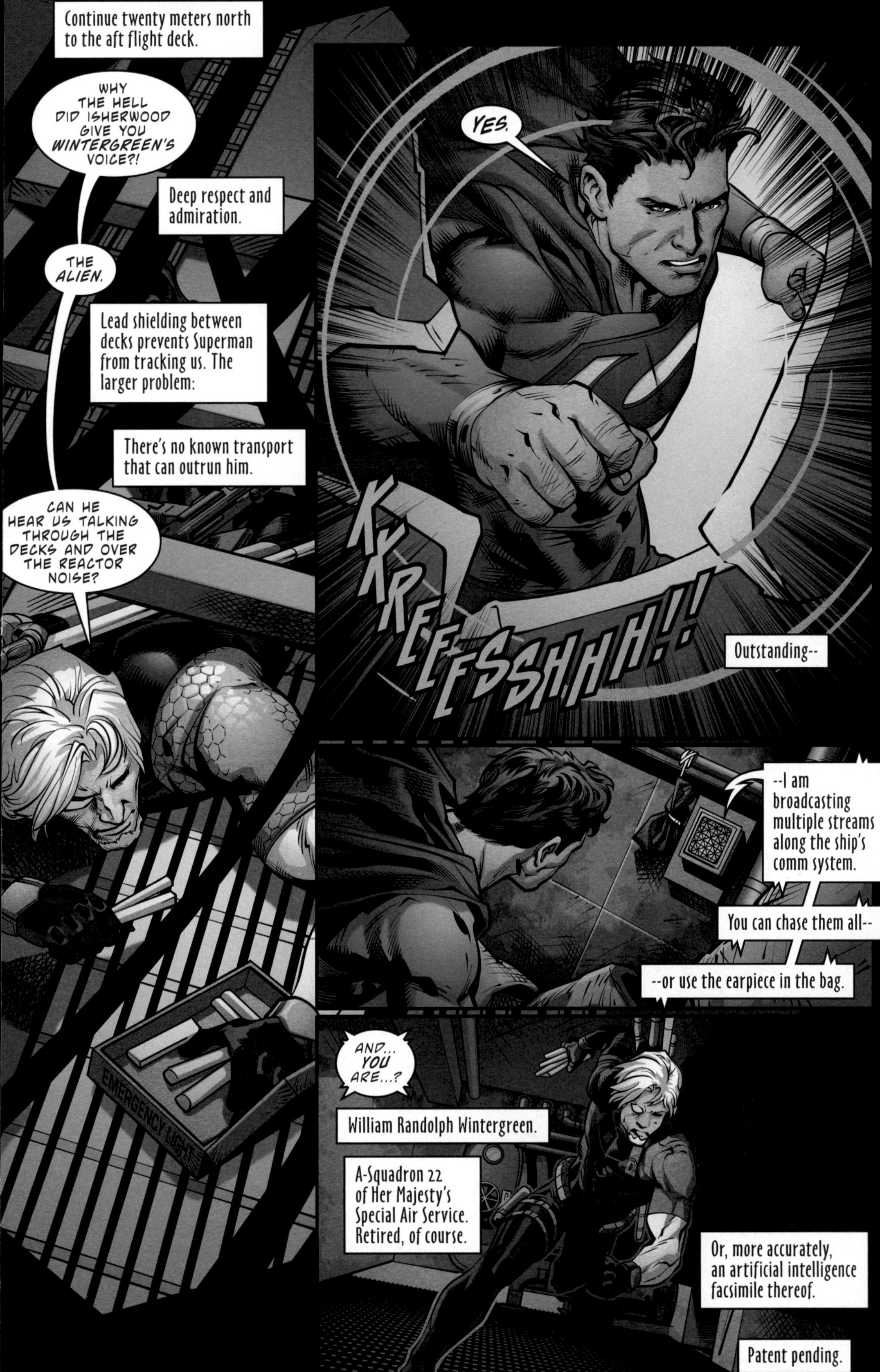
Continue twenty meters north to the aft flight deck.
WHY THE HELL DID ISHERWOOD GIVE YOU WINTERGREEN'S VOICE?!
Deep respect and admiration.
THE ALIEN.
Lead shielding between decks prevents Superman from tracking us. The larger problem:
There's no known transport that can outrun him.
CAN HE HEAR US TALKING THROUGH THE DECKS AND OVER THE REACTOR NOISE?
EMERGENCY LIGHT
YES.
KKREEESSHHH!!!
Outstanding--
--I am broadcasting multiple streams along the ship's comm system.
You can chase them all--
--or use the earpiece in the bag.
AND... YOU ARE...?
William Randolph Wintergreen.
A-Squadron 22 of Her Majesty's Special Air Service. Retired, of course.
Or, more accurately, an artificial intelligence facsimile thereof.
Patent pending.

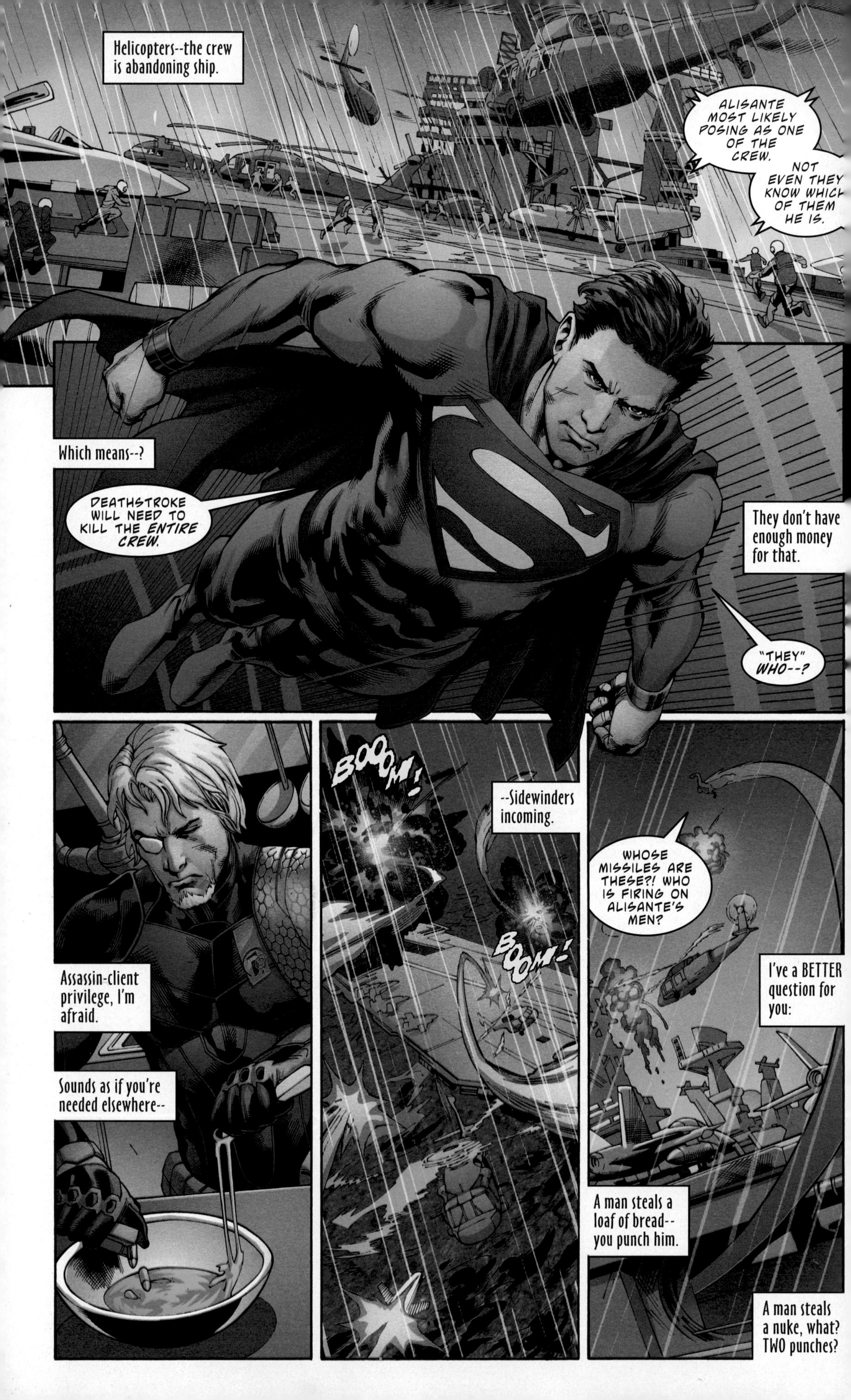
Helicopters--the crew is abandoning ship.
ALISANTE MOST LIKELY POSING AS ONE OF THE CREW.
NOT EVEN THEY KNOW WHICH OF THEM HE IS.
Which means--?
DEATHSTROKE WILL NEED TO KILL THE ENTIRE CREW.
They don't have enough money for that.
"THEY" WHO--?
Assassin-client privilege, I'm afraid.
Sounds as if you're needed elsewhere--
BOOOM!
--Sidewinders incoming.
BOOM!
WHOSE MISSILES ARE THESE?! WHO IS FIRING ON ALISANTE'S MEN?
I've a BETTER question for you:
A man steals a loaf of bread--you punch him.
A man steals a nuke, what? TWO punches?

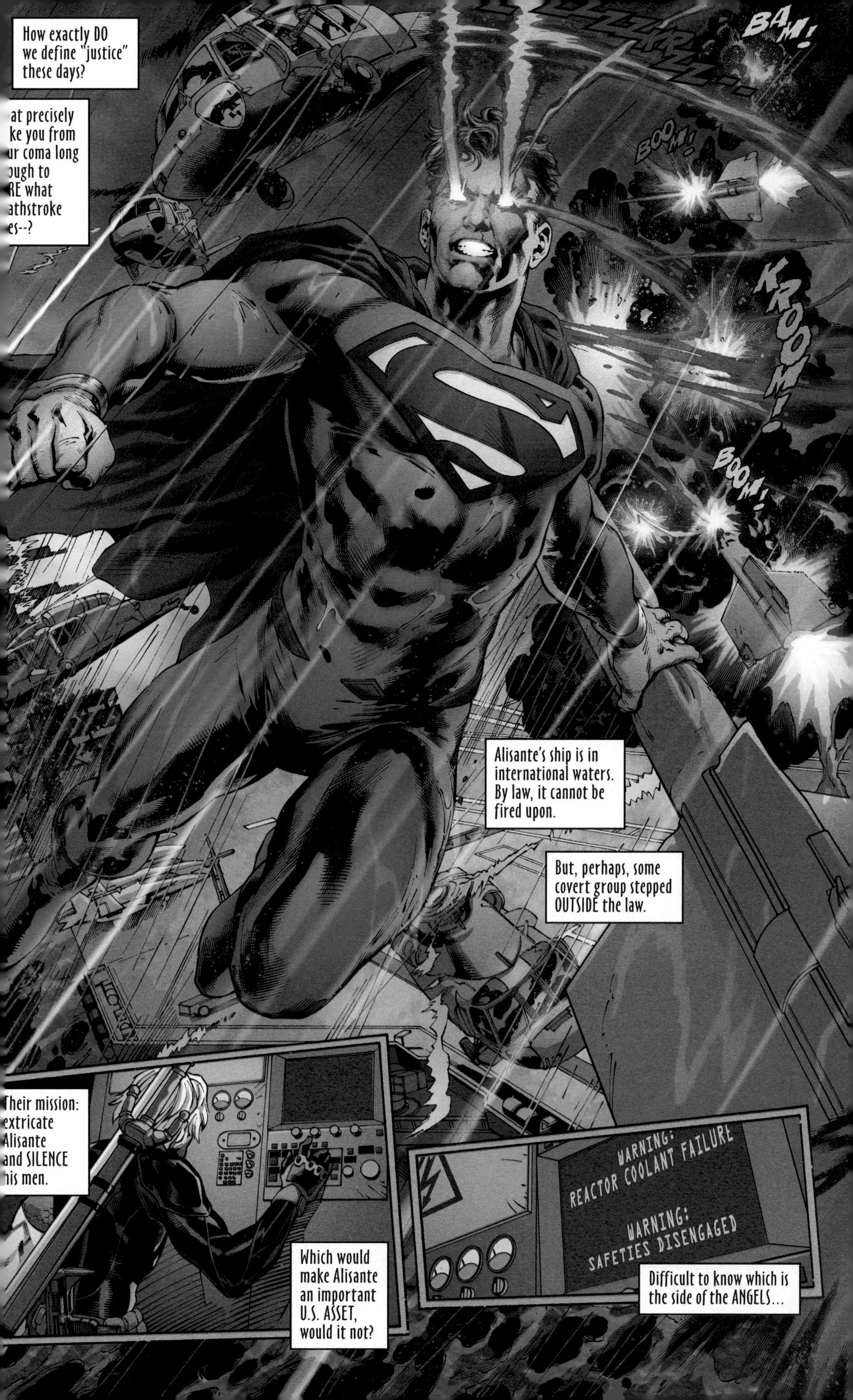
How exactly DO we define "justice" these days?
at precisely ke you from ur coma long ough to RE what athstroke es--?
BAM!
BOOM!
KROOOM!
BOOM!
Alisante's ship is in international waters. By law, it cannot be fired upon.
But, perhaps, some covert group stepped OUTSIDE the law.
Their mission: extricate Alisante and SILENCE his men.
WARNING: REACTOR COOLANT FAILURE
WARNING: SAFETIES DISENGAGED
Which would make Alisante an important U.S. ASSET, would it not?
Difficult to know which is the side of the ANGELS...

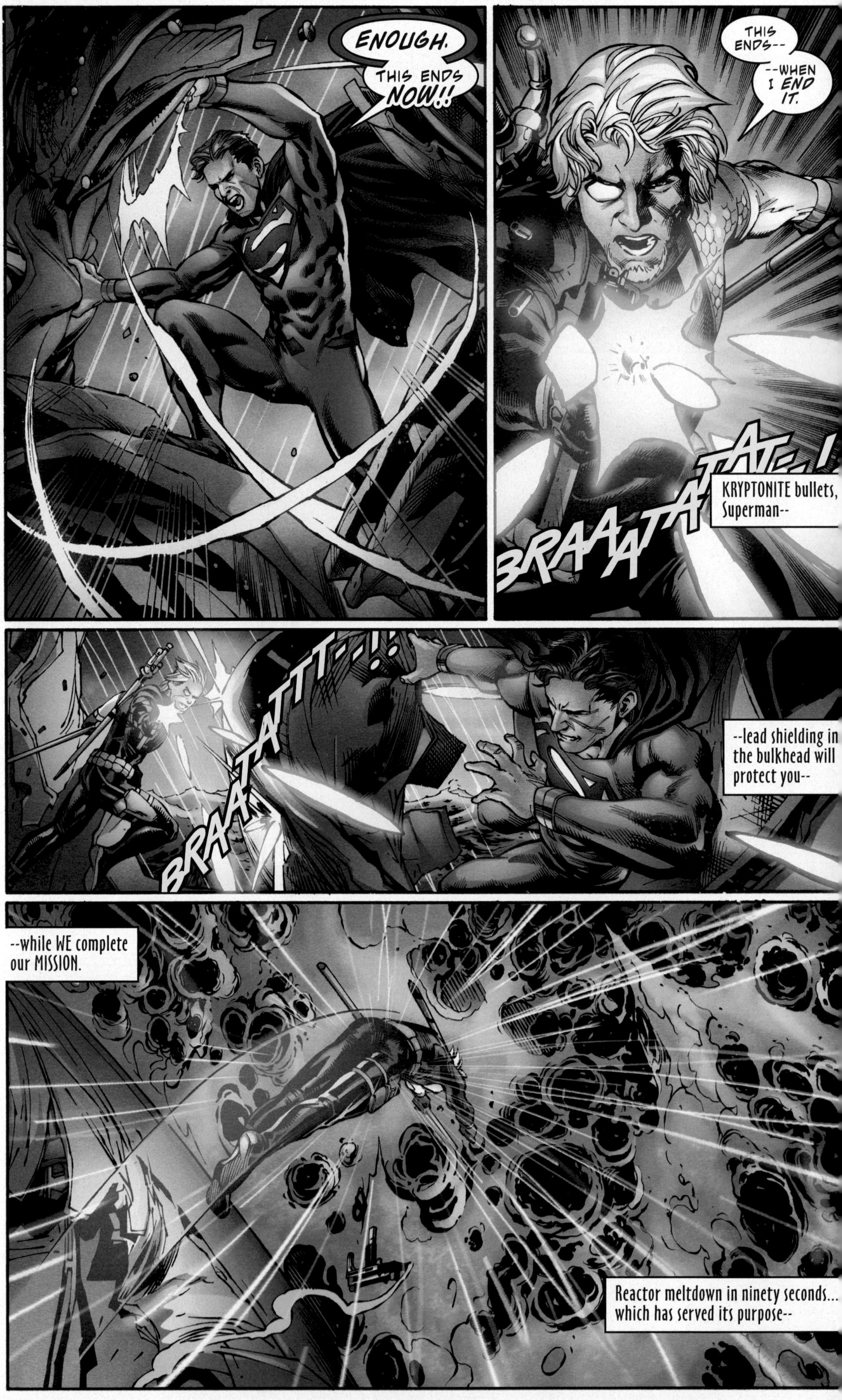
ENOUGH.
THIS ENDS NOW!!
THIS ENDS--
--WHEN I END IT.
BRAAAATATTAT--!
KRYPTONITE bullets, Superman--
BRAAATATTT--!!
--lead shielding in the bulkhead will protect you--
--while WE complete our MISSION.
Reactor meltdown in ninety seconds... which has served its purpose--

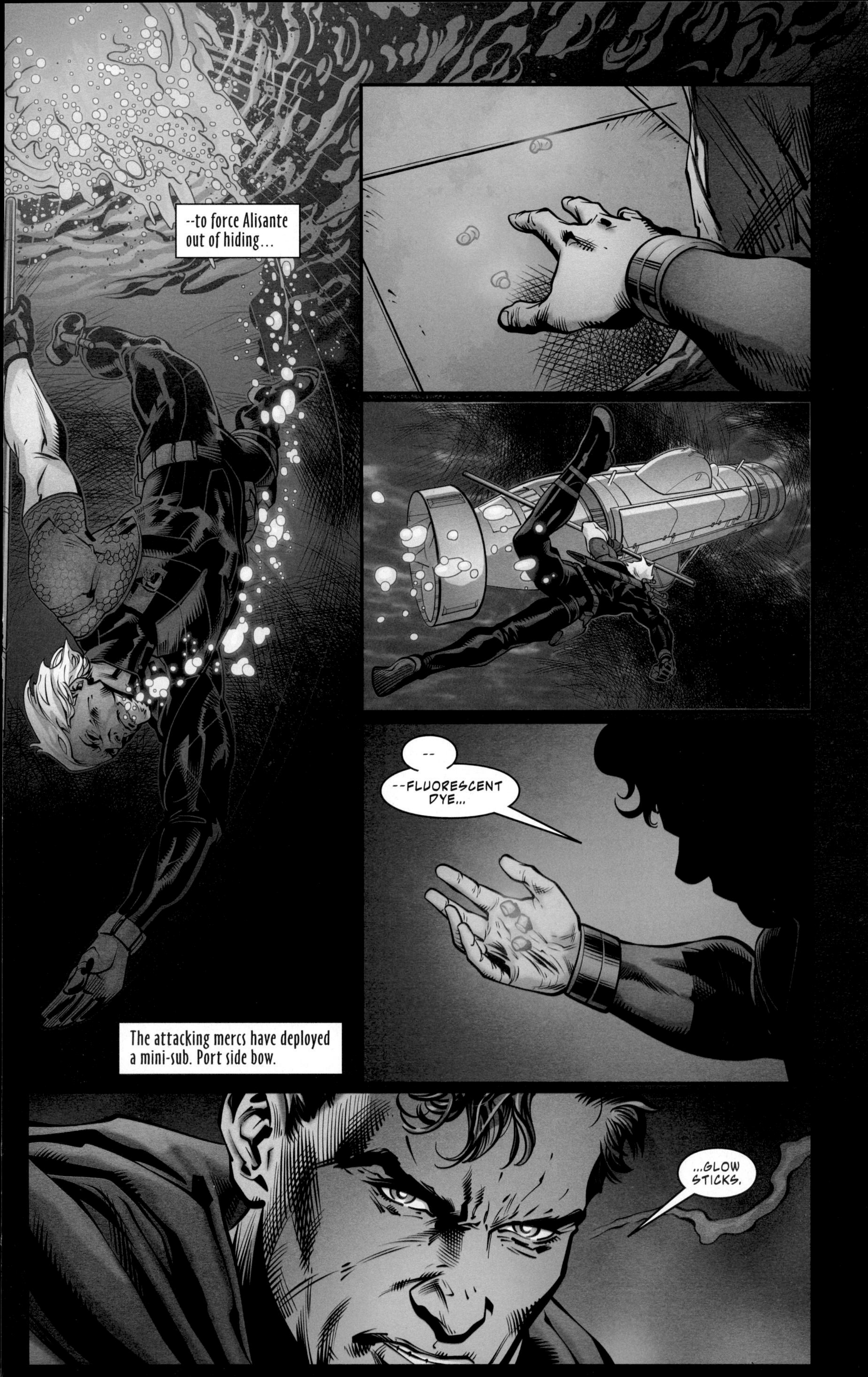
--to force Alisante out of hiding...
The attacking mercs have deployed a mini-sub. Port side bow.
--
--FLUORESCENT DYE...
...GLOW STICKS.

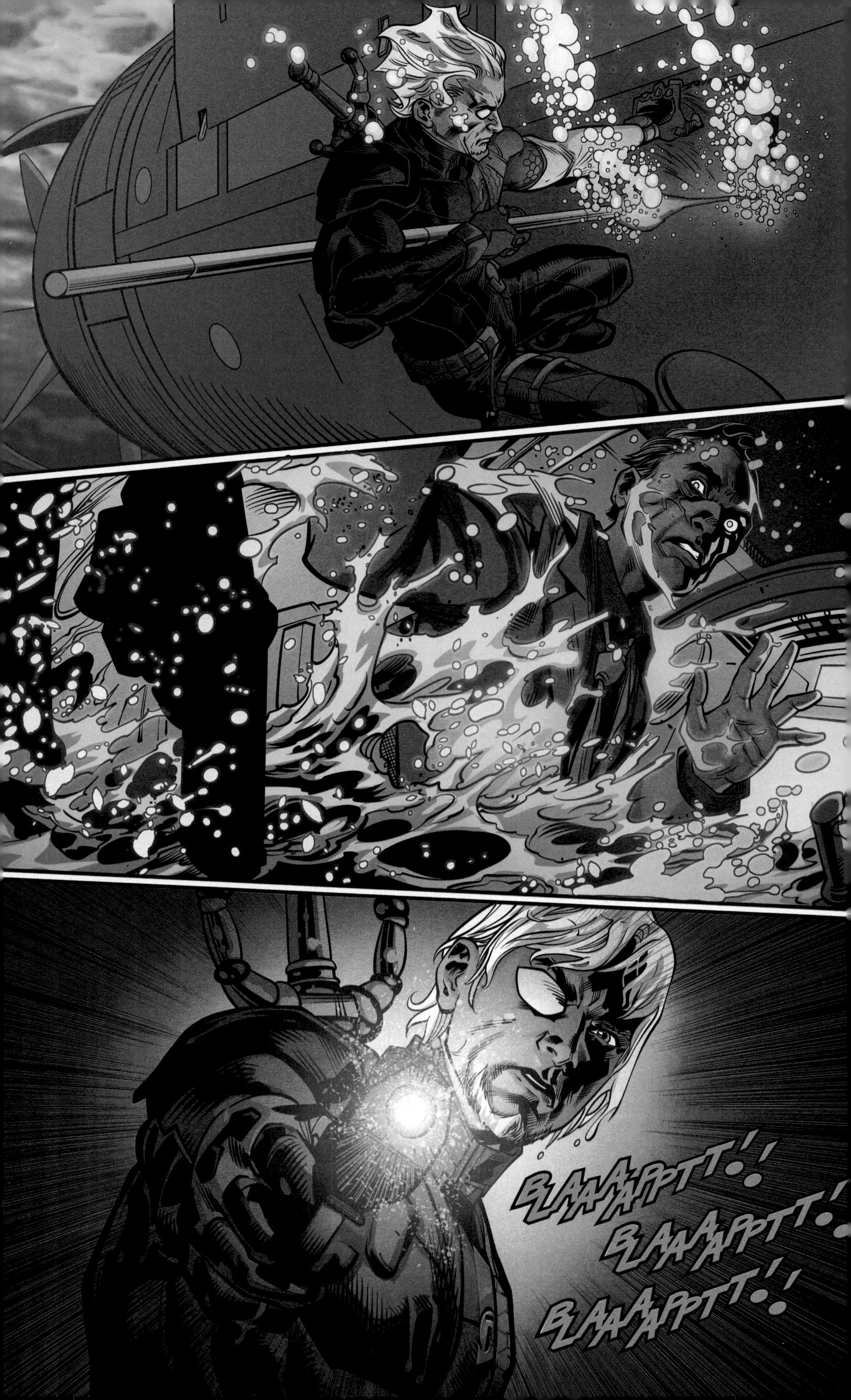
BLAAAAPPTT!!
BLAAAAPPTT!!
BLAAAAPPTT!!

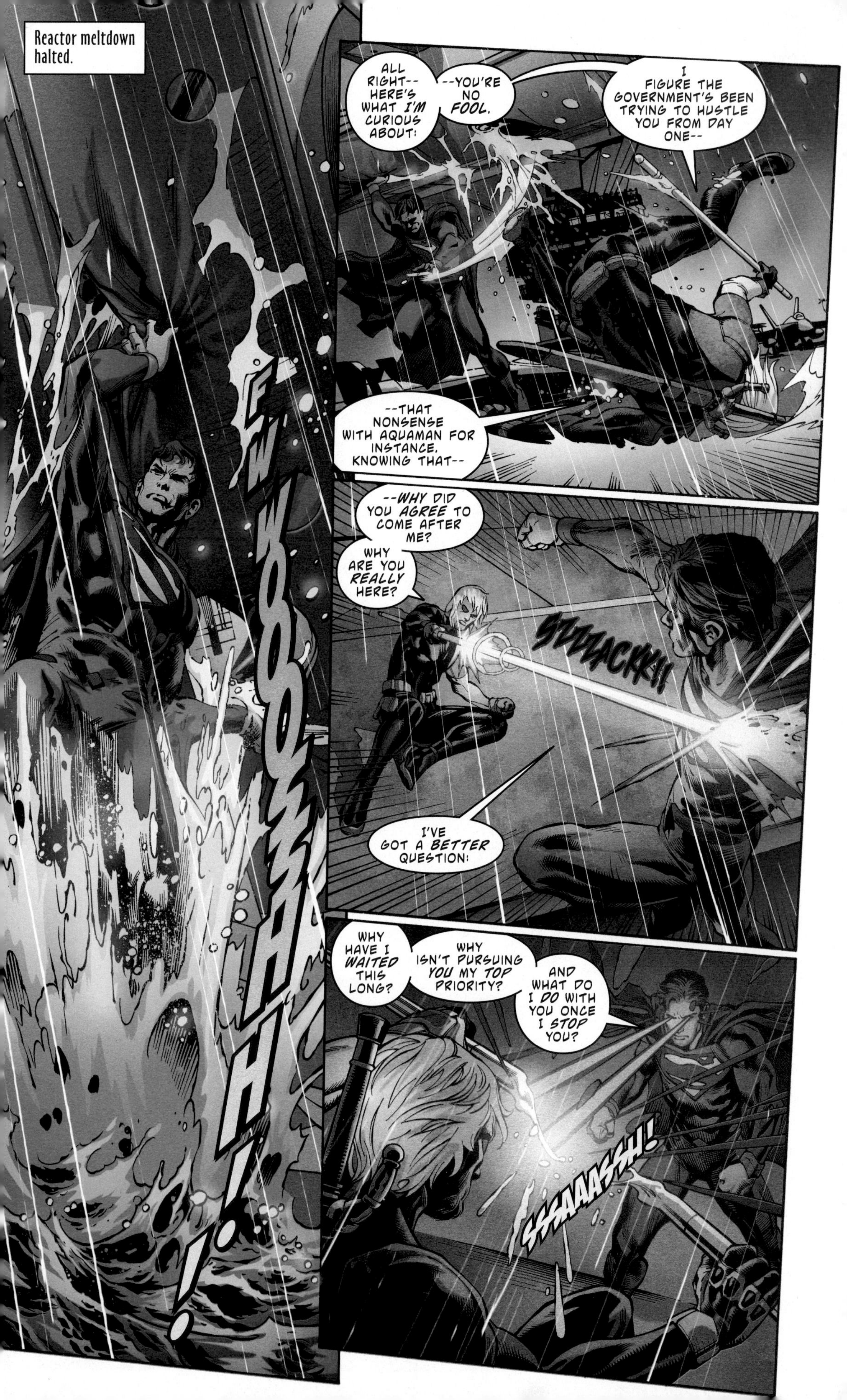

Reactor meltdown halted.
FWOOOOMMMAAHH!!
ALL RIGHT-- HERE'S WHAT I'M CURIOUS ABOUT:
--YOU'RE NO FOOL.
I FIGURE THE GOVERNMENT'S BEEN TRYING TO HUSTLE YOU FROM DAY ONE--
--THAT NONSENSE WITH AQUAMAN FOR INSTANCE. KNOWING THAT--
--WHY DID YOU AGREE TO COME AFTER ME?
WHY ARE YOU REALLY HERE?
SZZZACKK!!
I'VE GOT A BETTER QUESTION:
WHY HAVE I WAITED THIS LONG?
WHY ISN'T PURSUING YOU MY TOP PRIORITY?
AND WHAT DO I DO WITH YOU ONCE I STOP YOU?
SSSAAASSH!

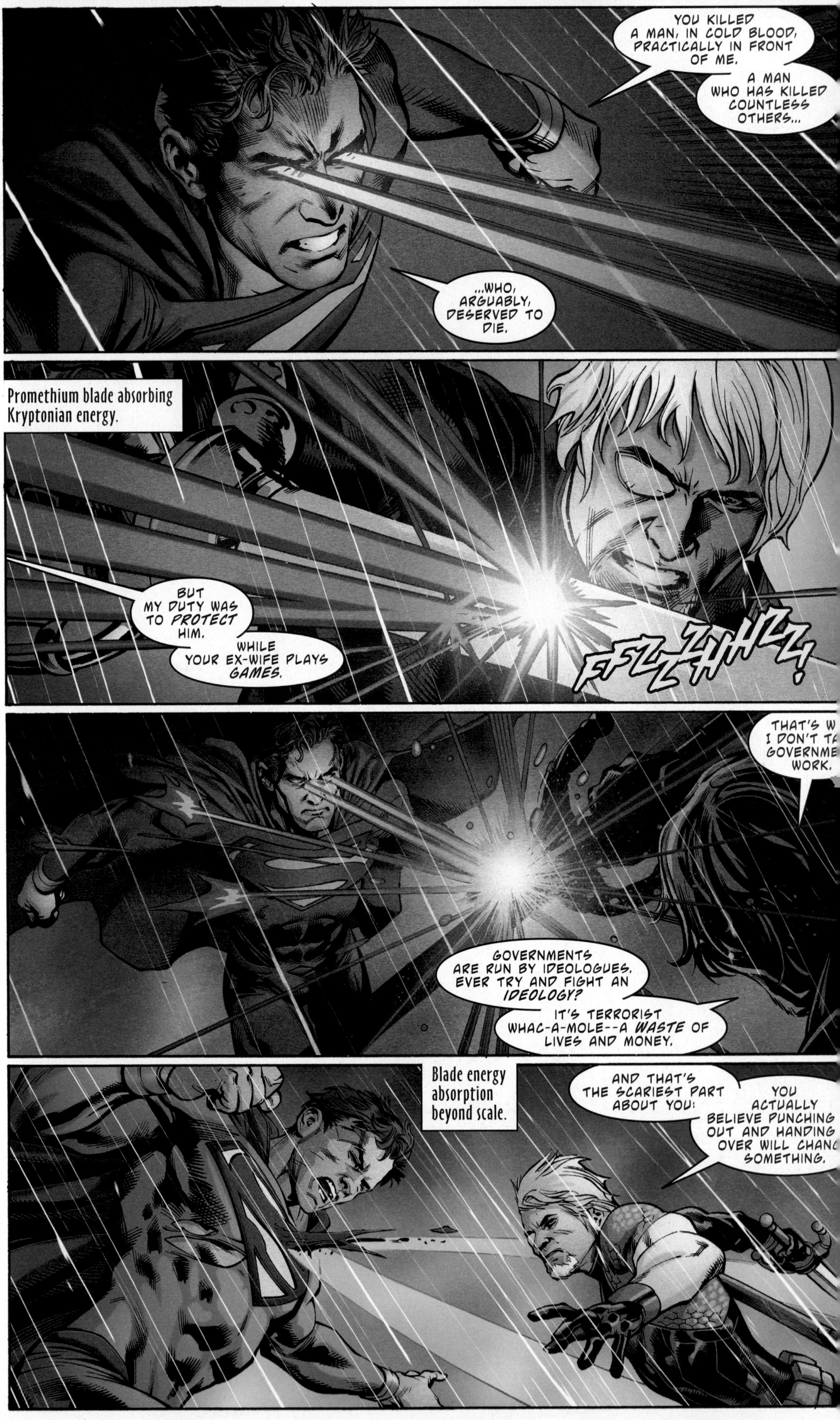
YOU KILLED A MAN, IN COLD BLOOD, PRACTICALLY IN FRONT OF ME.
A MAN WHO HAS KILLED COUNTLESS OTHERS...
...WHO, ARGUABLY, DESERVED TO DIE.
Promethium blade absorbing Kryptonian energy.
BUT MY DUTY WAS TO *PROTECT* HIM.
WHILE YOUR EX-WIFE PLAYS *GAMES.*
FFZZZHHZZ!
THAT'S W I DON'T TA GOVERNME WORK.
GOVERNMENTS ARE RUN BY IDEOLOGUES. EVER TRY AND FIGHT AN *IDEOLOGY?*
IT'S TERRORIST WHAC-A-MOLE--A *WASTE* OF LIVES AND MONEY.
Blade energy absorption beyond scale.
AND THAT'S THE SCARIEST PART ABOUT YOU:
YOU ACTUALLY BELIEVE PUNCHING OUT AND HANDING OVER WILL CHANG SOMETHING.

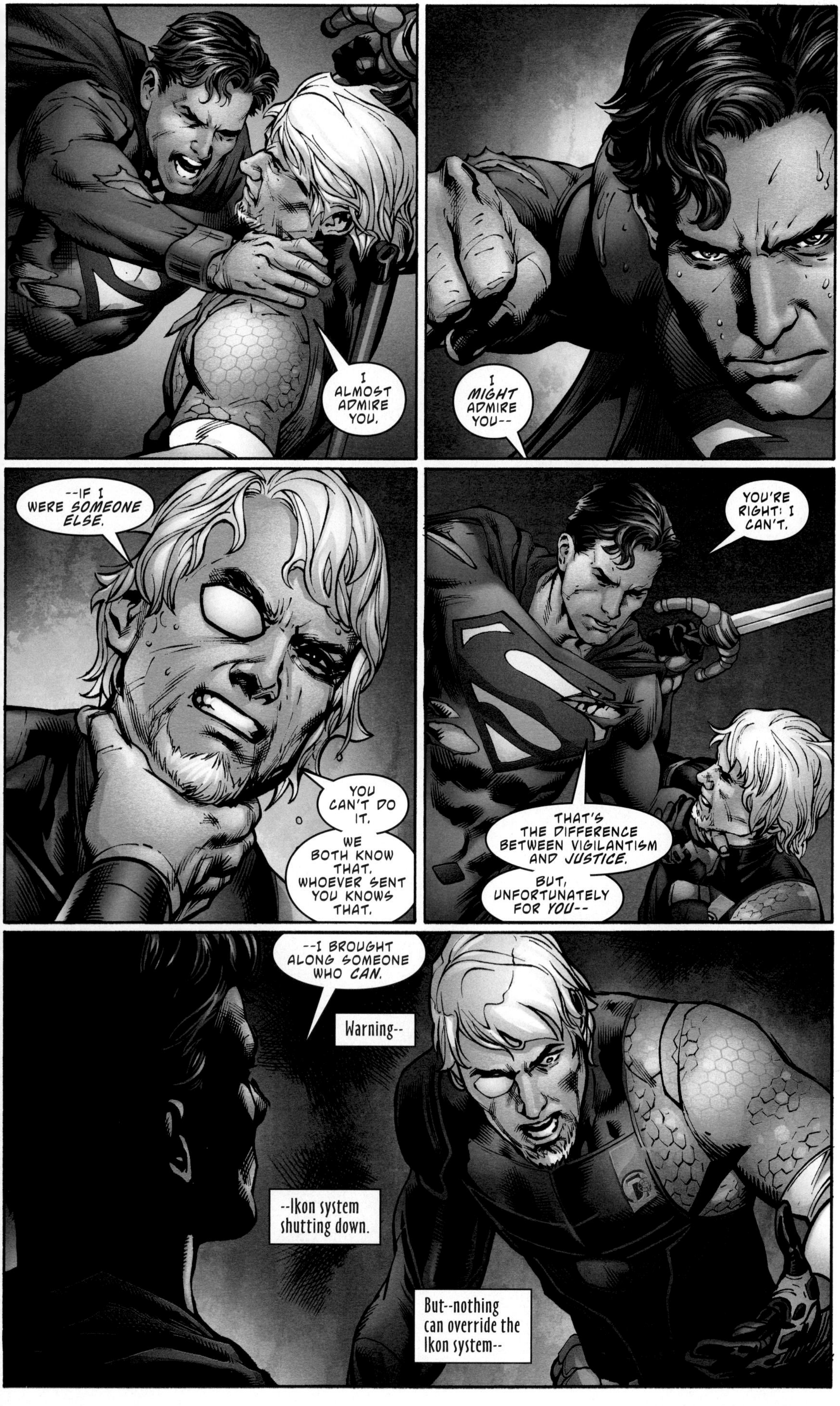
I ALMOST ADMIRE YOU.
I MIGHT ADMIRE YOU--
--IF I WERE SOMEONE ELSE.
YOU CAN'T DO IT.
WE BOTH KNOW THAT. WHOEVER SENT YOU KNOWS THAT.
YOU'RE RIGHT: I CAN'T.
THAT'S THE DIFFERENCE BETWEEN VIGILANTISM AND JUSTICE.
BUT, UNFORTUNATELY FOR YOU--
--I BROUGHT ALONG SOMEONE WHO CAN.
Warning--
--Ikon system shutting down.
But--nothing can override the Ikon system--

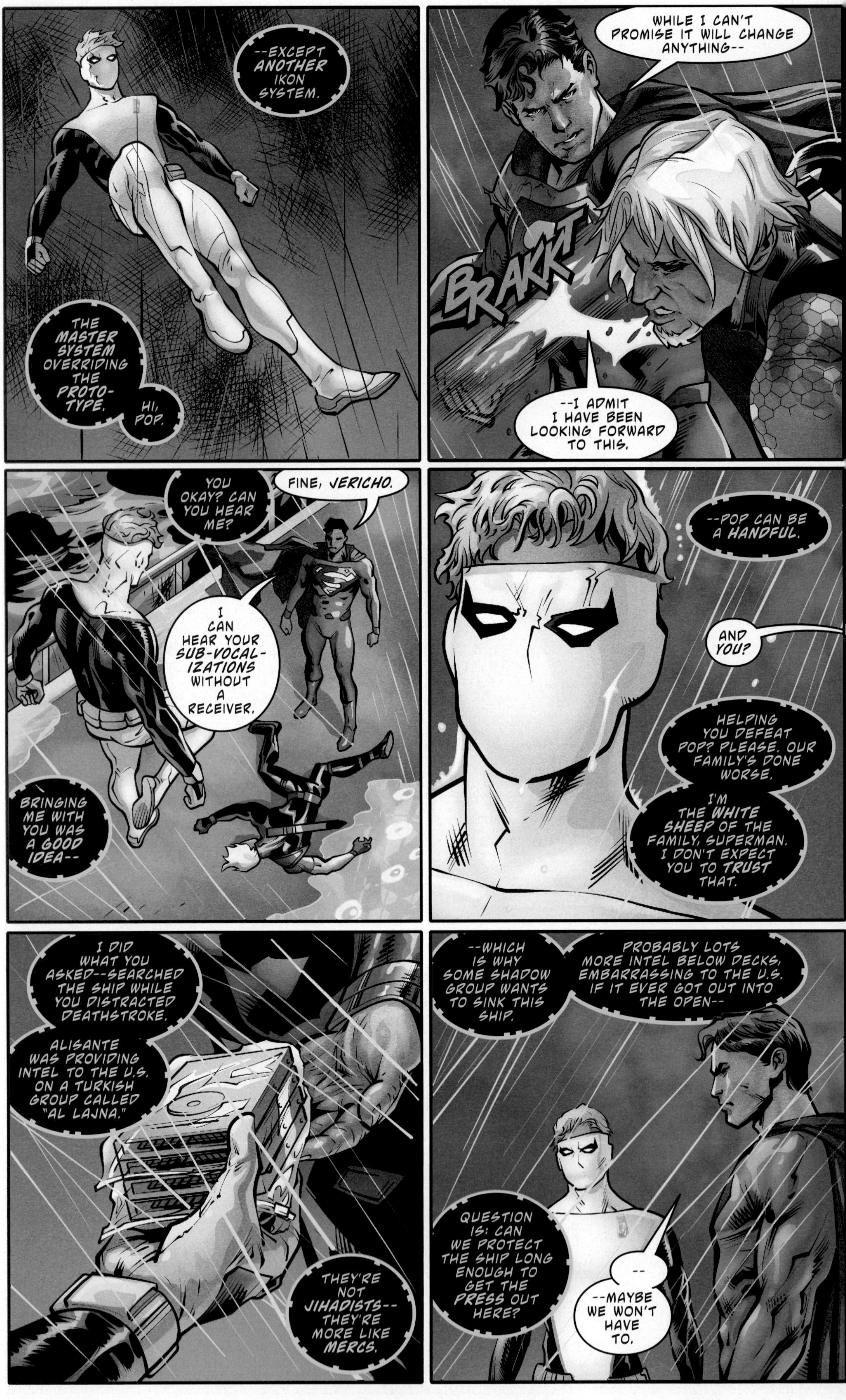
--EXCEPT ANOTHER IKON SYSTEM.
THE MASTER SYSTEM OVERRIDING THE PROTOTYPE.
HI, POP.
WHILE I CAN'T PROMISE IT WILL CHANGE ANYTHING--
BRAKKT
--I ADMIT I HAVE BEEN LOOKING FORWARD TO THIS.
YOU OKAY? CAN YOU HEAR ME?
FINE, JERICHO.
I CAN HEAR YOUR SUB-VOCALIZATIONS WITHOUT A RECEIVER.
BRINGING ME WITH YOU WAS A GOOD IDEA--
--POP CAN BE A HANDFUL.
AND YOU?
HELPING YOU DEFEAT POP? PLEASE. OUR FAMILY'S DONE WORSE.
I'M THE WHITE SHEEP OF THE FAMILY, SUPERMAN. I DON'T EXPECT YOU TO TRUST THAT.
I DID WHAT YOU ASKED--SEARCHED THE SHIP WHILE YOU DISTRACTED DEATHSTROKE.
ALISANTE WAS PROVIDING INTEL TO THE U.S. ON A TURKISH GROUP CALLED "AL LAJNA."
THEY'RE NOT JIHADISTS--THEY'RE MORE LIKE MERCS.
PROBABLY LOTS MORE INTEL BELOW DECKS, EMBARRASSING TO THE U.S. IF IT EVER GOT OUT INTO THE OPEN--
--WHICH IS WHY SOME SHADOW GROUP WANTS TO SINK THIS SHIP.
QUESTION IS: CAN WE PROTECT THE SHIP LONG ENOUGH TO GET THE PRESS OUT HERE?
--
--MAYBE WE WON'T HAVE TO.

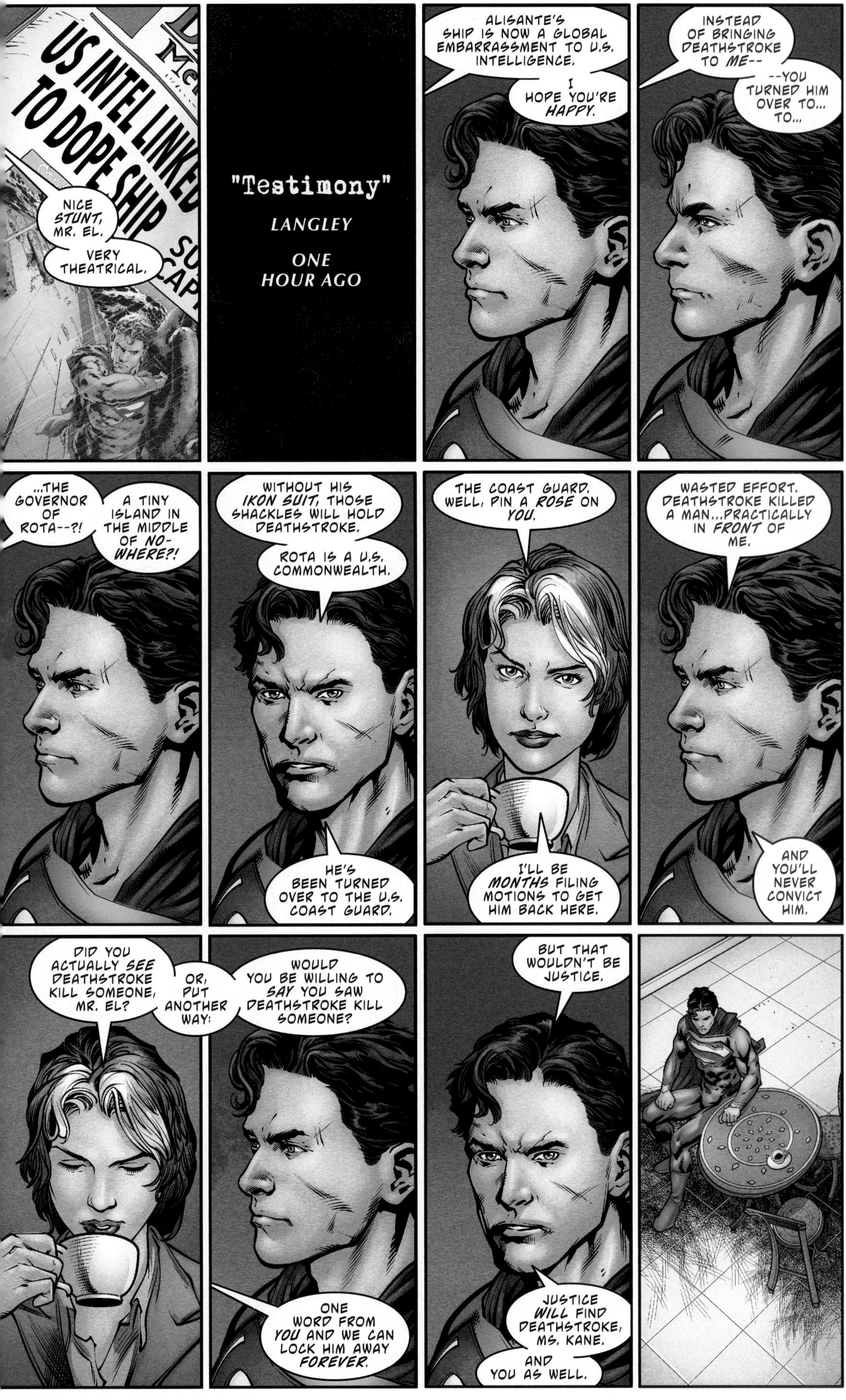
US INTEL LINKED TO DOPE SHIP
NICE STUNT, MR. EL.
VERY THEATRICAL.
"Testimony"
LANGLEY
ONE HOUR AGO
ALISANTE'S SHIP IS NOW A GLOBAL EMBARRASSMENT TO U.S. INTELLIGENCE.
I HOPE YOU'RE HAPPY.
INSTEAD OF BRINGING DEATHSTROKE TO ME--
--YOU TURNED HIM OVER TO... TO...
...THE GOVERNOR OF ROTA--?!
A TINY ISLAND IN THE MIDDLE OF NO-WHERE?!
WITHOUT HIS IKON SUIT, THOSE SHACKLES WILL HOLD DEATHSTROKE.
ROTA IS A U.S. COMMONWEALTH.
HE'S BEEN TURNED OVER TO THE U.S. COAST GUARD.
THE COAST GUARD. WELL, PIN A ROSE ON YOU.
I'LL BE MONTHS FILING MOTIONS TO GET HIM BACK HERE.
WASTED EFFORT. DEATHSTROKE KILLED A MAN...PRACTICALLY IN FRONT OF ME.
AND YOU'LL NEVER CONVICT HIM.
DID YOU ACTUALLY SEE DEATHSTROKE KILL SOMEONE, MR. EL?
OR, PUT ANOTHER WAY:
WOULD YOU BE WILLING TO SAY YOU SAW DEATHSTROKE KILL SOMEONE?
ONE WORD FROM YOU AND WE CAN LOCK HIM AWAY FOREVER.
BUT THAT WOULDN'T BE JUSTICE.
JUSTICE WILL FIND DEATHSTROKE, MS. KANE.
AND YOU AS WELL.

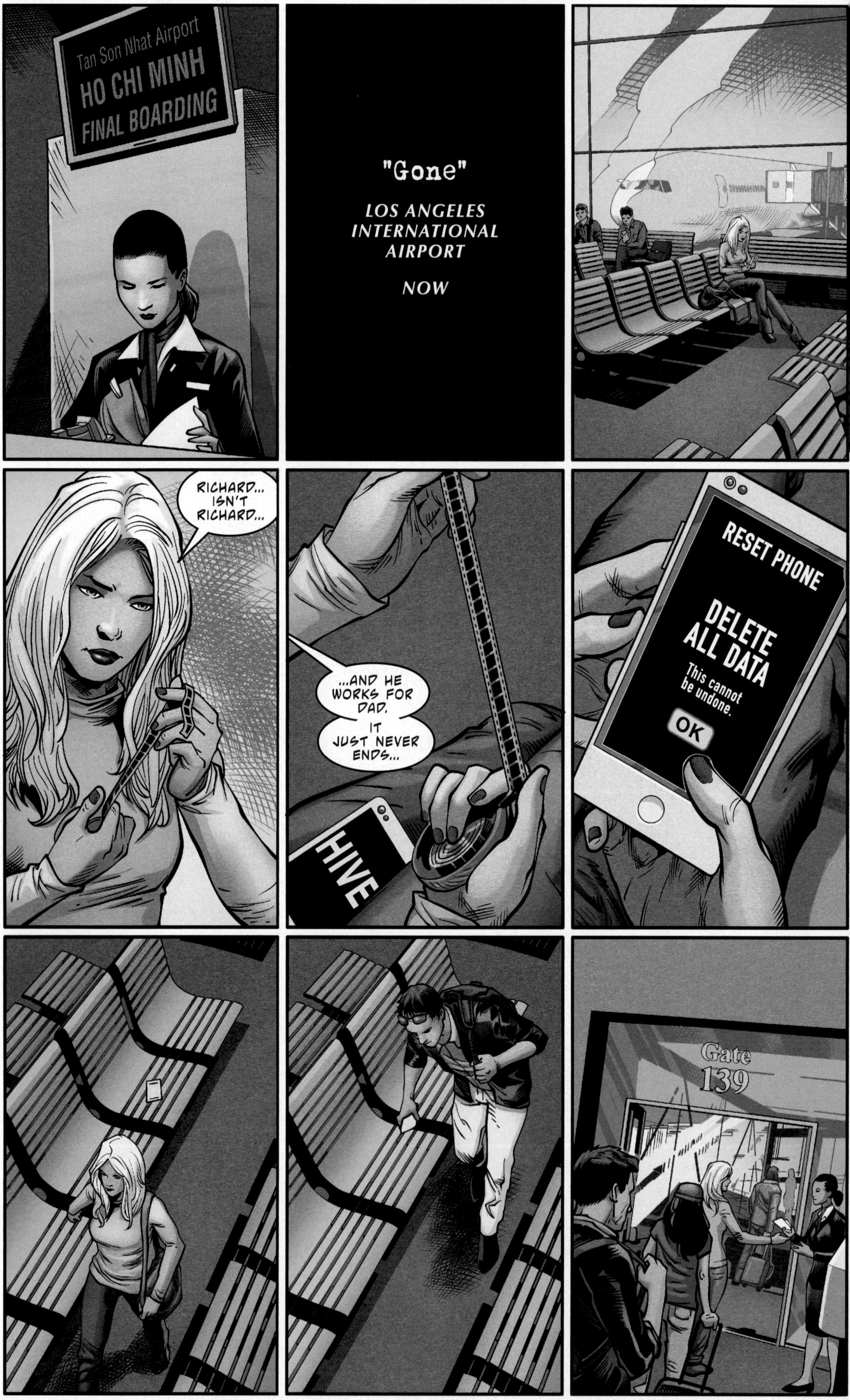
Tan Son Nhat Airport
HO CHI MINH
FINAL BOARDING
"Gone"
LOS ANGELES INTERNATIONAL AIRPORT
NOW
RICHARD... ISN'T RICHARD...
...AND HE WORKS FOR DAD.
IT JUST NEVER ENDS...
HIVE
RESET PHONE
DELETE ALL DATA
This cannot be undone.
OK
Gate
139

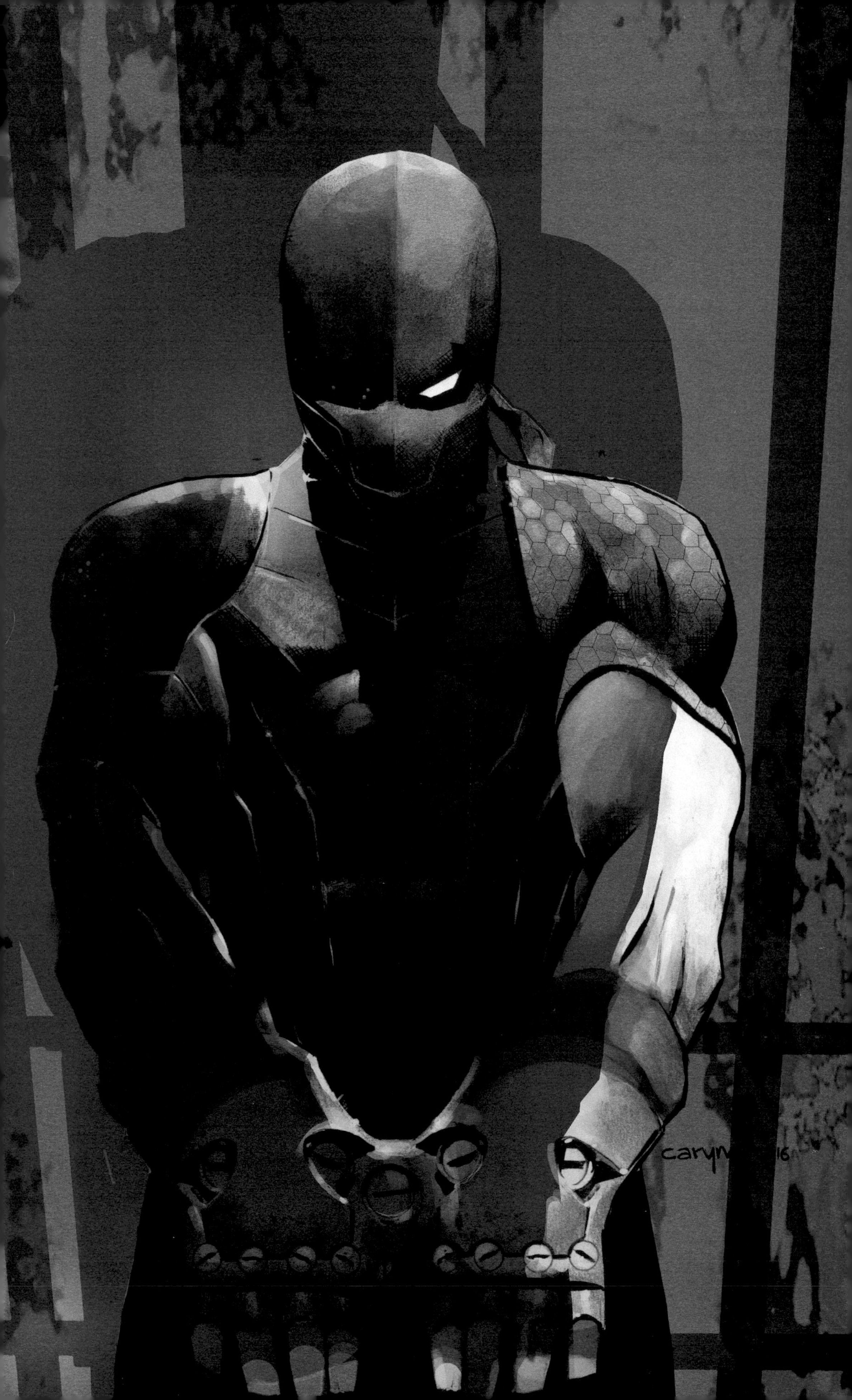

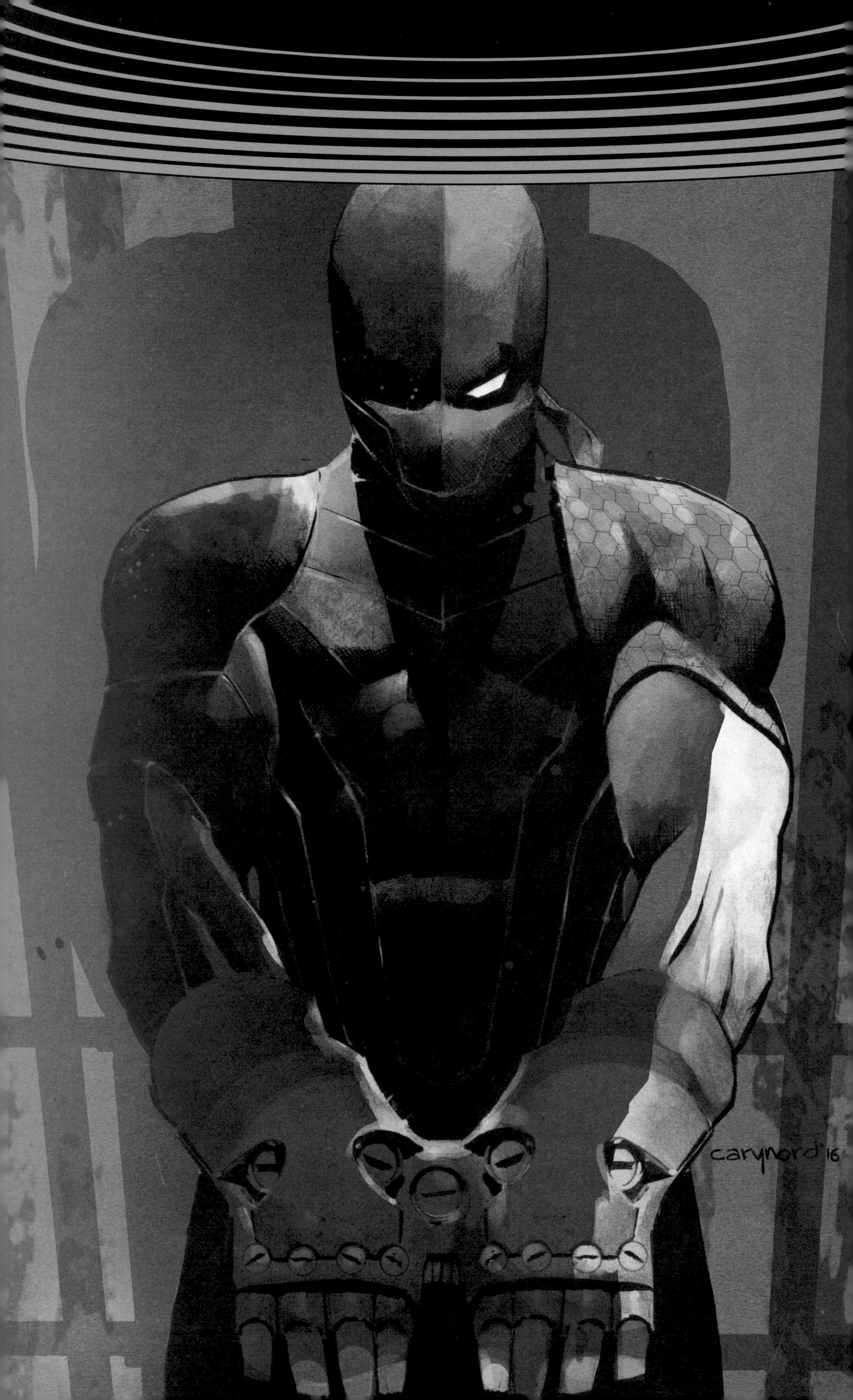
carynord '16

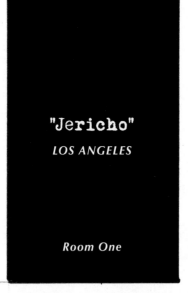

"Jericho"

LOS ANGELES

Room One

HOW LONG HAS HE BEEN WAITING?

THREE HOURS.

IT'S A LITTLE CREEPY.

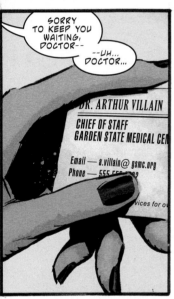

SORRY TO KEEP YOU WAITING, DOCTOR--

--UH... DOCTOR...

DR. ARTHUR VILLAIN

CHIEF OF STAFF
GARDEN STATE MEDICAL CEN

Email — a.villain@gsmc.org
Phone — 555-555-

...vices for ov

...VILLAIN...?

→SIGH←

IT'S WILL-HANE. IT'S FRENCH.

OF COURSE IT IS.

I'M ÉTIENNE, MR. WILSON'S AID.

HE'S AT LUNCH... IS THERE ANYTHING I CAN DO FOR YOU...?

NO.

--

OKAY, THEN.

I'LL BE BACK AS SOON AS JOSEPH RETURNS, SHOULDN'T BE LONG...

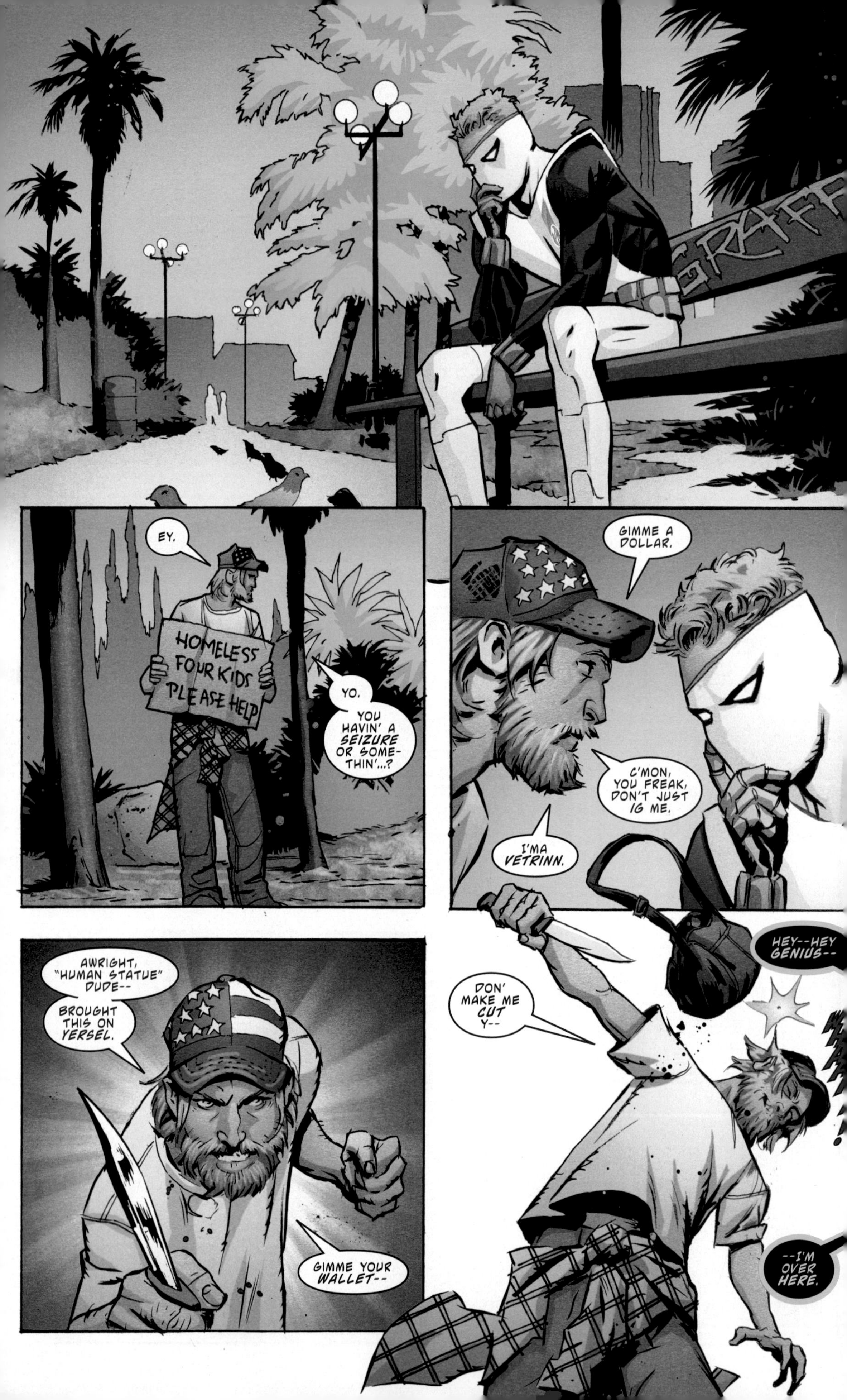
GRAFF
EY.
HOMELESS FOUR KIDS PLEASE HELP
YO.
YOU HAVIN' A SEIZURE OR SOME-THIN'...?
GIMME A DOLLAR.
C'MON, YOU FREAK, DON'T JUST IG ME.
I'MA VETRINN.
AWRIGHT, "HUMAN STATUE" DUDE--
BROUGHT THIS ON YERSEL.
GIMME YOUR WALLET--
DON' MAKE ME CUT Y--
HEY--HEY GENIUS--
--I'M OVER HERE.

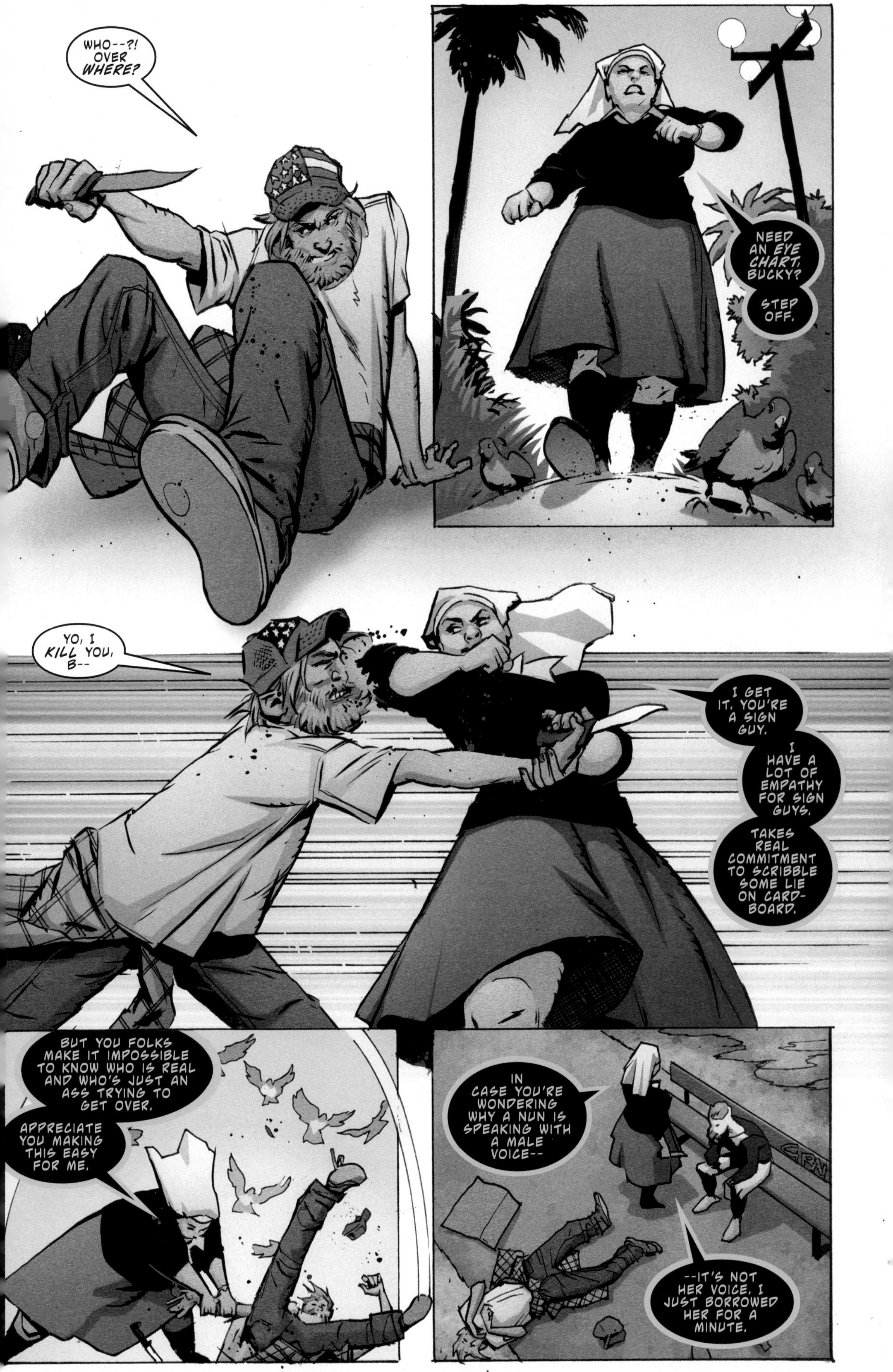

WHO--?! OVER WHERE?
NEED AN EYE CHART, BUCKY?
STEP OFF.
YO, I KILL YOU, B--
I GET IT, YOU'RE A SIGN GUY.
I HAVE A LOT OF EMPATHY FOR SIGN GUYS.
TAKES REAL COMMITMENT TO SCRIBBLE SOME LIE ON CARD-BOARD.
BUT YOU FOLKS MAKE IT IMPOSSIBLE TO KNOW WHO IS REAL AND WHO'S JUST AN ASS TRYING TO GET OVER.
APPRECIATE YOU MAKING THIS EASY FOR ME.
IN CASE YOU'RE WONDERING WHY A NUN IS SPEAKING WITH A MALE VOICE--
--IT'S NOT HER VOICE. I JUST BORROWED HER FOR A MINUTE.

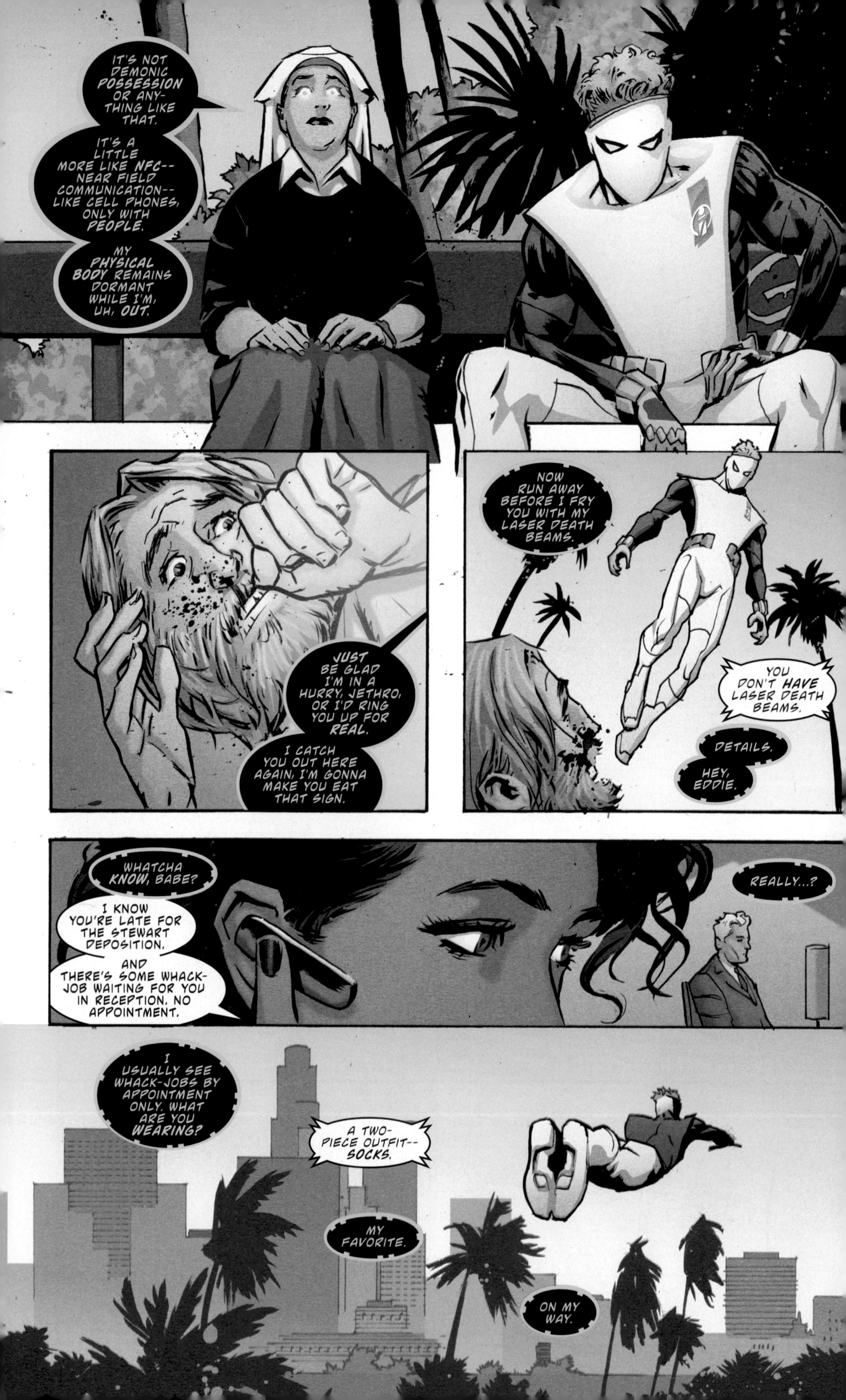
IT'S NOT DEMONIC POSSESSION OR ANYTHING LIKE THAT.
IT'S A LITTLE MORE LIKE NFC-- NEAR FIELD COMMUNICATION-- LIKE CELL PHONES, ONLY WITH PEOPLE.
MY PHYSICAL BODY REMAINS DORMANT WHILE I'M, UH, OUT.
JUST BE GLAD I'M IN A HURRY, JETHRO, OR I'D RING YOU UP FOR REAL.
I CATCH YOU OUT HERE AGAIN, I'M GONNA MAKE YOU EAT THAT SIGN.
NOW RUN AWAY BEFORE I FRY YOU WITH MY LASER DEATH BEAMS.
YOU DON'T HAVE LASER DEATH BEAMS.
DETAILS.
HEY, EDDIE.
WHATCHA KNOW, BABE?
I KNOW YOU'RE LATE FOR THE STEWART DEPOSITION.
AND THERE'S SOME WHACK-JOB WAITING FOR YOU IN RECEPTION. NO APPOINTMENT.
REALLY...?
I USUALLY SEE WHACK-JOBS BY APPOINTMENT ONLY. WHAT ARE YOU WEARING?
A TWO-PIECE OUTFIT-- SOCKS.
MY FAVORITE.
ON MY WAY.

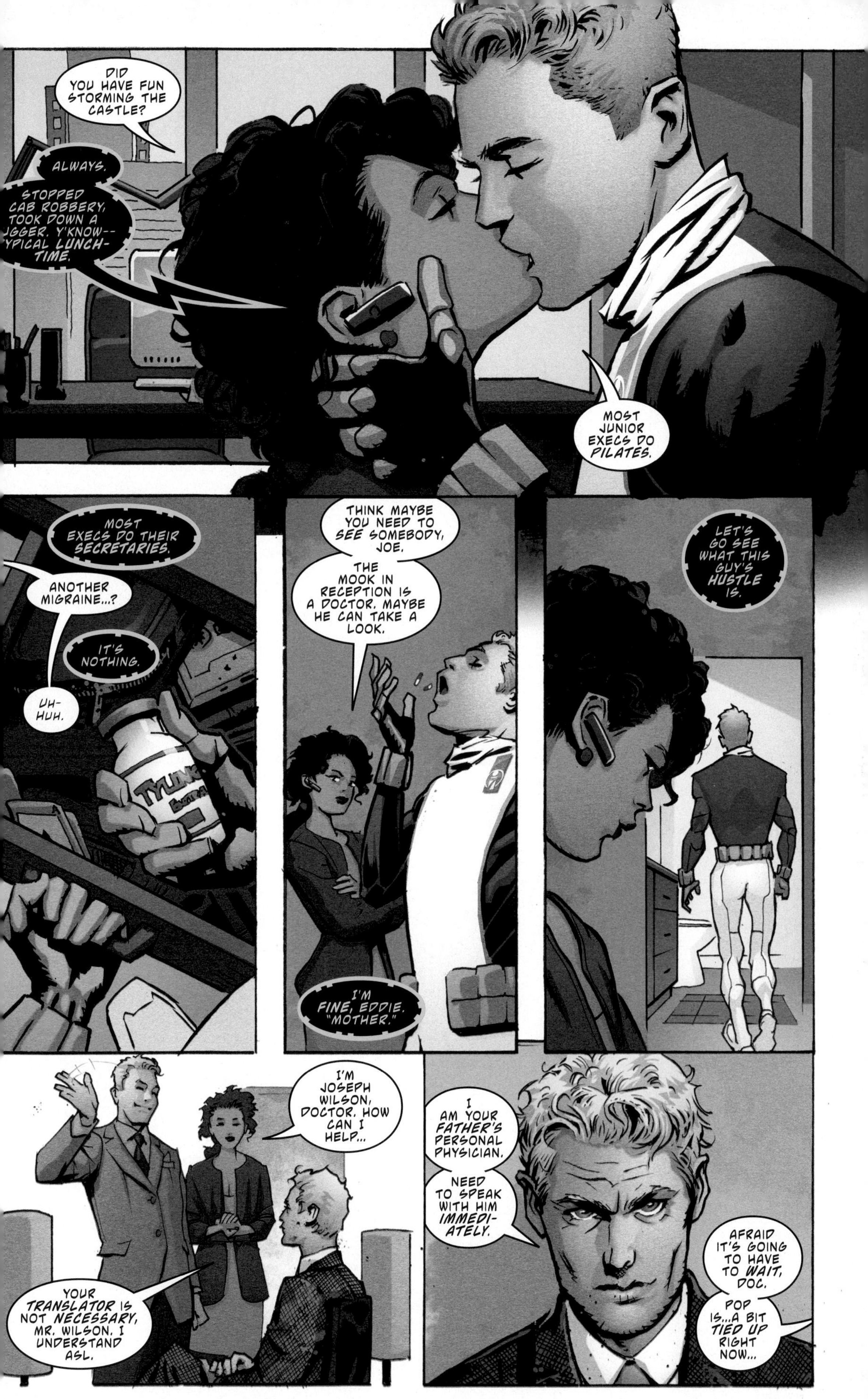
DID YOU HAVE FUN STORMING THE CASTLE?
ALWAYS.
STOPPED CAB ROBBERY, TOOK DOWN A UGGER. Y'KNOW-- YPICAL LUNCH-TIME.
MOST JUNIOR EXECS DO PILATES.
MOST EXECS DO THEIR SECRETARIES.
ANOTHER MIGRAINE...?
IT'S NOTHING.
UH-HUH.
THINK MAYBE YOU NEED TO SEE SOMEBODY, JOE.
THE MOOK IN RECEPTION IS A DOCTOR. MAYBE HE CAN TAKE A LOOK.
I'M FINE, EDDIE. "MOTHER."
LET'S GO SEE WHAT THIS GUY'S HUSTLE IS.
I'M JOSEPH WILSON, DOCTOR. HOW CAN I HELP...
YOUR TRANSLATOR IS NOT NECESSARY, MR. WILSON. I UNDERSTAND ASL.
I AM YOUR FATHER'S PERSONAL PHYSICIAN.
NEED TO SPEAK WITH HIM IMMEDI-ATELY.
AFRAID IT'S GOING TO HAVE TO WAIT, DOC.
POP IS...A BIT TIED UP RIGHT NOW...

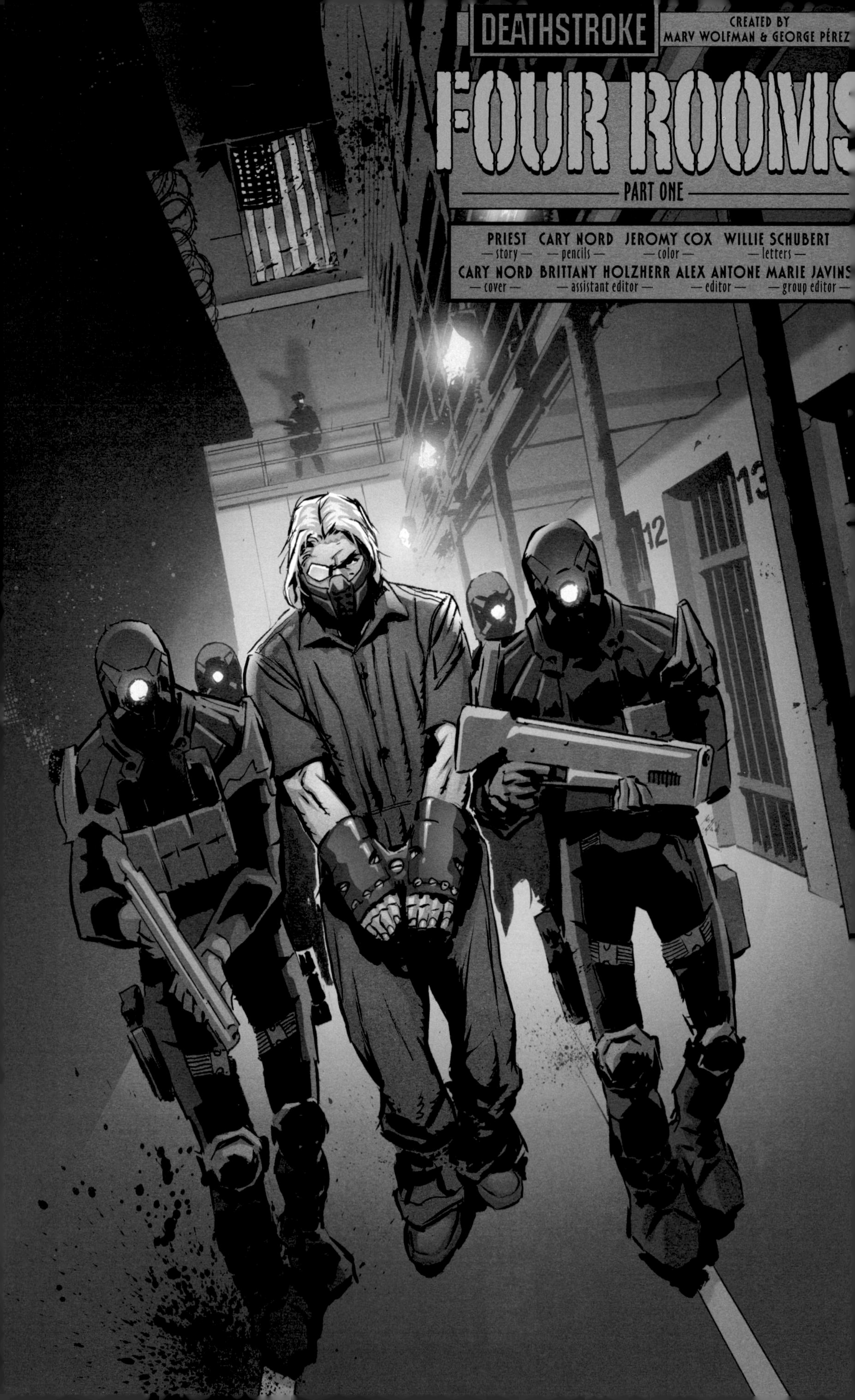
DEATHSTROKE
CREATED BY
MARV WOLFMAN & GEORGE PÉREZ
FOUR ROOMS
PART ONE
PRIEST — story —
CARY NORD — pencils —
JEROMY COX — color —
WILLIE SCHUBERT — letters —
CARY NORD — cover —
BRITTANY HOLZHERR — assistant editor —
ALEX ANTONE — editor —
MARIE JAVINS — group editor —
12
13

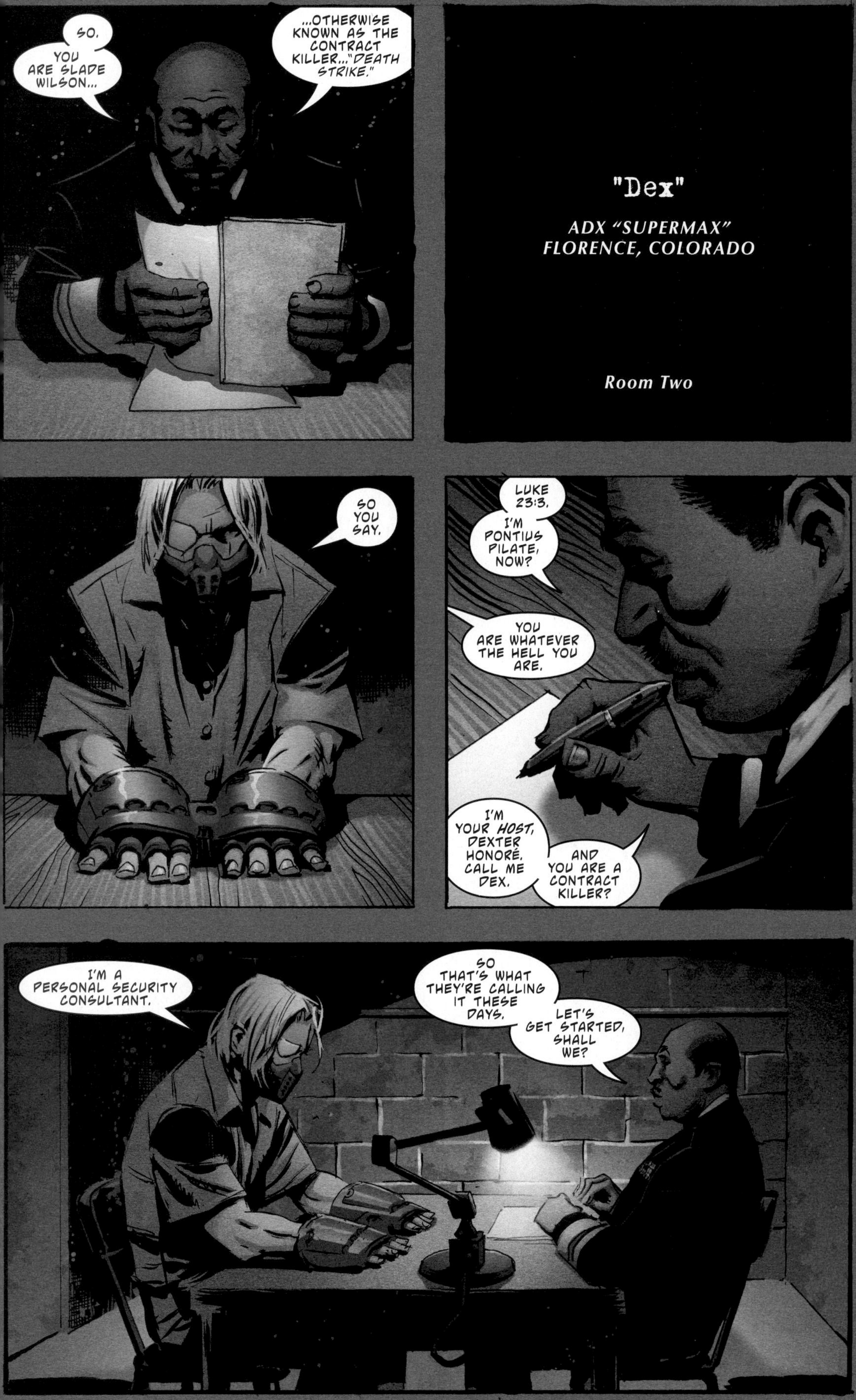
SO. YOU ARE SLADE WILSON...
...OTHERWISE KNOWN AS THE CONTRACT KILLER..."DEATH STRIKE."
"Dex"
ADX "SUPERMAX"
FLORENCE, COLORADO
Room Two
SO YOU SAY.
LUKE 23:3. I'M PONTIUS PILATE, NOW?
YOU ARE WHATEVER THE HELL YOU ARE.
I'M YOUR HOST, DEXTER HONORÉ. CALL ME DEX.
AND YOU ARE A CONTRACT KILLER?
I'M A PERSONAL SECURITY CONSULTANT.
SO THAT'S WHAT THEY'RE CALLING IT THESE DAYS.
LET'S GET STARTED, SHALL WE?

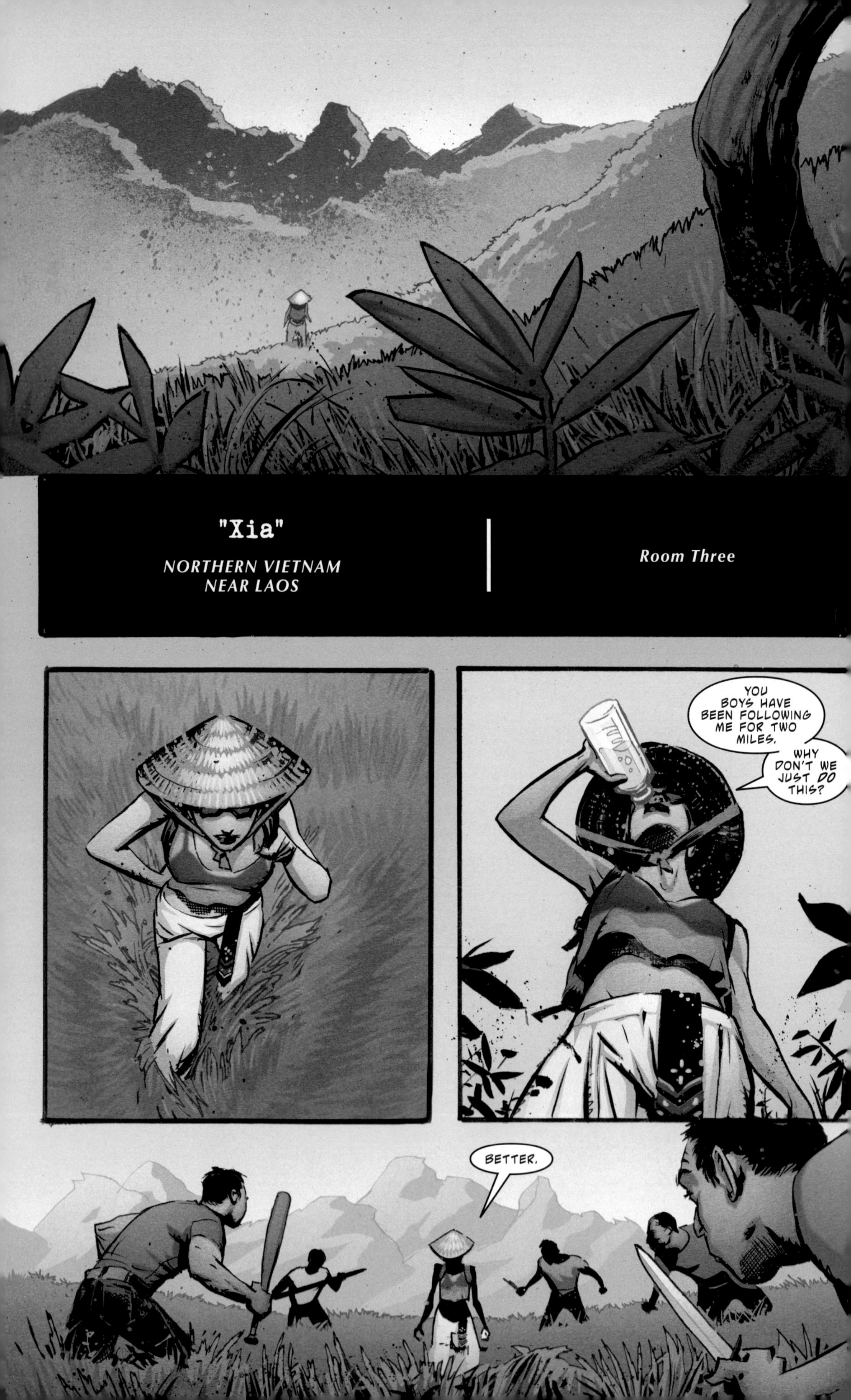
"Xia"
NORTHERN VIETNAM
NEAR LAOS
Room Three
YOU BOYS HAVE BEEN FOLLOWING ME FOR TWO MILES.
WHY DON'T WE JUST DO THIS?
BETTER.

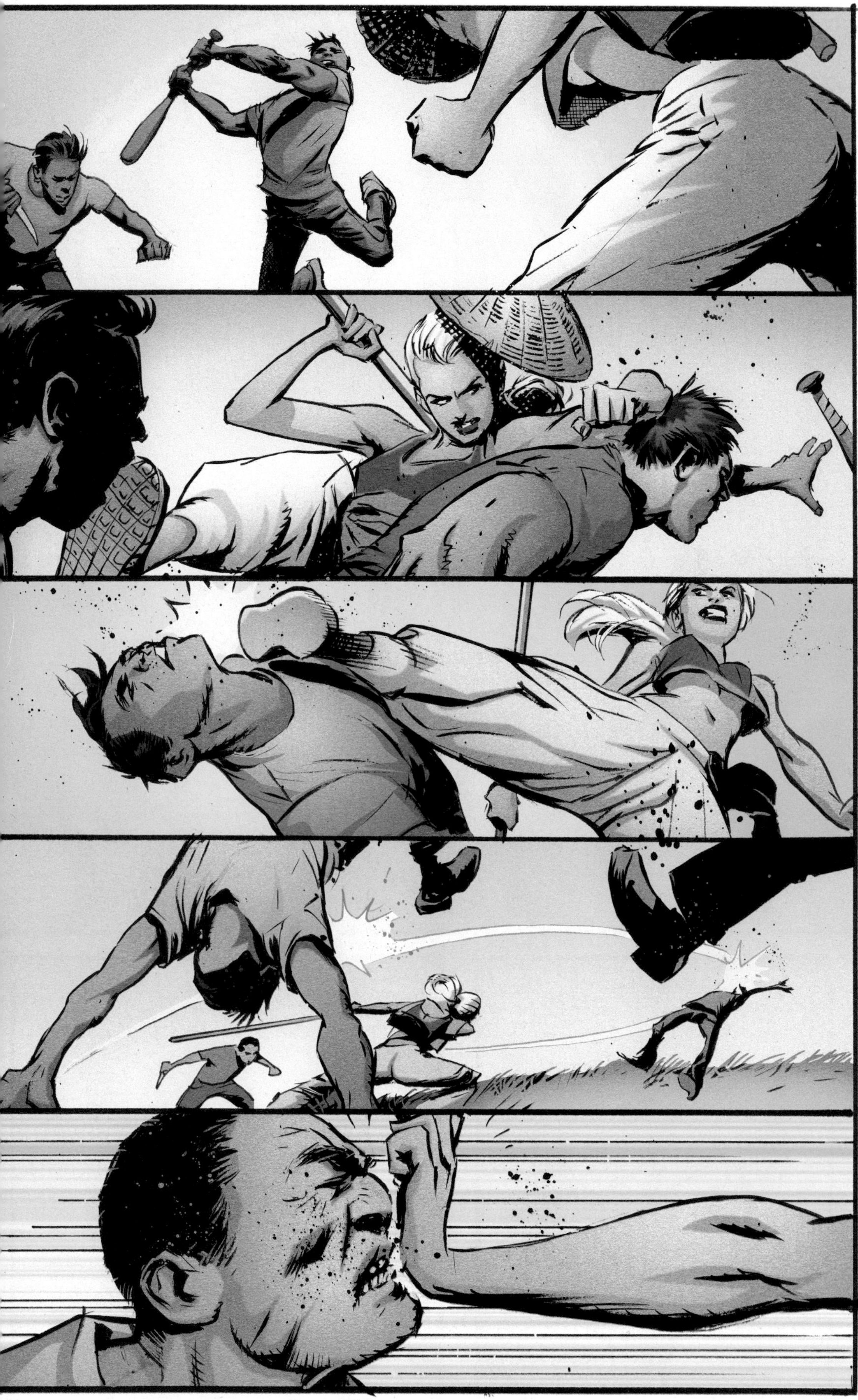

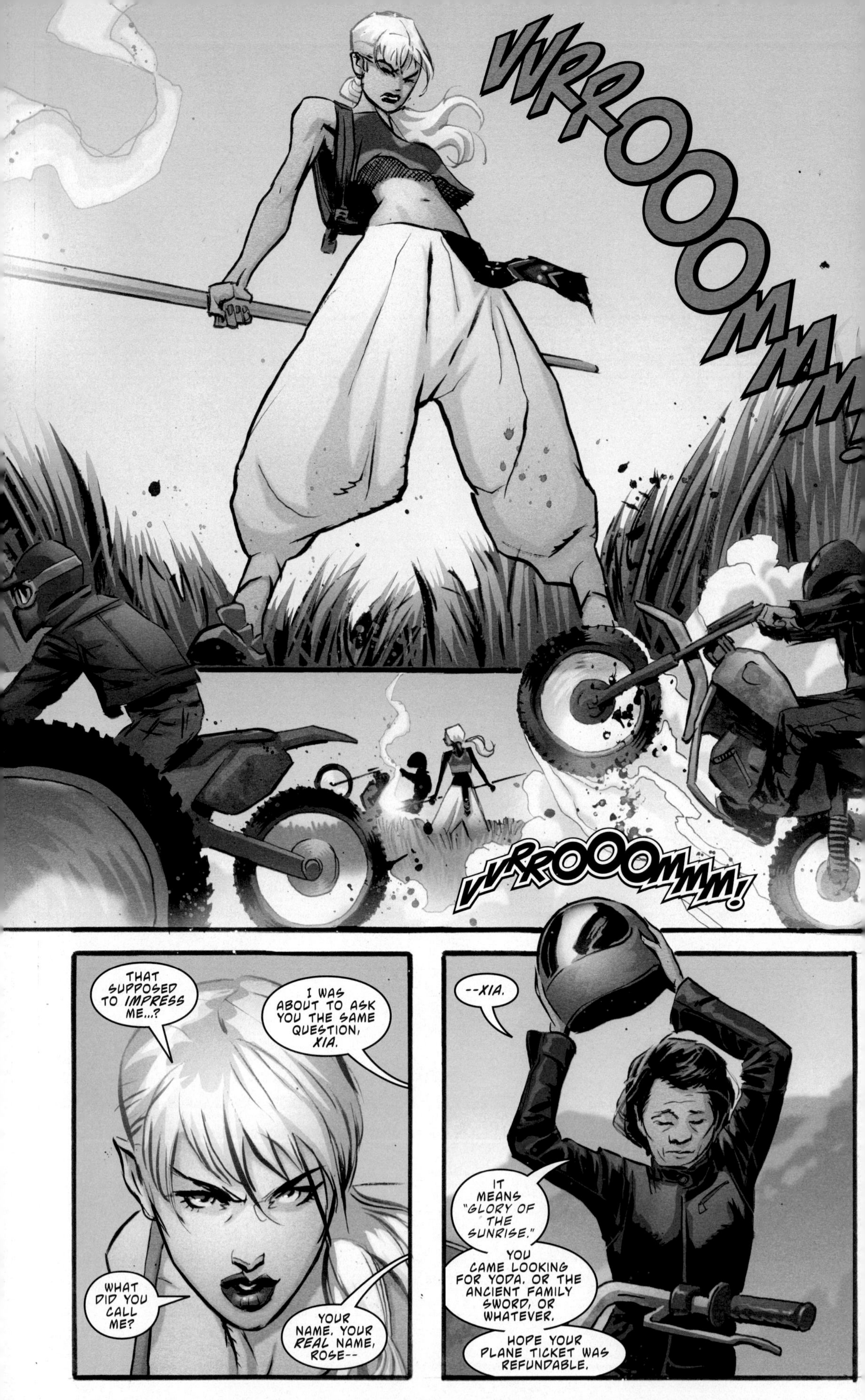
VVRROOOOMMM!
VVRROOOOMMMM!
THAT SUPPOSED TO *IMPRESS* ME...?
I WAS ABOUT TO ASK YOU THE SAME QUESTION, *XIA.*
WHAT DID YOU CALL ME?
YOUR NAME. YOUR *REAL* NAME, ROSE--
--XIA.
IT MEANS "GLORY OF THE SUNRISE."
YOU CAME LOOKING FOR YODA. OR THE ANCIENT FAMILY SWORD, OR WHATEVER.
HOPE YOUR PLANE TICKET WAS REFUNDABLE.

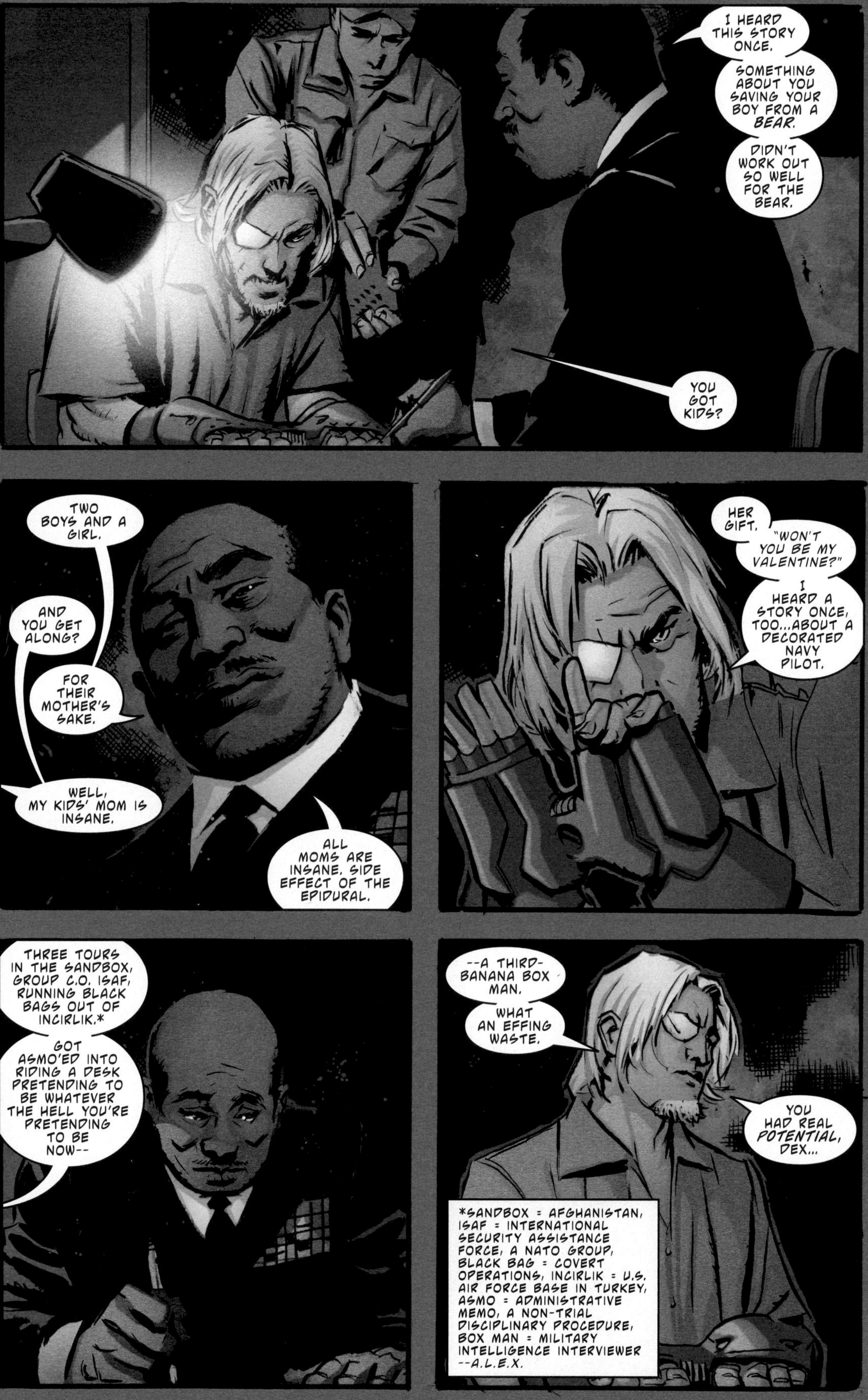
I HEARD THIS STORY ONCE.
SOMETHING ABOUT YOU SAVING YOUR BOY FROM A BEAR.
DIDN'T WORK OUT SO WELL FOR THE BEAR.
YOU GOT KIDS?
TWO BOYS AND A GIRL.
AND YOU GET ALONG?
FOR THEIR MOTHER'S SAKE.
WELL, MY KIDS' MOM IS INSANE.
ALL MOMS ARE INSANE. SIDE EFFECT OF THE EPIDURAL.
HER GIFT.
"WON'T YOU BE MY VALENTINE?"
I HEARD A STORY ONCE, TOO...ABOUT A DECORATED NAVY PILOT.
THREE TOURS IN THE SANDBOX, GROUP C.O. ISAF, RUNNING BLACK BAGS OUT OF INCIRLIK.*
GOT ASMO'ED INTO RIDING A DESK PRETENDING TO BE WHATEVER THE HELL YOU'RE PRETENDING TO BE NOW--
--A THIRD-BANANA BOX MAN.
WHAT AN EFFING WASTE.
YOU HAD REAL POTENTIAL, DEX...
*SANDBOX = AFGHANISTAN, ISAF = INTERNATIONAL SECURITY ASSISTANCE FORCE, A NATO GROUP, BLACK BAG = COVERT OPERATIONS, INCIRLIK = U.S. AIR FORCE BASE IN TURKEY, ASMO = ADMINISTRATIVE MEMO, A NON-TRIAL DISCIPLINARY PROCEDURE, BOX MAN = MILITARY INTELLIGENCE INTERVIEWER --A.L.E.X.

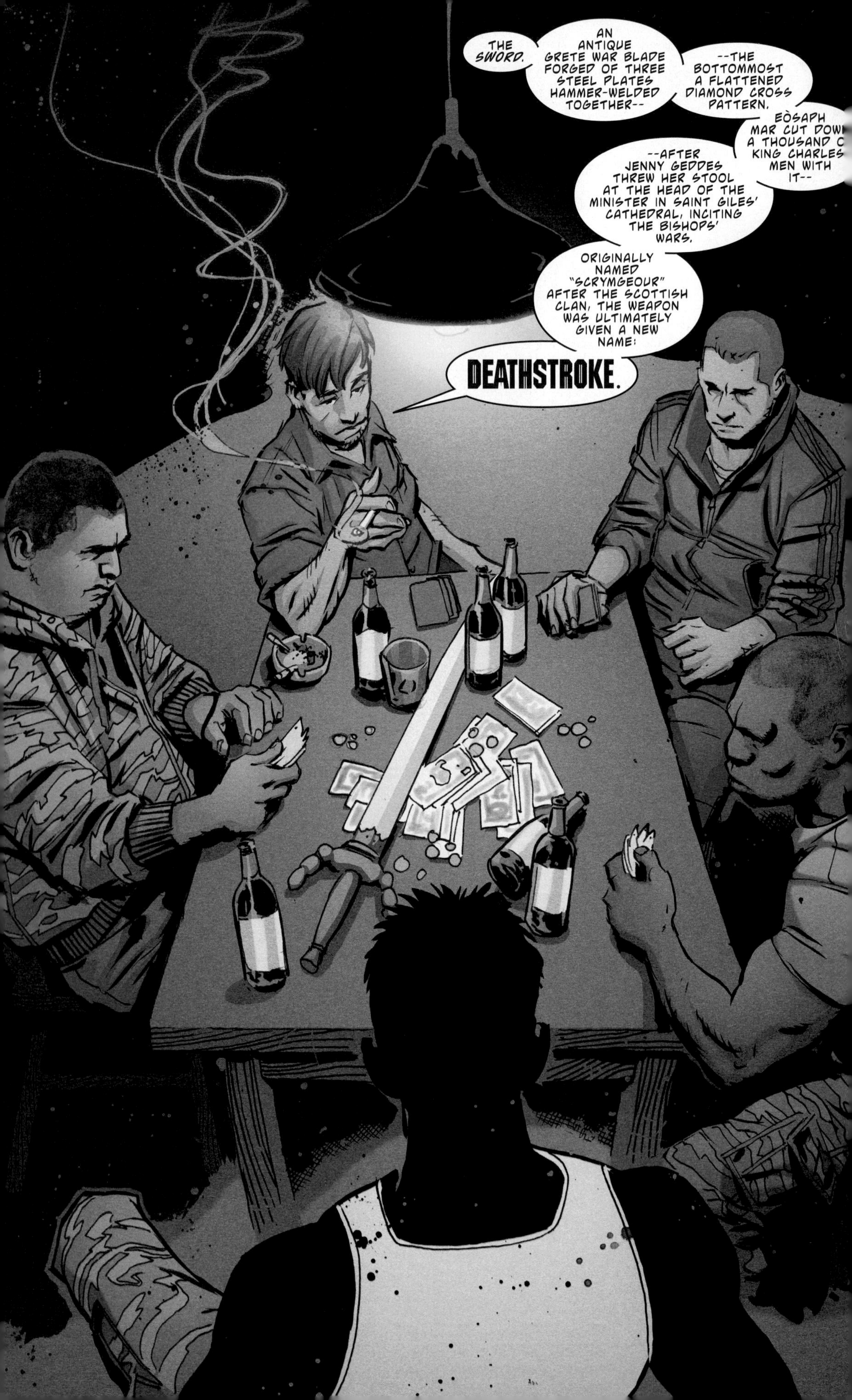
THE SWORD.
AN ANTIQUE GRETE WAR BLADE FORGED OF THREE STEEL PLATES HAMMER-WELDED TOGETHER--
--THE BOTTOMMOST A FLATTENED DIAMOND CROSS PATTERN.
EÒSAPH MAR CUT DOWN A THOUSAND OF KING CHARLES' MEN WITH IT--
--AFTER JENNY GEDDES THREW HER STOOL AT THE HEAD OF THE MINISTER IN SAINT GILES' CATHEDRAL, INCITING THE BISHOPS' WARS.
ORIGINALLY NAMED "SCRYMGEOUR" AFTER THE SCOTTISH CLAN, THE WEAPON WAS ULTIMATELY GIVEN A NEW NAME:
DEATHSTROKE.

OR, AT LEAST, THAT'S THE STORY OUR CROAT MATE TELLS OL' FREDRIC.

OR ARE YOU A *SERB?* WHO CAN TELL.

WHO GIVES A FLOCK.

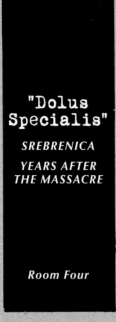

"Dolus Specialis"

SREBRENICA

YEARS AFTER THE MASSACRE

Room Four

EIGHTEEN HOURS OF *BAD HANDS,* HE BETS THE FAMILY HEIRLOOM.

RUBBISH. THING'S STAMPED "MADE IN TAIWAN."

TWO HUNNERD, FREDRIC. WHAT ABOUT *YOU,* SURFER BOY?

FULL BOAT, BELG.

QUEENS FULL OF NINES.

TI VARAO.

CAN'T BE SURE MATE, BUTTUH THIN 'AT LIKELY TRANSLATES TO "BOLLOCKS"...

OH PLEASE, RAX--

--IT'S HIS FAMILY SWORD. 'ES OBVIOUSLY AN EXPERT--

EY, YO, YOU REALLY DON'T WANNA BE *DOIN'* THIS--

SKRIGM-SKRAKKTT!

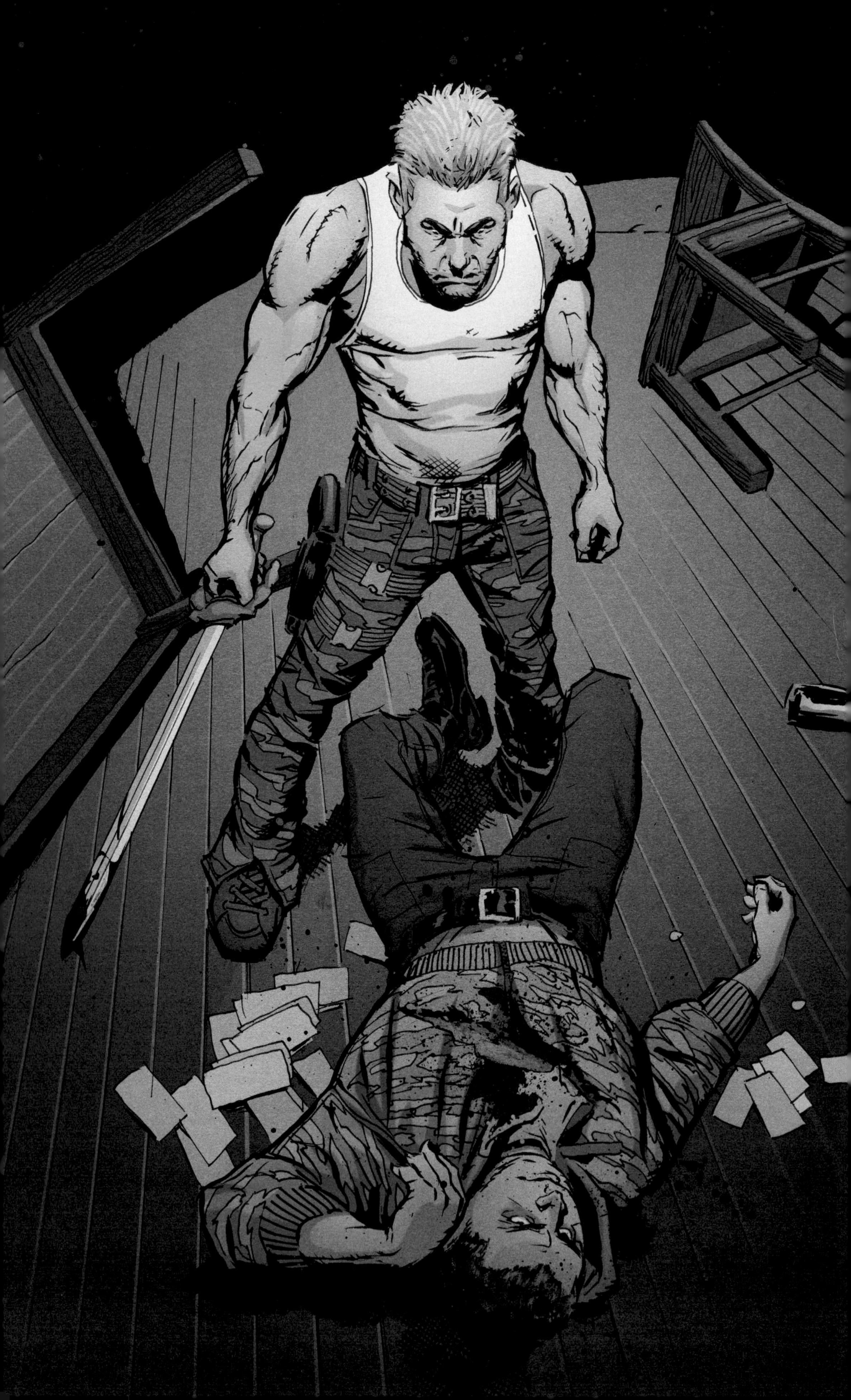

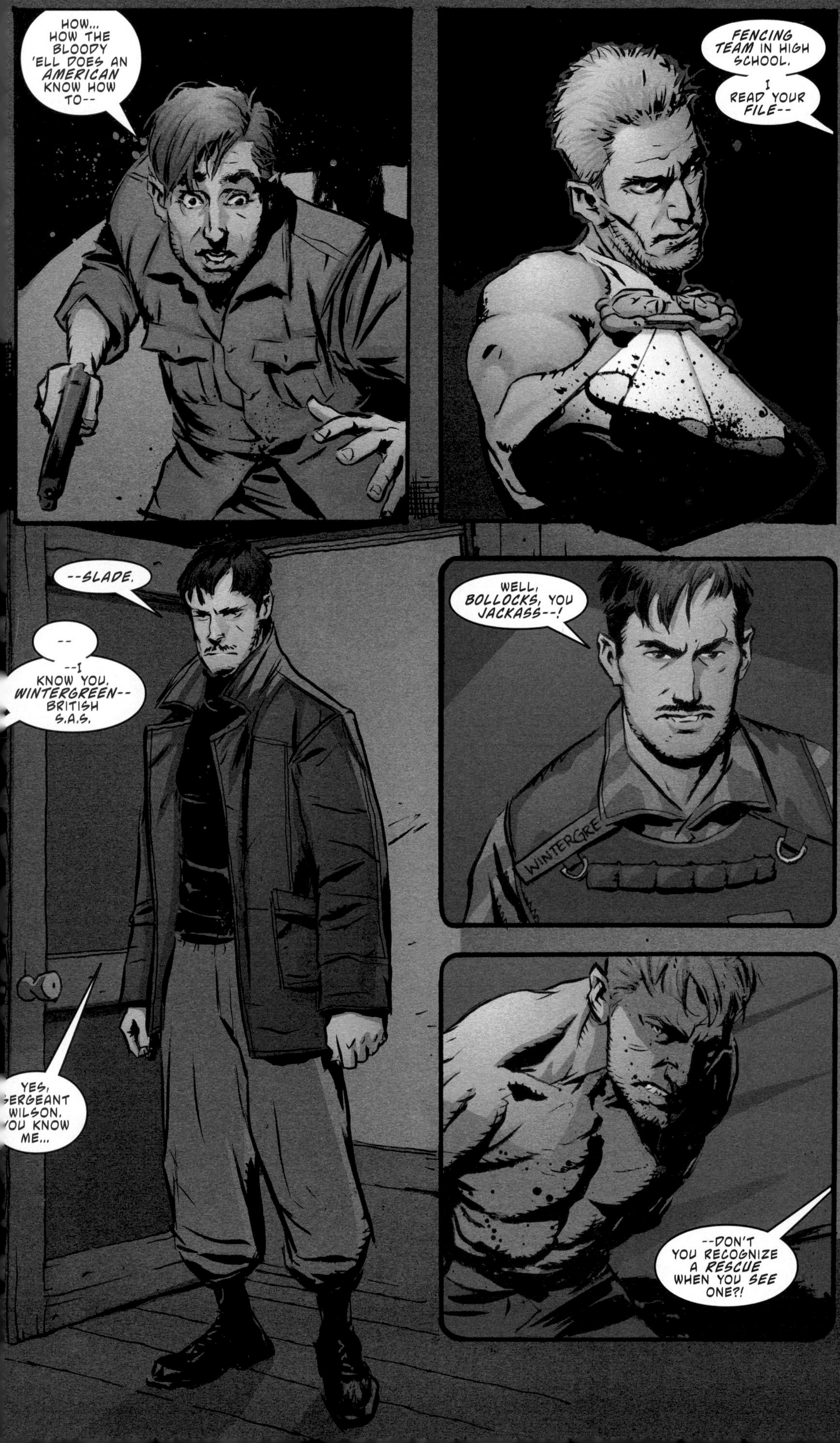
HOW... HOW THE BLOODY 'ELL DOES AN *AMERICAN* KNOW HOW TO--
FENCING TEAM IN HIGH SCHOOL.
I READ YOUR *FILE*--
--SLADE.
--
--I KNOW YOU. *WINTERGREEN*-- BRITISH S.A.S.
YES, SERGEANT WILSON. YOU KNOW ME...
WELL, *BOLLOCKS,* YOU *JACKASS*--!
WINTERGRE
--DON'T YOU RECOGNIZE A *RESCUE* WHEN YOU SEE ONE?!

"DEATHSTROKE," HUH...

NOW WE MEET AGAIN. DIFFERENT CONTINENT, SAME *RUBBISH!*

YOU ARE *AWOL*, SERGEANT.

LET'S GET *ON* WITH IT, MAJOR.

HOW, FREDRIC?

THE *YANKEE WANKER* KILLED OUR *FOURTH.*

THEN HE'LL HAVE TO TAKE THE DEAD MAN'S PLACE.

GENERAL DRAGAS IS ON HIS WAY.

DRAGAS, HUH?

THE CHIMP WHO ORDERED THE *MASSACRE* OF BOSNIAN MUSLIMS.

DRAGAS' BEEN INDICTED ON *WAR CRIMES.*

WE'VE ORDERS TO ARREST HIM.

RIGHT. YOU, THE DEAD CROAT AND YOUR LOUDMOUTH BETTY THERE.

ORDERS FROM *WHO?* THE *FRENCH* RUN THIS NATO FORCE.

IT'S *ILLEGAL* FOR YOU TO EVEN *BE* HERE.

US.

YOU MEAN IT'S ILLEGAL FOR *EITHER* OF US TO BE HERE.

FIVE MILLION BOUNTY ON DRAGAS' HEAD.

THEN WE *UNDERSTAND* EACH OTHER.

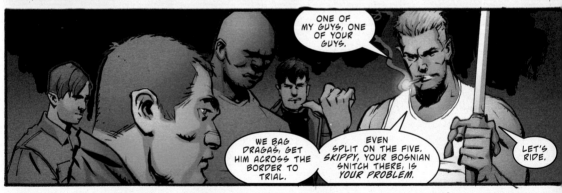

ONE OF MY GUYS, ONE OF YOUR GUYS.

WE BAG DRAGAS, GET HIM ACROSS THE BORDER TO TRIAL.

EVEN SPLIT ON THE FIVE, *SKIPPY.* YOUR BOSNIAN SNITCH THERE, IS *YOUR PROBLEM.*

LET'S RIDE.

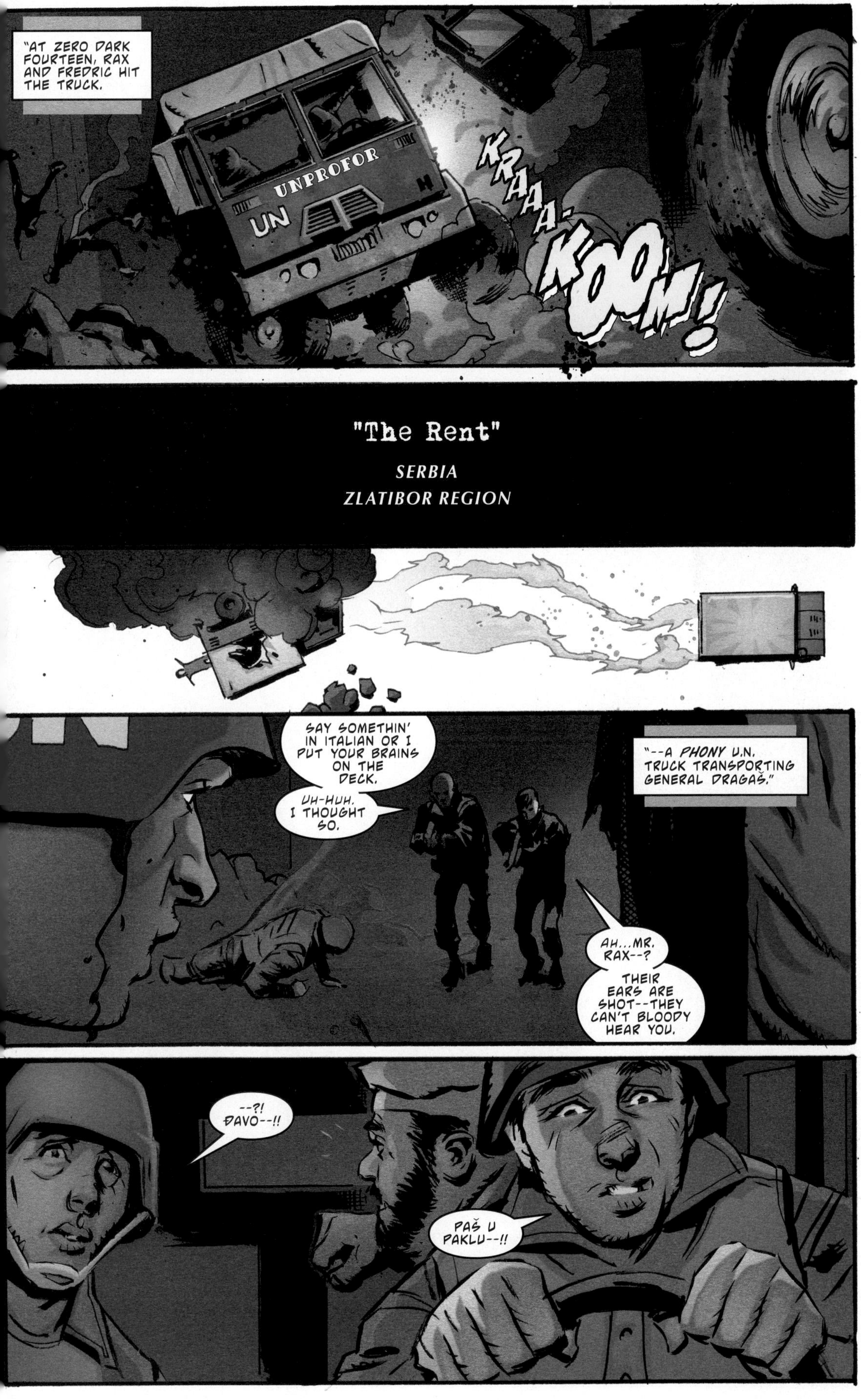
"AT ZERO DARK FOURTEEN, RAX AND FREDRIC HIT THE TRUCK.
UNPROFOR
UN
KRAAA-KOOM!
"The Rent"
SERBIA
ZLATIBOR REGION
SAY SOMETHIN' IN ITALIAN OR I PUT YOUR BRAINS ON THE DECK.
UH-HUH. I THOUGHT SO.
"--A PHONY U.N. TRUCK TRANSPORTING GENERAL DRAGAŠ."
AH...MR. RAX--?
THEIR EARS ARE SHOT--THEY CAN'T BLOODY HEAR YOU.
--?! ĐAVO--!!
PAŠ U PAKLU--!!

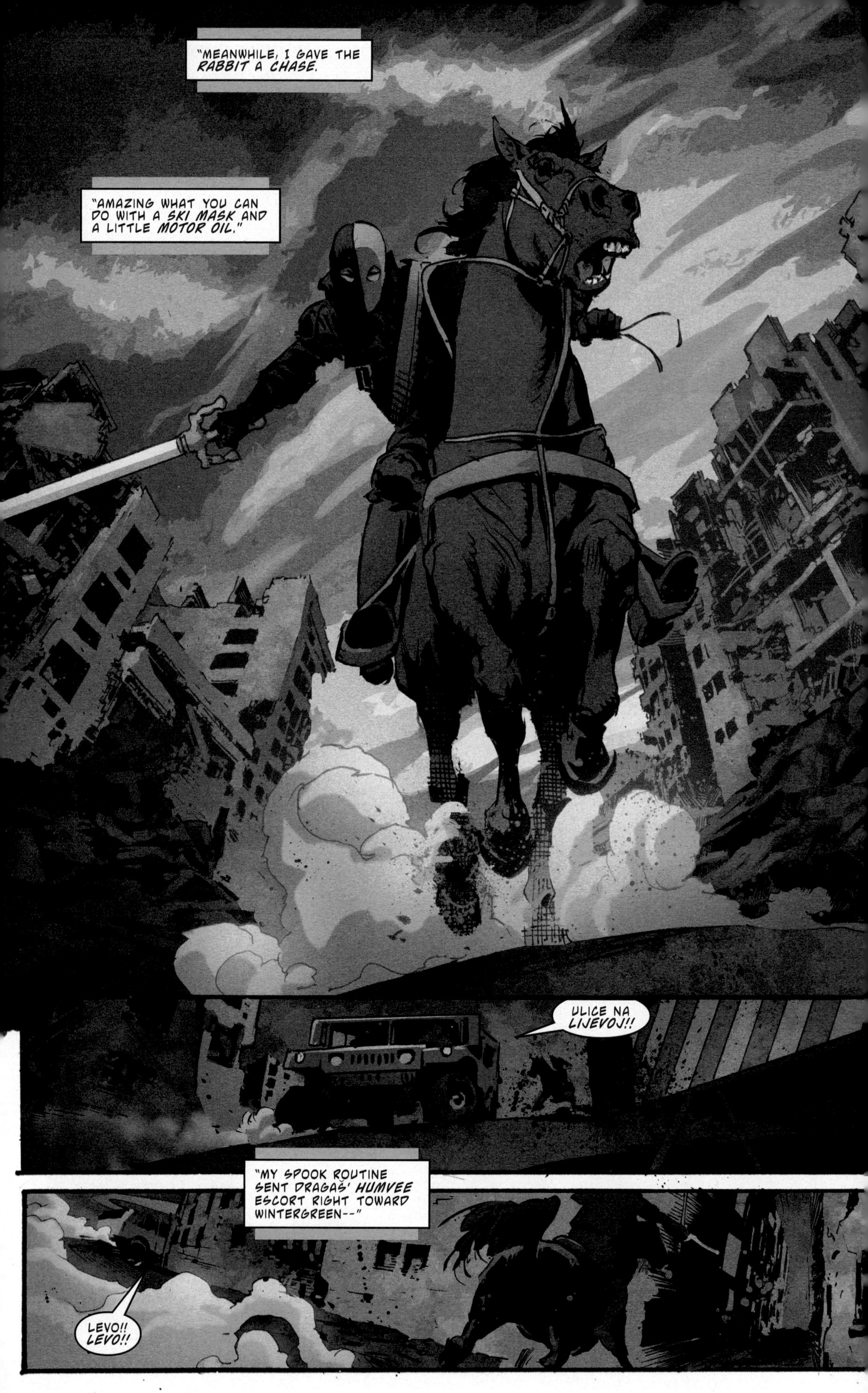
"MEANWHILE, I GAVE THE RABBIT A CHASE.
"AMAZING WHAT YOU CAN DO WITH A SKI MASK AND A LITTLE MOTOR OIL."
ULICE NA LIJEVOJ!!
"MY SPOOK ROUTINE SENT DRAGAŠ' HUMVEE ESCORT RIGHT TOWARD WINTERGREEN--"
LEVO!! LEVO!!

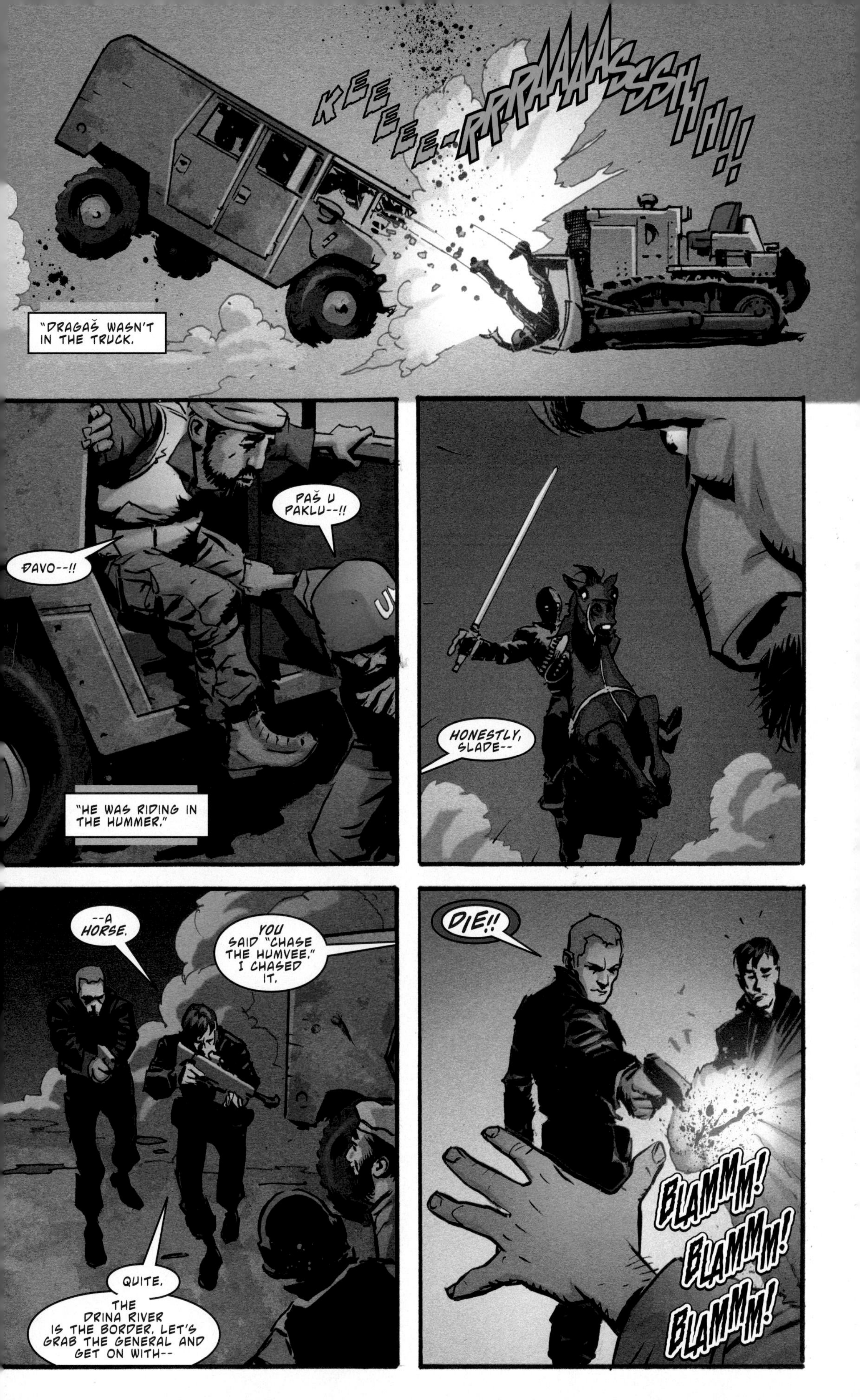
KEEEEE-RRRAAAASSSHH!!
"DRAGAŠ WASN'T IN THE TRUCK.
PAŠ U PAKLU--!!
ĐAVO--!!
"HE WAS RIDING IN THE HUMMER."
HONESTLY, SLADE--
--A HORSE.
YOU SAID "CHASE THE HUMVEE." I CHASED IT.
QUITE.
THE DRINA RIVER IS THE BORDER. LET'S GRAB THE GENERAL AND GET ON WITH--
DIE!!
BLAMMM! BLAMMM! BLAMMM!

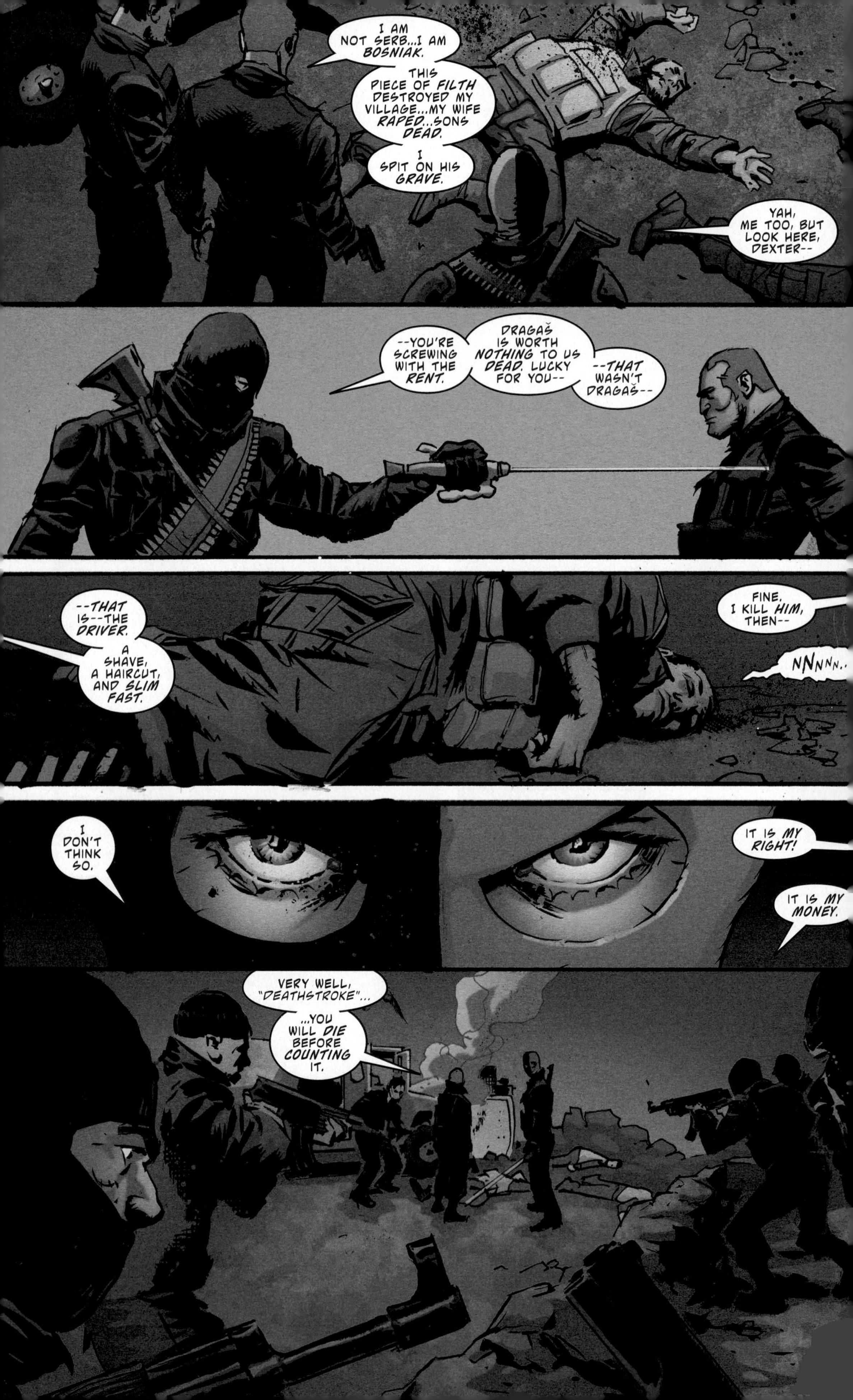
I AM NOT SERB...I AM *BOSNIAK*.
THIS PIECE OF *FILTH* DESTROYED MY VILLAGE...MY WIFE *RAPED*...SONS *DEAD*.
I SPIT ON HIS *GRAVE*.
YAH, ME TOO, BUT LOOK HERE, DEXTER--
--YOU'RE SCREWING WITH THE *RENT*.
DRAGAŠ IS WORTH *NOTHING* TO US *DEAD*. LUCKY FOR YOU--
--*THAT* WASN'T DRAGAŠ--
--*THAT* IS--THE *DRIVER*.
A SHAVE, A HAIRCUT, AND *SLIM FAST*.
FINE, I KILL *HIM*, THEN--
NNNNN..
I DON'T THINK SO.
IT IS *MY RIGHT!*
IT IS MY *MONEY*.
VERY WELL, "*DEATHSTROKE*"...
...YOU WILL *DIE* BEFORE *COUNTING* IT.

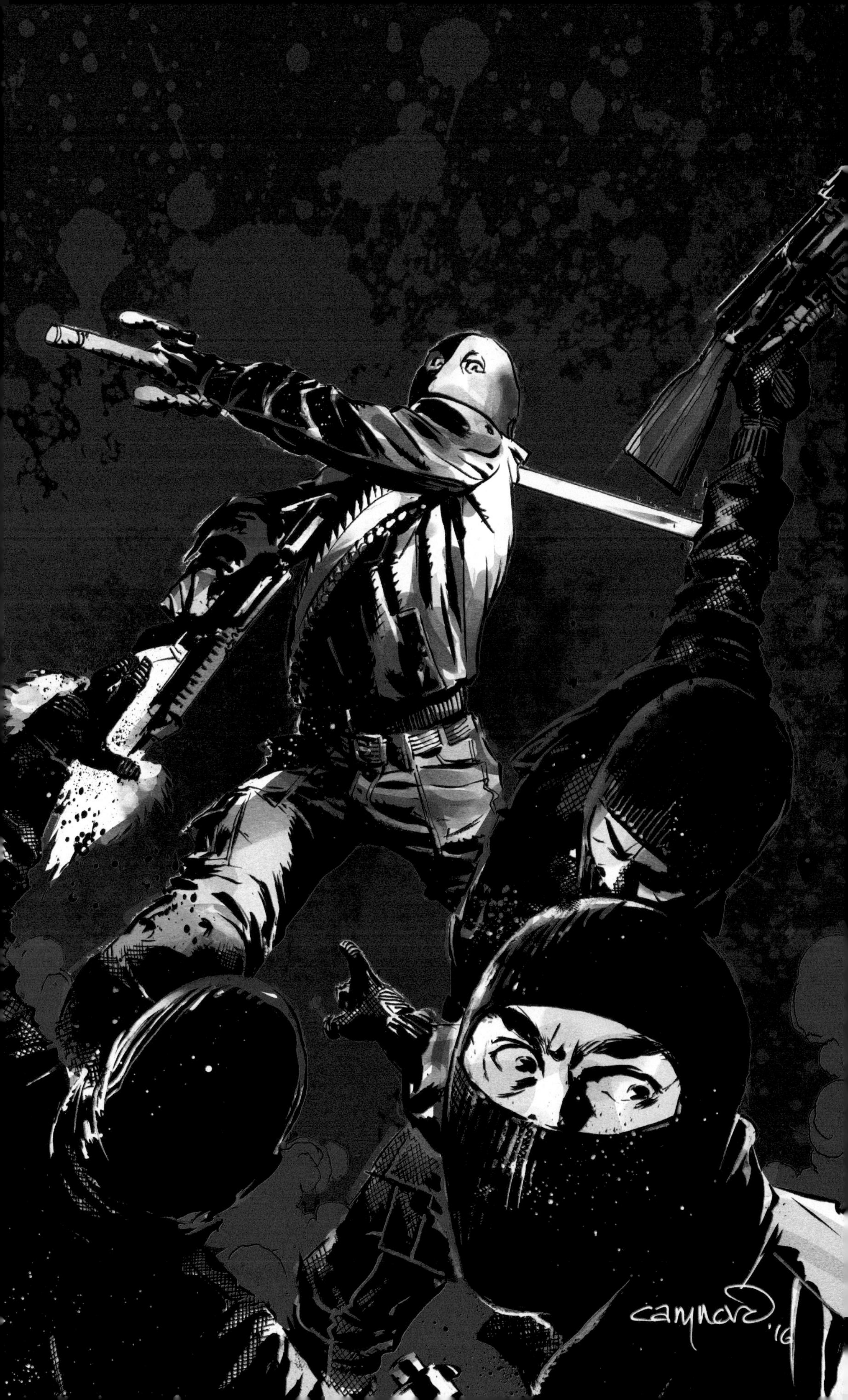

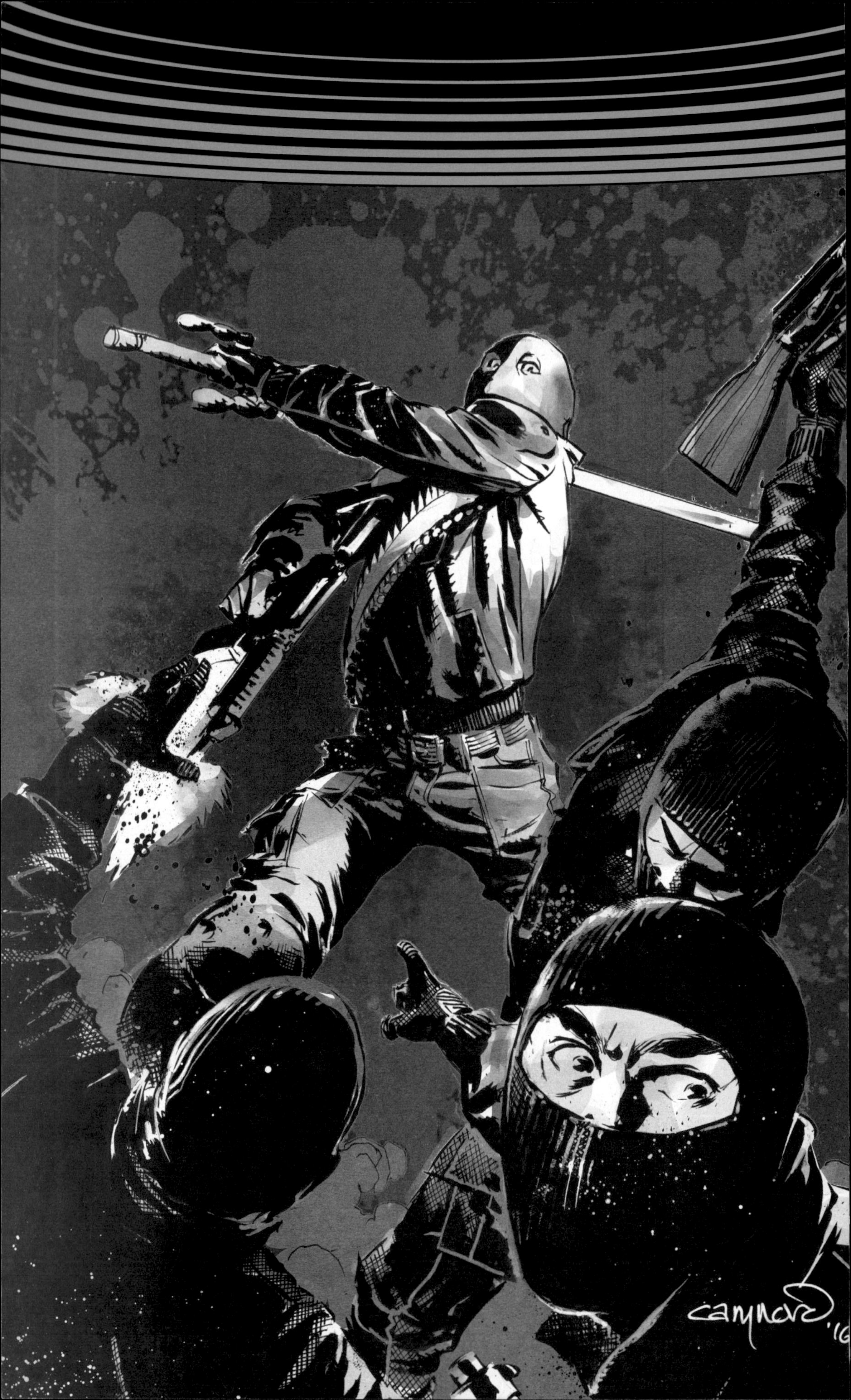

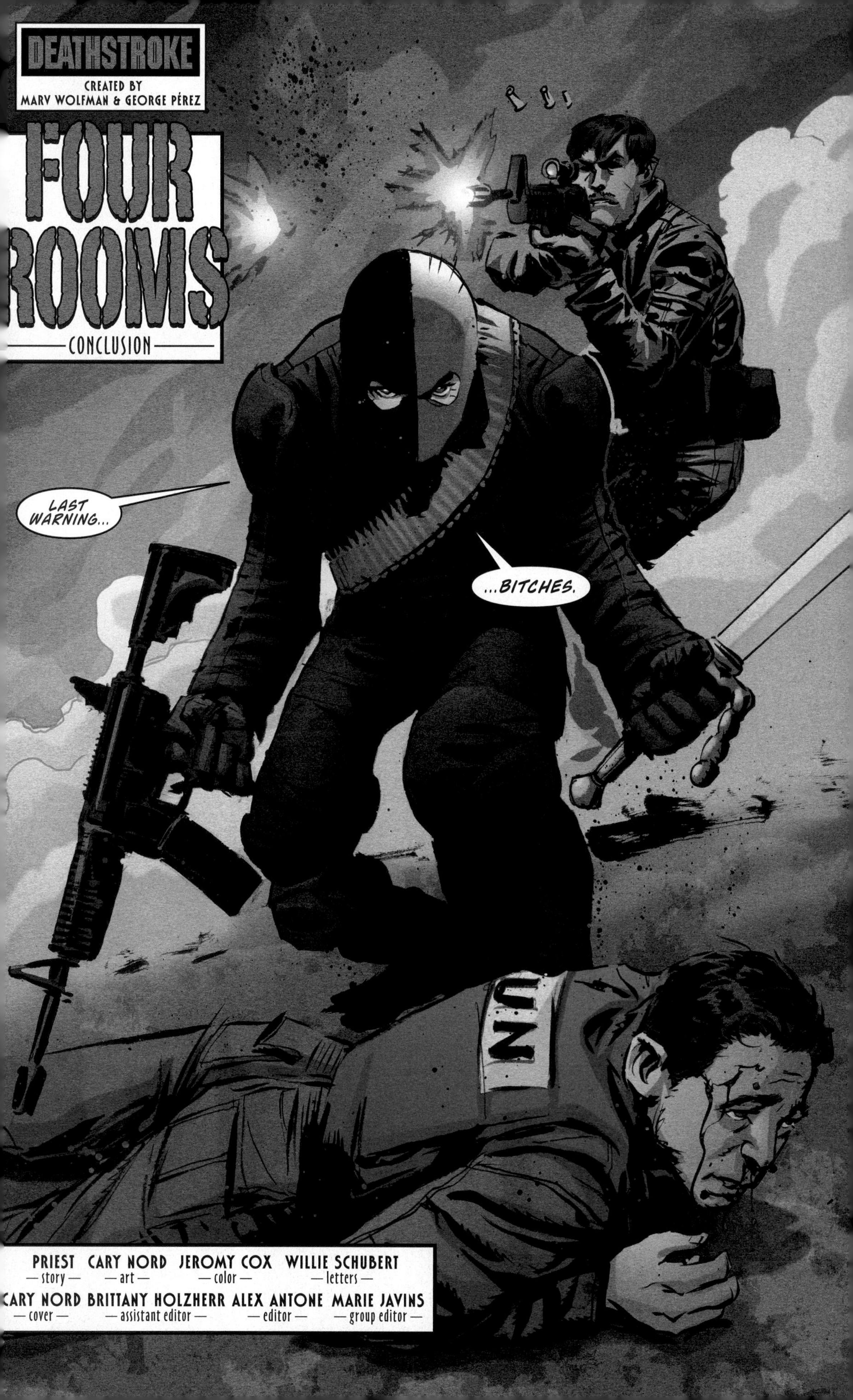
DEATHSTROKE
CREATED BY
MARV WOLFMAN & GEORGE PÉREZ
FOUR ROOMS
CONCLUSION
LAST WARNING...
...BITCHES.
UN
PRIEST — story — CARY NORD — art — JEROMY COX — color — WILLIE SCHUBERT — letters —
CARY NORD — cover — BRITTANY HOLZHERR — assistant editor — ALEX ANTONE — editor — MARIE JAVINS — group editor —

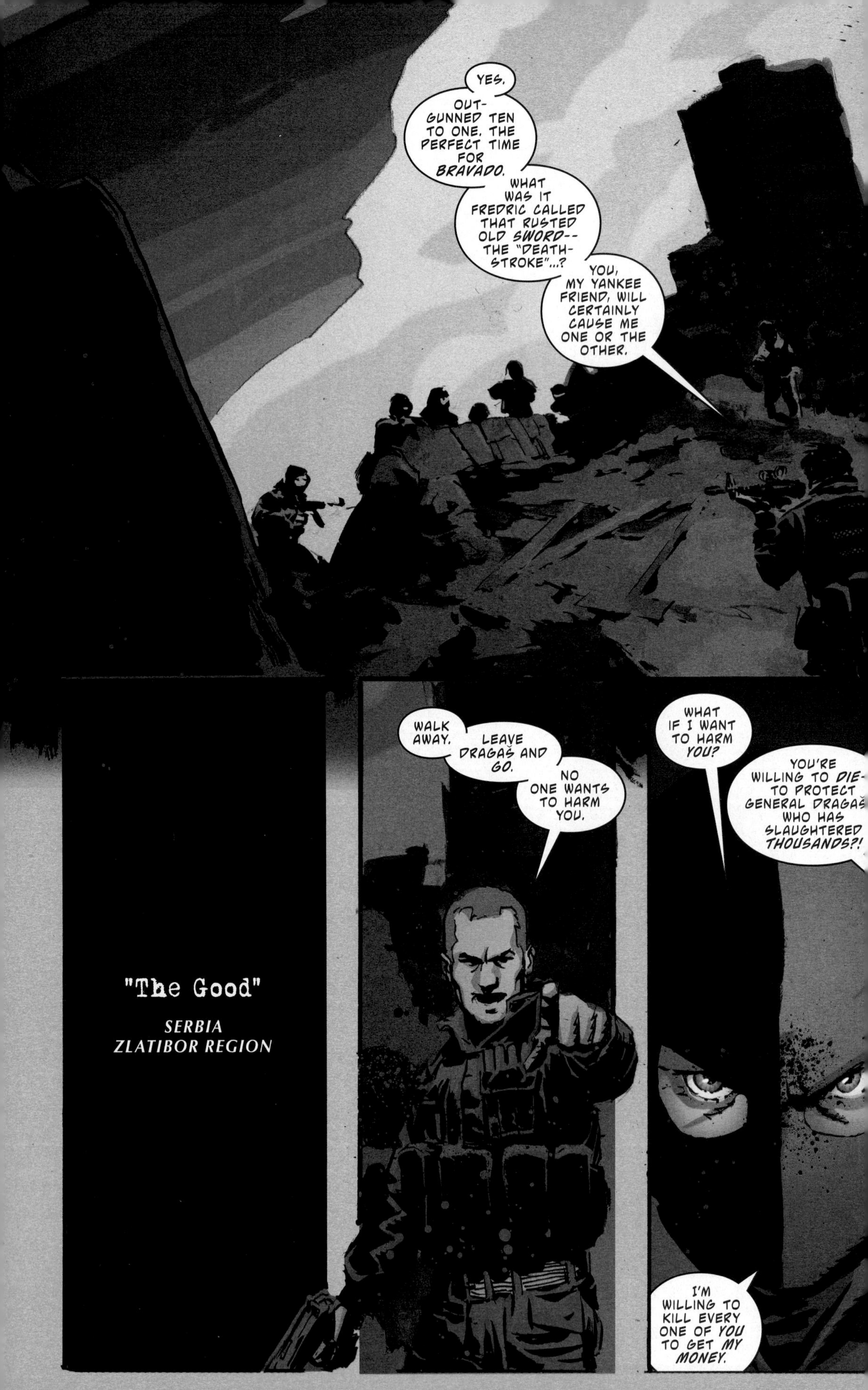
YES.
OUT-GUNNED TEN TO ONE. THE PERFECT TIME FOR BRAVADO.
WHAT WAS IT FREDRIC CALLED THAT RUSTED OLD SWORD-- THE "DEATH-STROKE"...?
YOU, MY YANKEE FRIEND, WILL CERTAINLY CAUSE ME ONE OR THE OTHER.
"The Good"
SERBIA
ZLATIBOR REGION
WALK AWAY.
LEAVE DRAGAŠ AND GO.
NO ONE WANTS TO HARM YOU.
WHAT IF I WANT TO HARM YOU?
YOU'RE WILLING TO DIE-- TO PROTECT GENERAL DRAGAŠ WHO HAS SLAUGHTERED THOUSANDS?!
I'M WILLING TO KILL EVERY ONE OF YOU TO GET MY MONEY.

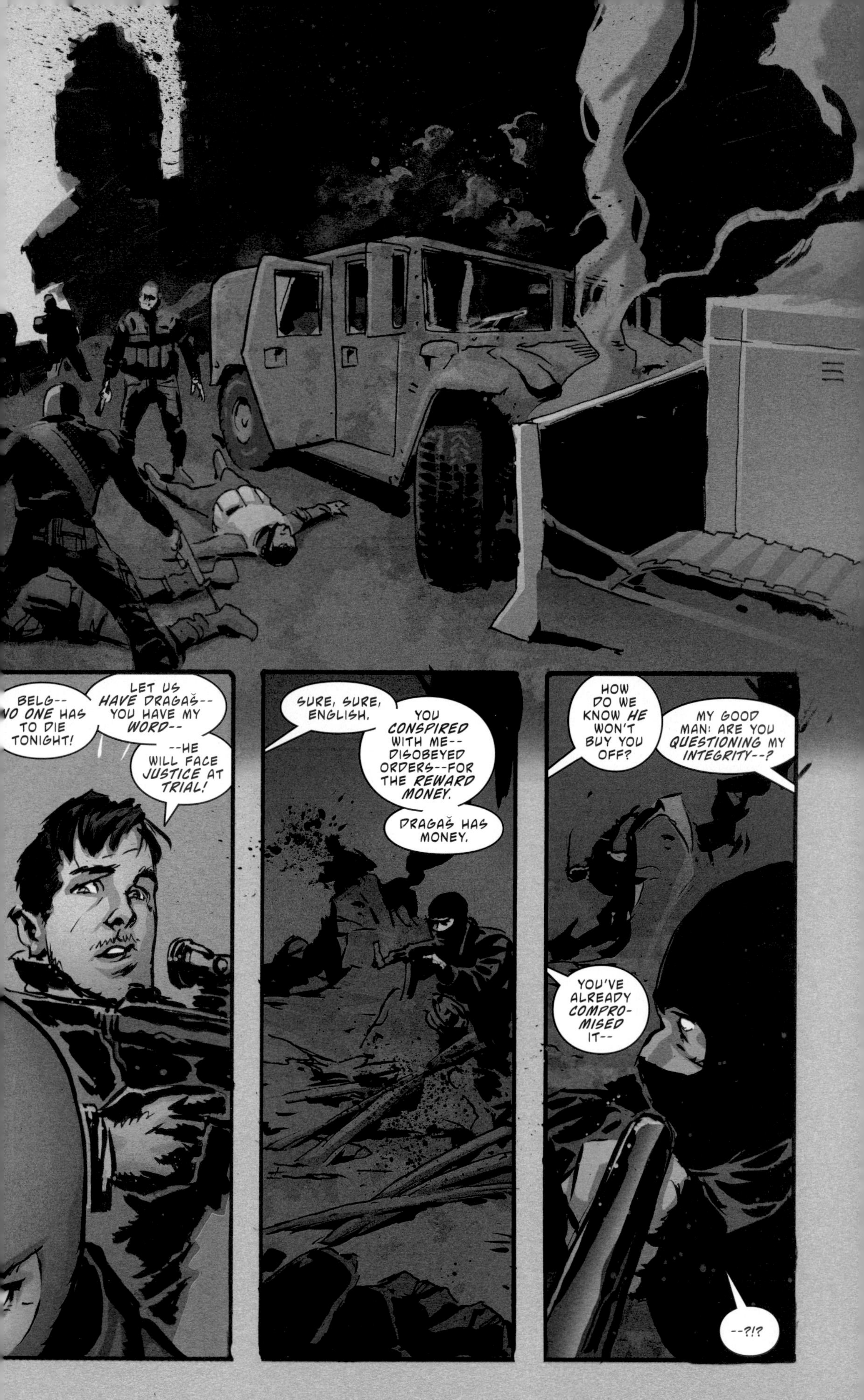
BELG-- NO ONE HAS TO DIE TONIGHT!
LET US HAVE DRAGAŠ-- YOU HAVE MY WORD--
--HE WILL FACE JUSTICE AT TRIAL!
SURE, SURE, ENGLISH.
YOU CONSPIRED WITH ME-- DISOBEYED ORDERS--FOR THE REWARD MONEY.
DRAGAŠ HAS MONEY.
HOW DO WE KNOW HE WON'T BUY YOU OFF?
MY GOOD MAN: ARE YOU QUESTIONING MY INTEGRITY--?
YOU'VE ALREADY COMPRO-MISED IT--
--?!?

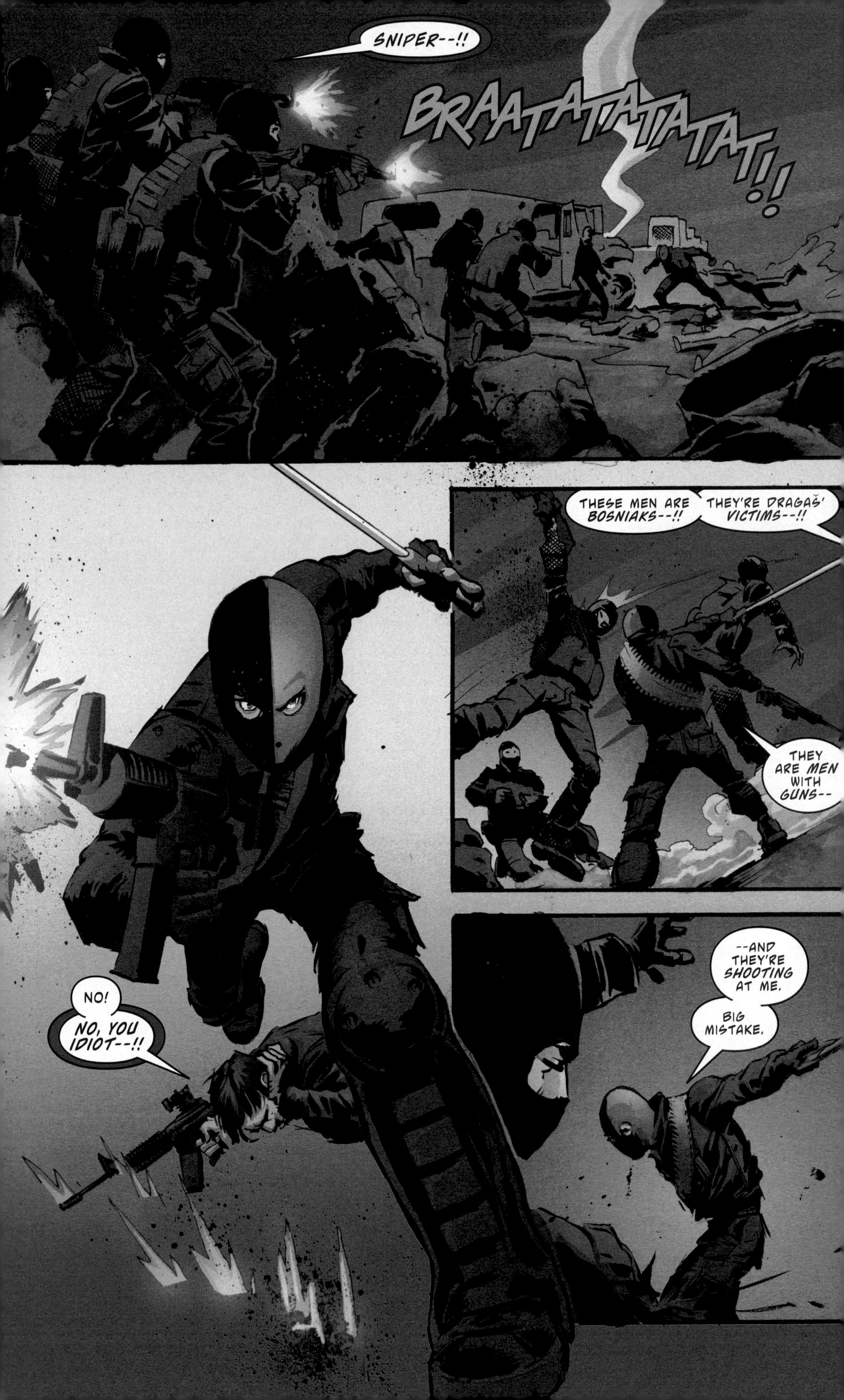
SNIPER--!!
BRAATATATATATAT!!
THESE MEN ARE BOSNIAKS--!!
THEY'RE DRAGAŠ' VICTIMS--!!
THEY ARE MEN WITH GUNS--
--AND THEY'RE SHOOTING AT ME.
BIG MISTAKE.
NO!
NO, YOU IDIOT--!!

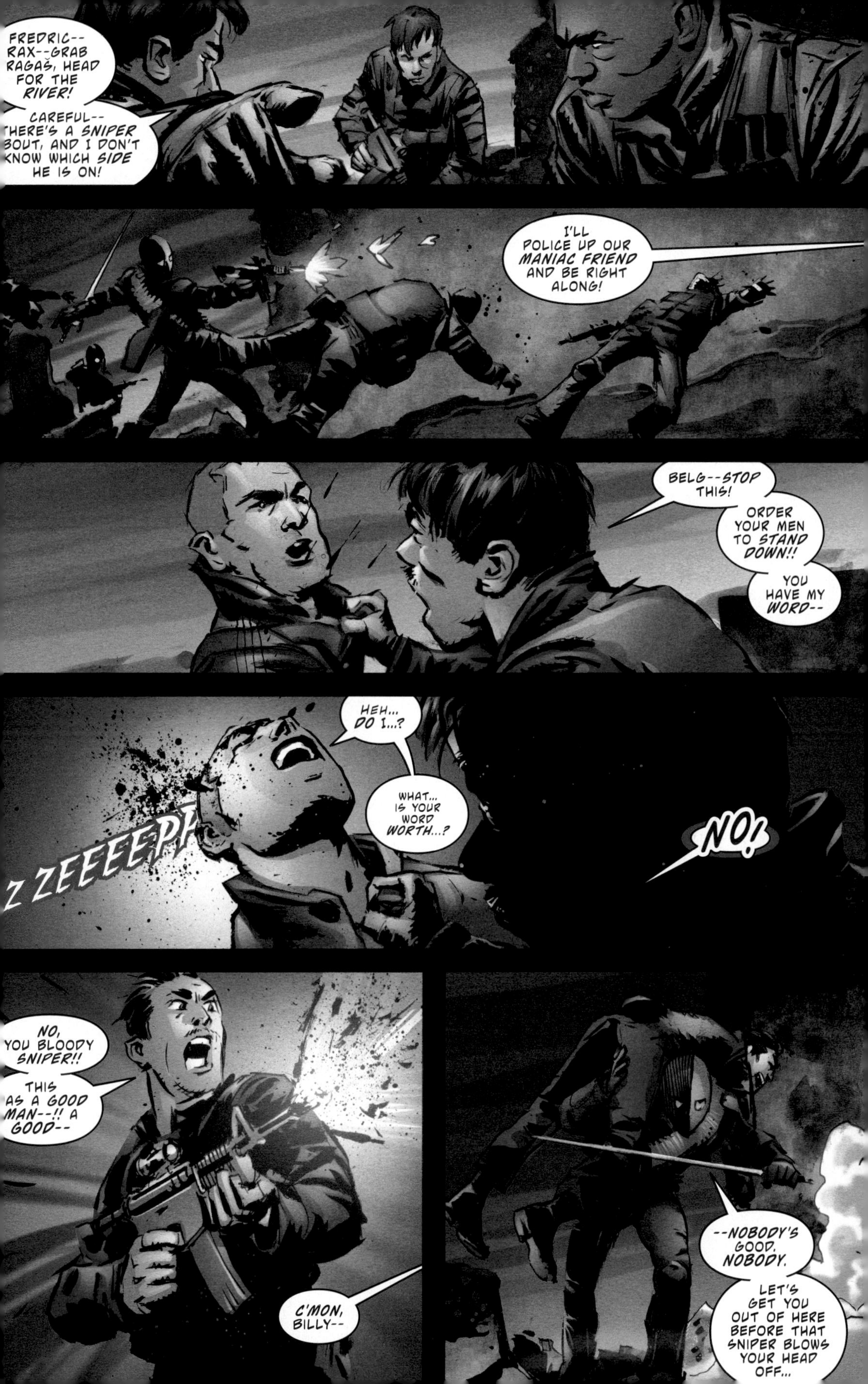
FREDRIC--RAX--GRAB RAGAŠ, HEAD FOR THE RIVER!
CAREFUL--THERE'S A SNIPER 'BOUT, AND I DON'T KNOW WHICH SIDE HE IS ON!
I'LL POLICE UP OUR MANIAC FRIEND AND BE RIGHT ALONG!
BELG--STOP THIS!
ORDER YOUR MEN TO STAND DOWN!!
YOU HAVE MY WORD--
HEH... DO I...?
WHAT... IS YOUR WORD WORTH...?
ZZEEEEEPP
NO!
NO, YOU BLOODY SNIPER!!
THIS WAS A GOOD MAN--!! A GOOD--
C'MON, BILLY--
--NOBODY'S GOOD. NOBODY.
LET'S GET YOU OUT OF HERE BEFORE THAT SNIPER BLOWS YOUR HEAD OFF...

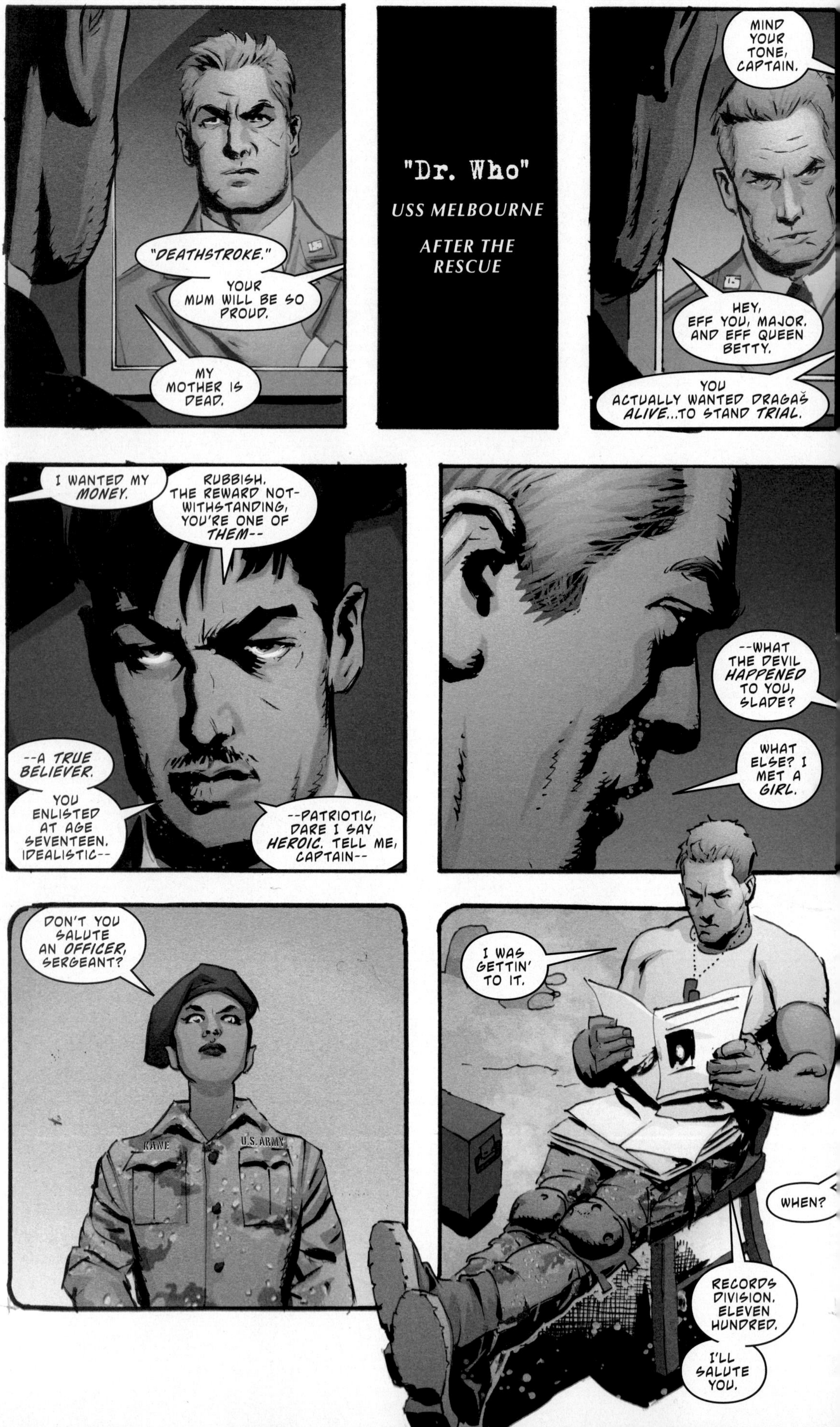
"DEATHSTROKE."
YOUR MUM WILL BE SO PROUD.
MY MOTHER IS DEAD.
"Dr. Who"
USS MELBOURNE
AFTER THE RESCUE
MIND YOUR TONE, CAPTAIN.
HEY, EFF YOU, MAJOR. AND EFF QUEEN BETTY.
YOU ACTUALLY WANTED DRAGAŠ ALIVE...TO STAND TRIAL.
I WANTED MY MONEY.
RUBBISH. THE REWARD NOT-WITHSTANDING, YOU'RE ONE OF THEM--
--A TRUE BELIEVER.
YOU ENLISTED AT AGE SEVENTEEN. IDEALISTIC--
--PATRIOTIC, DARE I SAY HEROIC. TELL ME, CAPTAIN--
--WHAT THE DEVIL HAPPENED TO YOU, SLADE?
WHAT ELSE? I MET A GIRL.
DON'T YOU SALUTE AN OFFICER, SERGEANT?
KANE
U.S. ARMY
I WAS GETTIN' TO IT.
WHEN?
RECORDS DIVISION. ELEVEN HUNDRED.
I'LL SALUTE YOU.

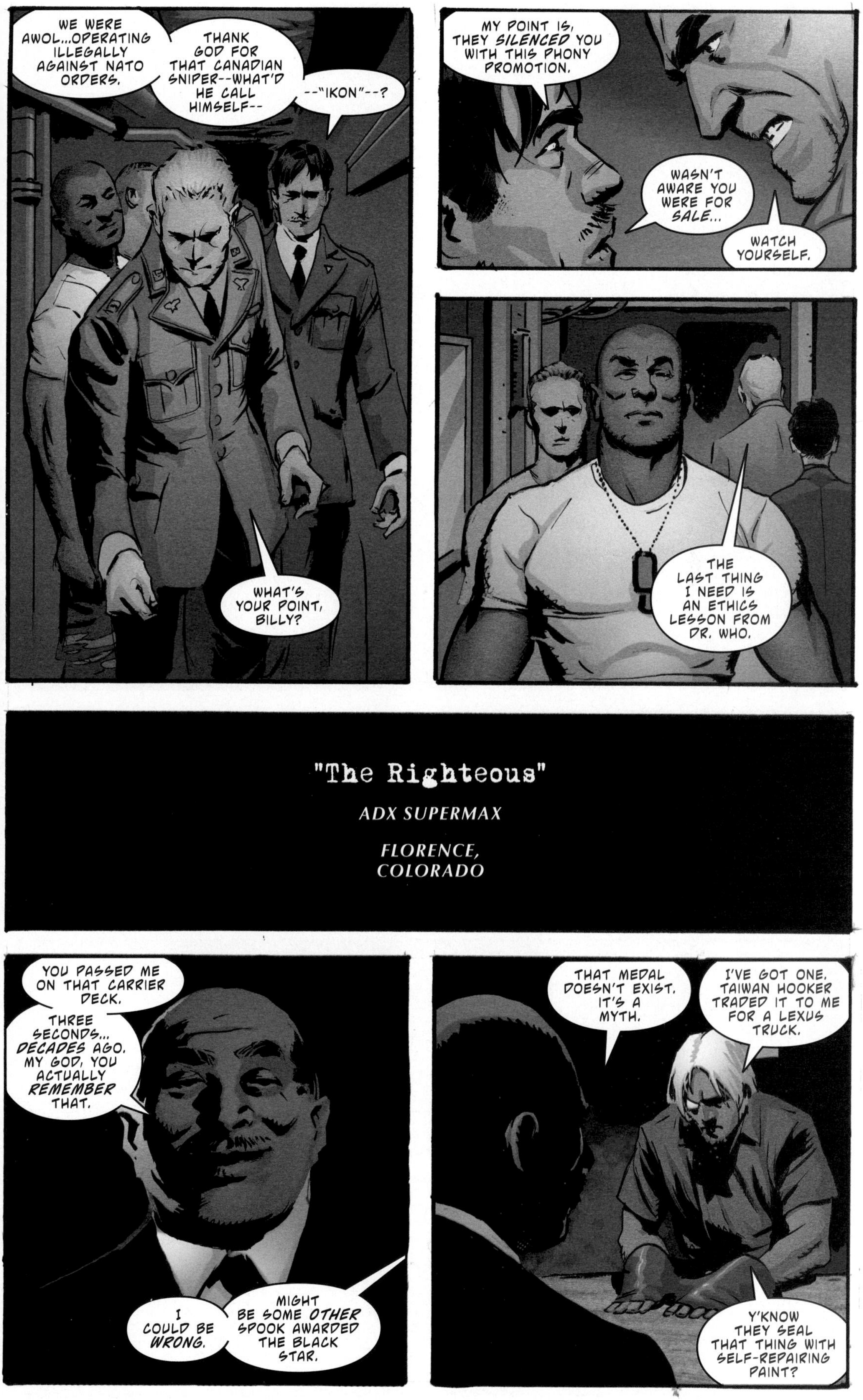
WE WERE AWOL...OPERATING ILLEGALLY AGAINST NATO ORDERS.
THANK GOD FOR THAT CANADIAN SNIPER--WHAT'D HE CALL HIMSELF--
--"IKON"--?
WHAT'S YOUR POINT, BILLY?
MY POINT IS, THEY SILENCED YOU WITH THIS PHONY PROMOTION.
WASN'T AWARE YOU WERE FOR SALE...
WATCH YOURSELF.
THE LAST THING I NEED IS AN ETHICS LESSON FROM DR. WHO.
"The Righteous"
ADX SUPERMAX
FLORENCE, COLORADO
YOU PASSED ME ON THAT CARRIER DECK.
THREE SECONDS... DECADES AGO. MY GOD, YOU ACTUALLY REMEMBER THAT.
I COULD BE WRONG.
MIGHT BE SOME OTHER SPOOK AWARDED THE BLACK STAR.
THAT MEDAL DOESN'T EXIST. IT'S A MYTH.
I'VE GOT ONE. TAIWAN HOOKER TRADED IT TO ME FOR A LEXUS TRUCK.
Y'KNOW THEY SEAL THAT THING WITH SELF-REPAIRING PAINT?

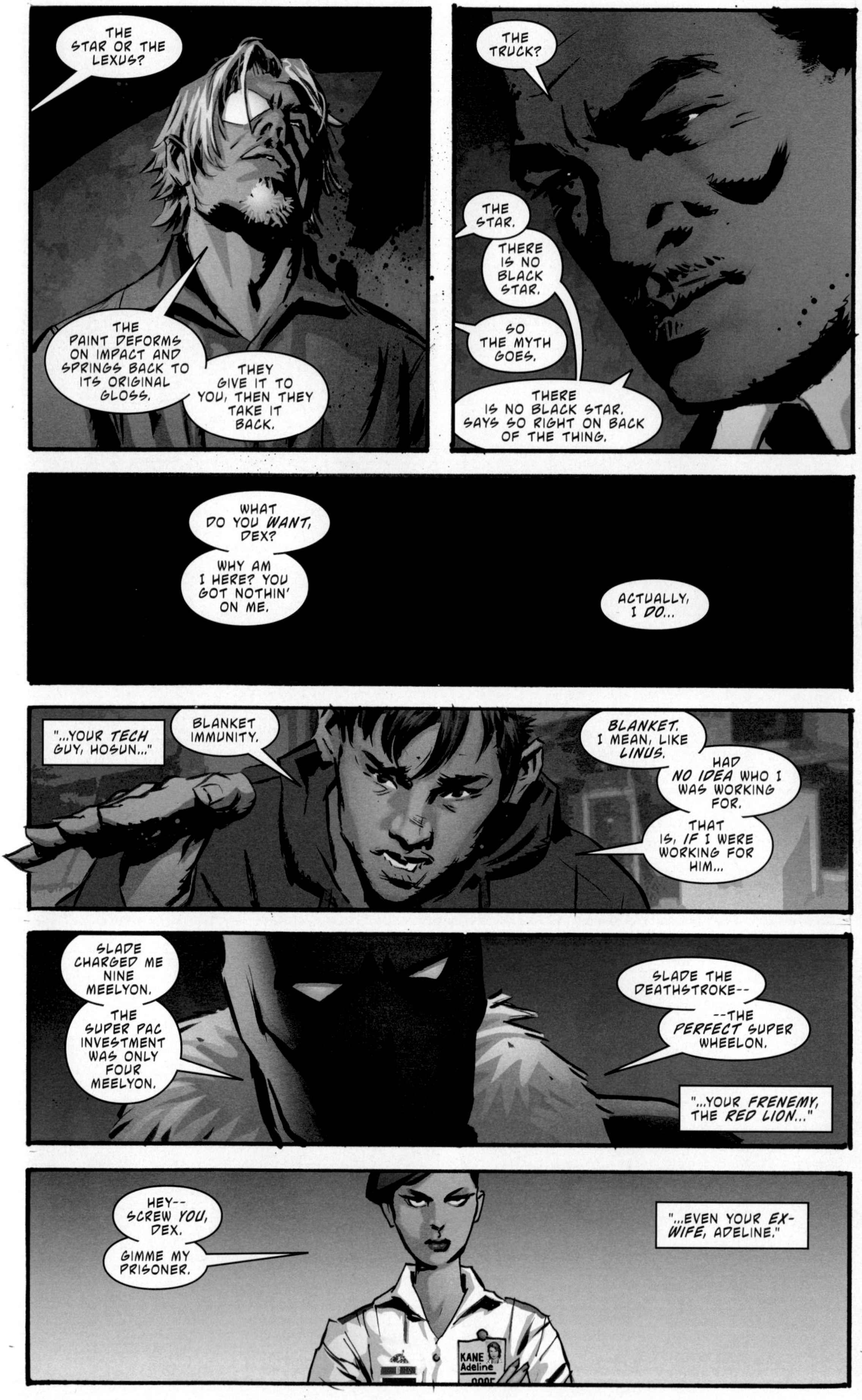
THE STAR OR THE LEXUS?
THE TRUCK?
THE STAR.
THERE IS NO BLACK STAR.
SO THE MYTH GOES.
THERE IS NO BLACK STAR. SAYS SO RIGHT ON BACK OF THE THING.
THE PAINT DEFORMS ON IMPACT AND SPRINGS BACK TO ITS ORIGINAL GLOSS.
THEY GIVE IT TO YOU, THEN THEY TAKE IT BACK.
WHAT DO YOU WANT, DEX?
WHY AM I HERE? YOU GOT NOTHIN' ON ME.
ACTUALLY, I DO...
"...YOUR TECH GUY, HOSUN..."
BLANKET IMMUNITY.
BLANKET. I MEAN, LIKE LINUS.
HAD NO IDEA WHO I WAS WORKING FOR.
THAT IS, IF I WERE WORKING FOR HIM...
SLADE CHARGED ME NINE MEELYON.
THE SUPER PAC INVESTMENT WAS ONLY FOUR MEELYON.
SLADE THE DEATHSTROKE--
--THE PERFECT SUPER WHEELON.
"...YOUR FRENEMY, THE RED LION..."
HEY--SCREW YOU, DEX.
GIMME MY PRISONER.
"...EVEN YOUR EX-WIFE, ADELINE."
KANE Adeline

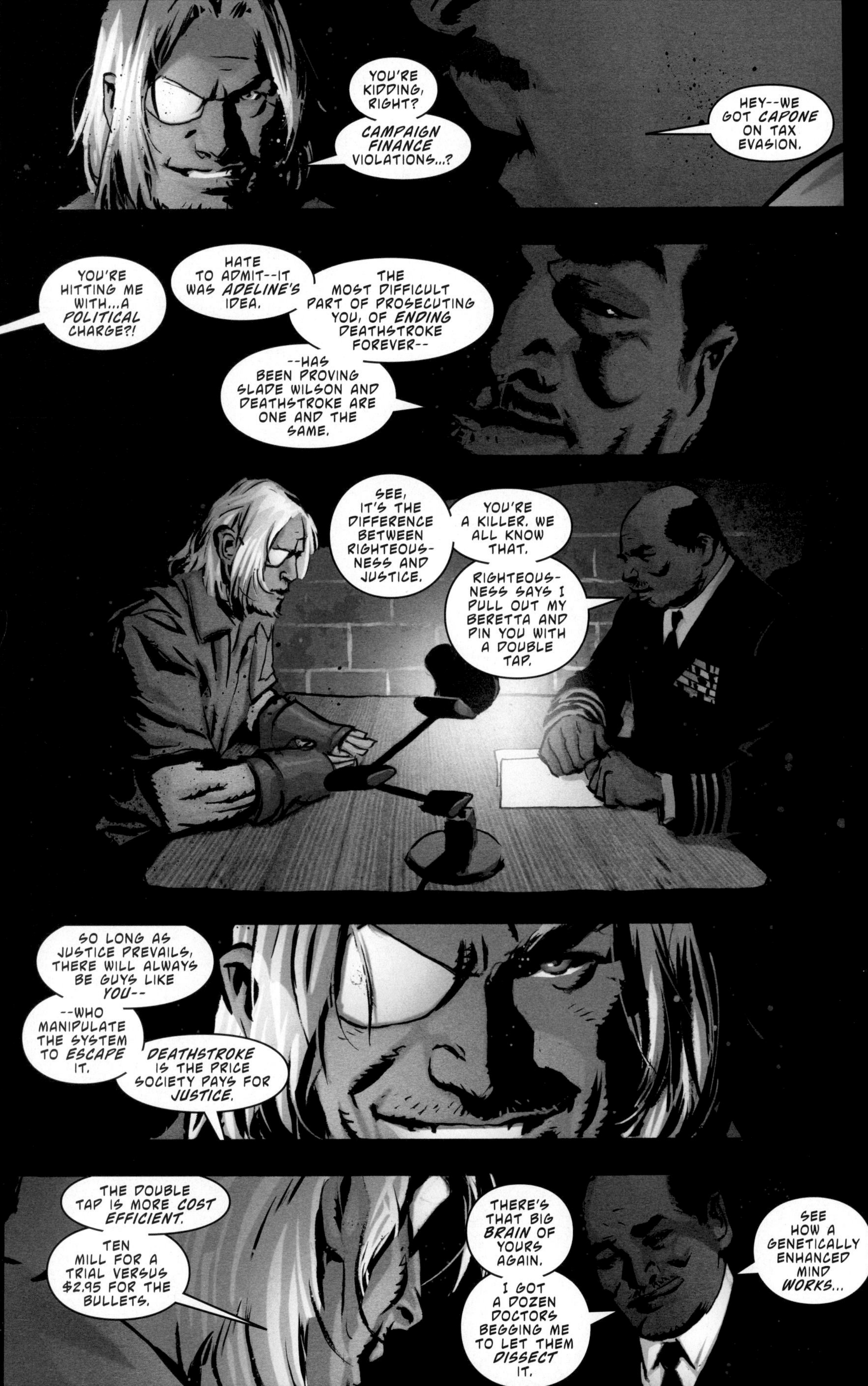
YOU'RE KIDDING, RIGHT?
CAMPAIGN FINANCE VIOLATIONS...?
HEY--WE GOT CAPONE ON TAX EVASION.
YOU'RE HITTING ME WITH...A POLITICAL CHARGE?!
HATE TO ADMIT--IT WAS ADELINE'S IDEA.
THE MOST DIFFICULT PART OF PROSECUTING YOU, OF ENDING DEATHSTROKE FOREVER--
--HAS BEEN PROVING SLADE WILSON AND DEATHSTROKE ARE ONE AND THE SAME.
SEE, IT'S THE DIFFERENCE BETWEEN RIGHTEOUS-NESS AND JUSTICE.
YOU'RE A KILLER. WE ALL KNOW THAT.
RIGHTEOUS-NESS SAYS I PULL OUT MY BERETTA AND PIN YOU WITH A DOUBLE TAP.
SO LONG AS JUSTICE PREVAILS, THERE WILL ALWAYS BE GUYS LIKE YOU--
--WHO MANIPULATE THE SYSTEM TO ESCAPE IT.
DEATHSTROKE IS THE PRICE SOCIETY PAYS FOR JUSTICE.
THE DOUBLE TAP IS MORE COST EFFICIENT.
TEN MILL FOR A TRIAL VERSUS $2.95 FOR THE BULLETS.
THERE'S THAT BIG BRAIN OF YOURS AGAIN.
I GOT A DOZEN DOCTORS BEGGING ME TO LET THEM DISSECT IT.
SEE HOW A GENETICALLY ENHANCED MIND WORKS...

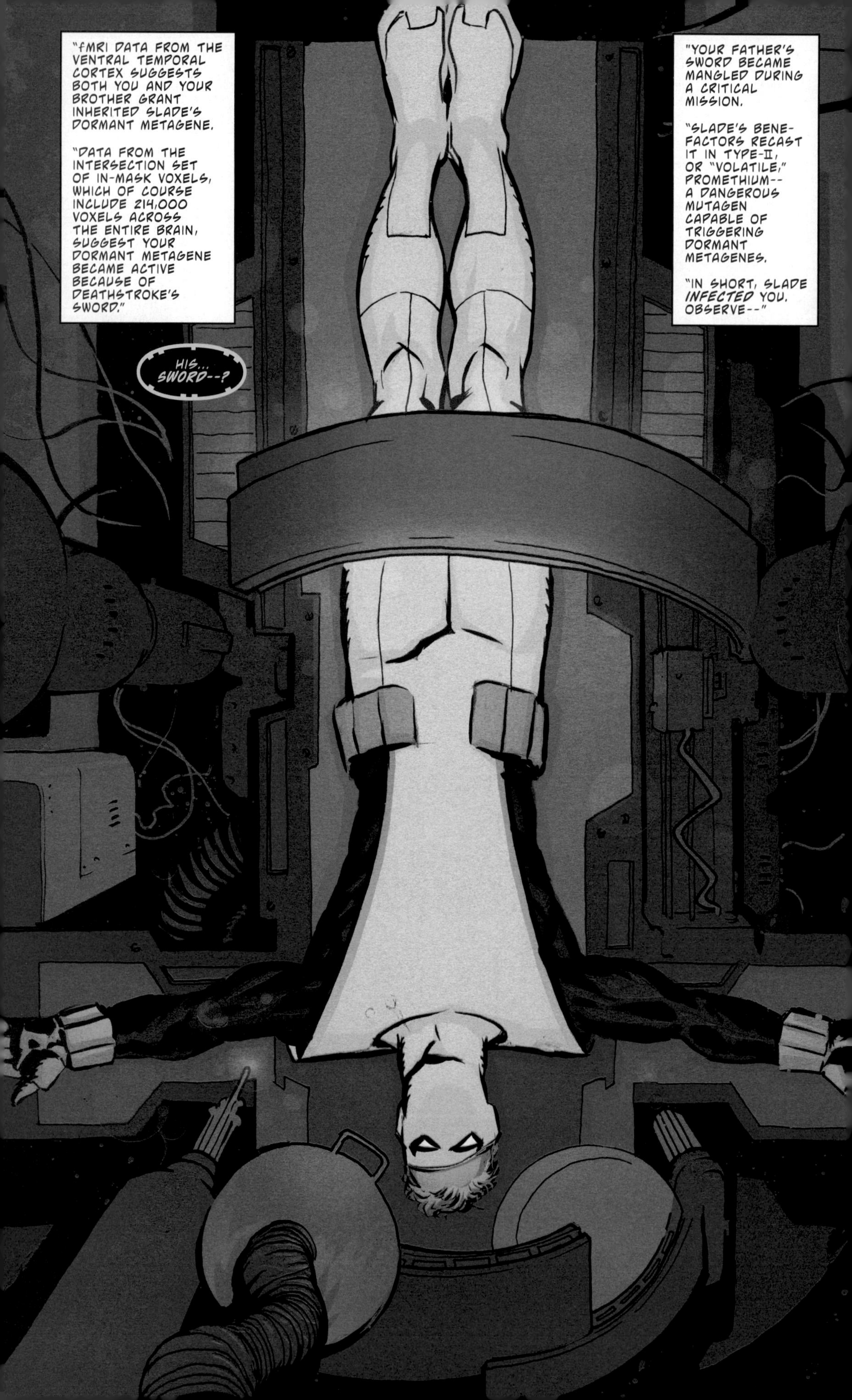
"fMRI DATA FROM THE VENTRAL TEMPORAL CORTEX SUGGESTS BOTH YOU AND YOUR BROTHER GRANT INHERITED SLADE'S DORMANT METAGENE.
"DATA FROM THE INTERSECTION SET OF IN-MASK VOXELS, WHICH OF COURSE INCLUDE 214,000 VOXELS ACROSS THE ENTIRE BRAIN, SUGGEST YOUR DORMANT METAGENE BECAME ACTIVE BECAUSE OF DEATHSTROKE'S SWORD."
HIS... SWORD--?
"YOUR FATHER'S SWORD BECAME MANGLED DURING A CRITICAL MISSION.
"SLADE'S BENE-FACTORS RECAST IT IN TYPE-II, OR "VOLATILE," PROMETHIUM-- A DANGEROUS MUTAGEN CAPABLE OF TRIGGERING DORMANT METAGENES.
"IN SHORT, SLADE *INFECTED* YOU. OBSERVE--"

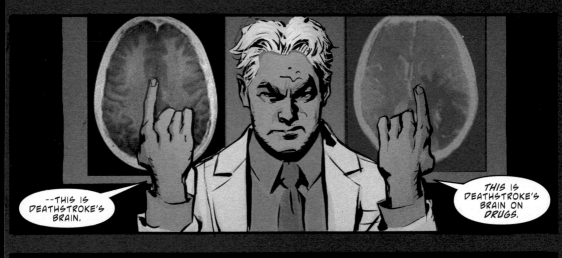

--THIS IS DEATHSTROKE'S BRAIN.

THIS IS DEATHSTROKE'S BRAIN ON DRUGS.

"Jericho"

JERSEY CITY MEDICAL CENTER

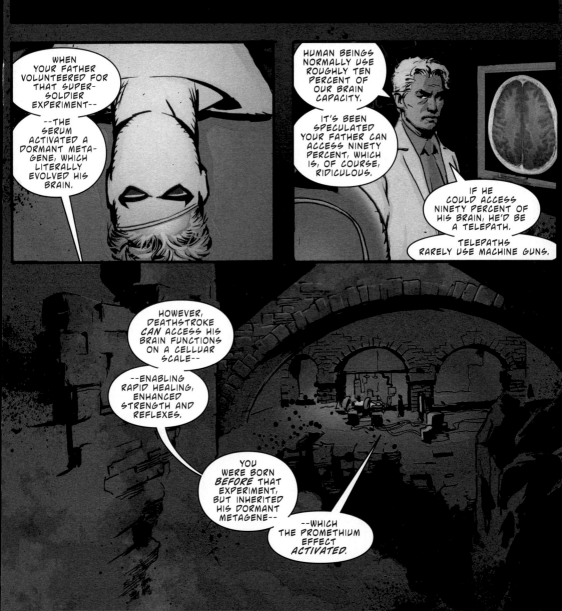

WHEN YOUR FATHER VOLUNTEERED FOR THAT SUPER-SOLDIER EXPERIMENT--

--THE SERUM ACTIVATED A DORMANT META-GENE, WHICH LITERALLY EVOLVED HIS BRAIN.

HUMAN BEINGS NORMALLY USE ROUGHLY TEN PERCENT OF OUR BRAIN CAPACITY.

IT'S BEEN SPECULATED YOUR FATHER CAN ACCESS NINETY PERCENT, WHICH IS, OF COURSE, RIDICULOUS.

IF HE COULD ACCESS NINETY PERCENT OF HIS BRAIN, HE'D BE A TELEPATH.

TELEPATHS RARELY USE MACHINE GUNS.

HOWEVER, DEATHSTROKE CAN ACCESS HIS BRAIN FUNCTIONS ON A CELLULAR SCALE--

--ENABLING RAPID HEALING, ENHANCED STRENGTH AND REFLEXES.

YOU WERE BORN BEFORE THAT EXPERIMENT, BUT INHERITED HIS DORMANT METAGENE--

--WHICH THE PROMETHIUM EFFECT ACTIVATED.

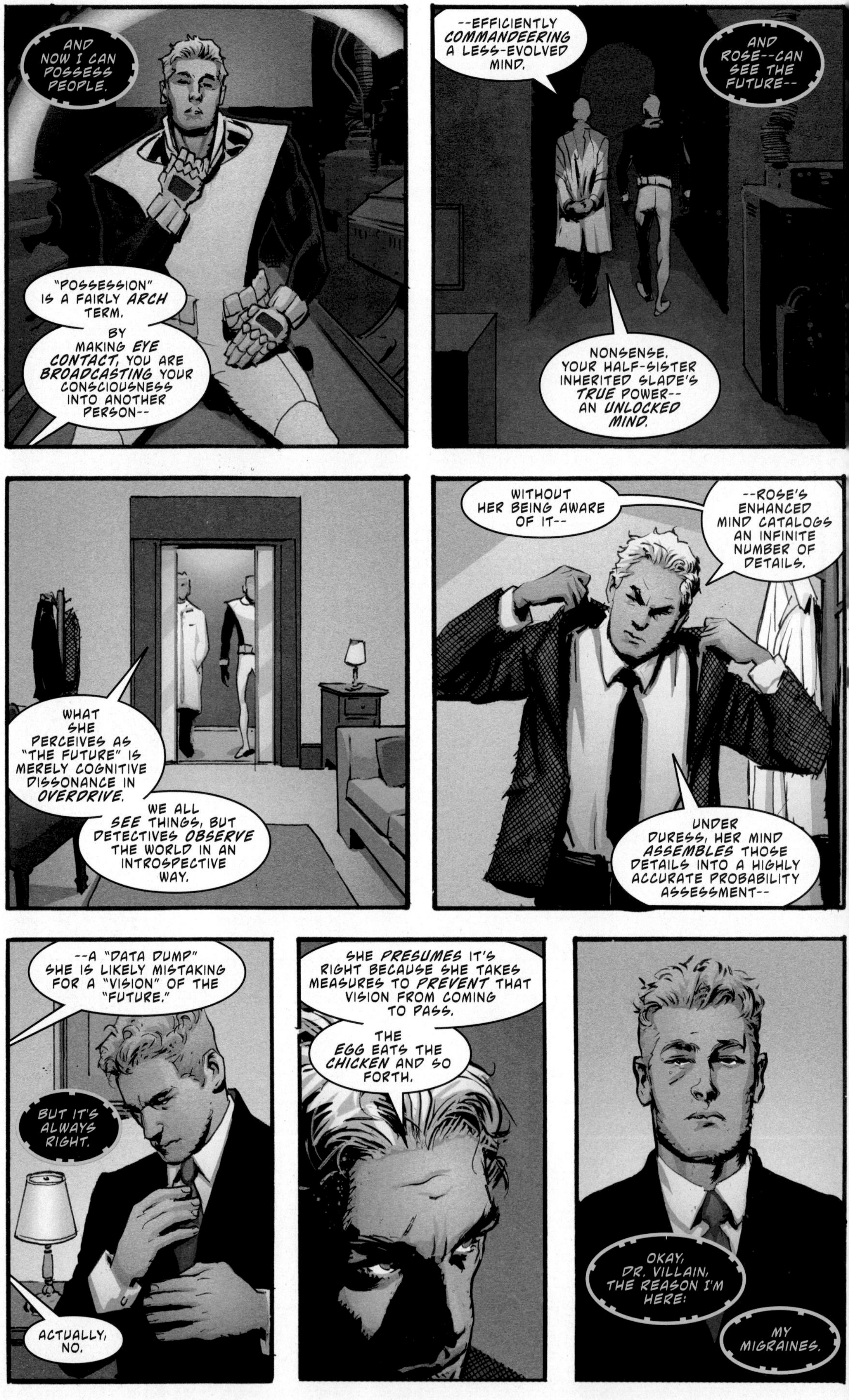
AND NOW I CAN POSSESS PEOPLE.
"POSSESSION" IS A FAIRLY ARCH TERM.
BY MAKING EYE CONTACT, YOU ARE BROADCASTING YOUR CONSCIOUSNESS INTO ANOTHER PERSON--
--EFFICIENTLY COMMANDEERING A LESS-EVOLVED MIND.
AND ROSE--CAN SEE THE FUTURE--
NONSENSE. YOUR HALF-SISTER INHERITED SLADE'S TRUE POWER--AN UNLOCKED MIND.
WHAT SHE PERCEIVES AS "THE FUTURE" IS MERELY COGNITIVE DISSONANCE IN OVERDRIVE.
WE ALL SEE THINGS, BUT DETECTIVES OBSERVE THE WORLD IN AN INTROSPECTIVE WAY.
WITHOUT HER BEING AWARE OF IT--
--ROSE'S ENHANCED MIND CATALOGS AN INFINITE NUMBER OF DETAILS.
UNDER DURESS, HER MIND ASSEMBLES THOSE DETAILS INTO A HIGHLY ACCURATE PROBABILITY ASSESSMENT--
--A "DATA DUMP" SHE IS LIKELY MISTAKING FOR A "VISION" OF THE "FUTURE."
BUT IT'S ALWAYS RIGHT.
ACTUALLY, NO.
SHE PRESUMES IT'S RIGHT BECAUSE SHE TAKES MEASURES TO PREVENT THAT VISION FROM COMING TO PASS.
THE EGG EATS THE CHICKEN AND SO FORTH.
OKAY, DR. VILLAIN, THE REASON I'M HERE:
MY MIGRAINES.

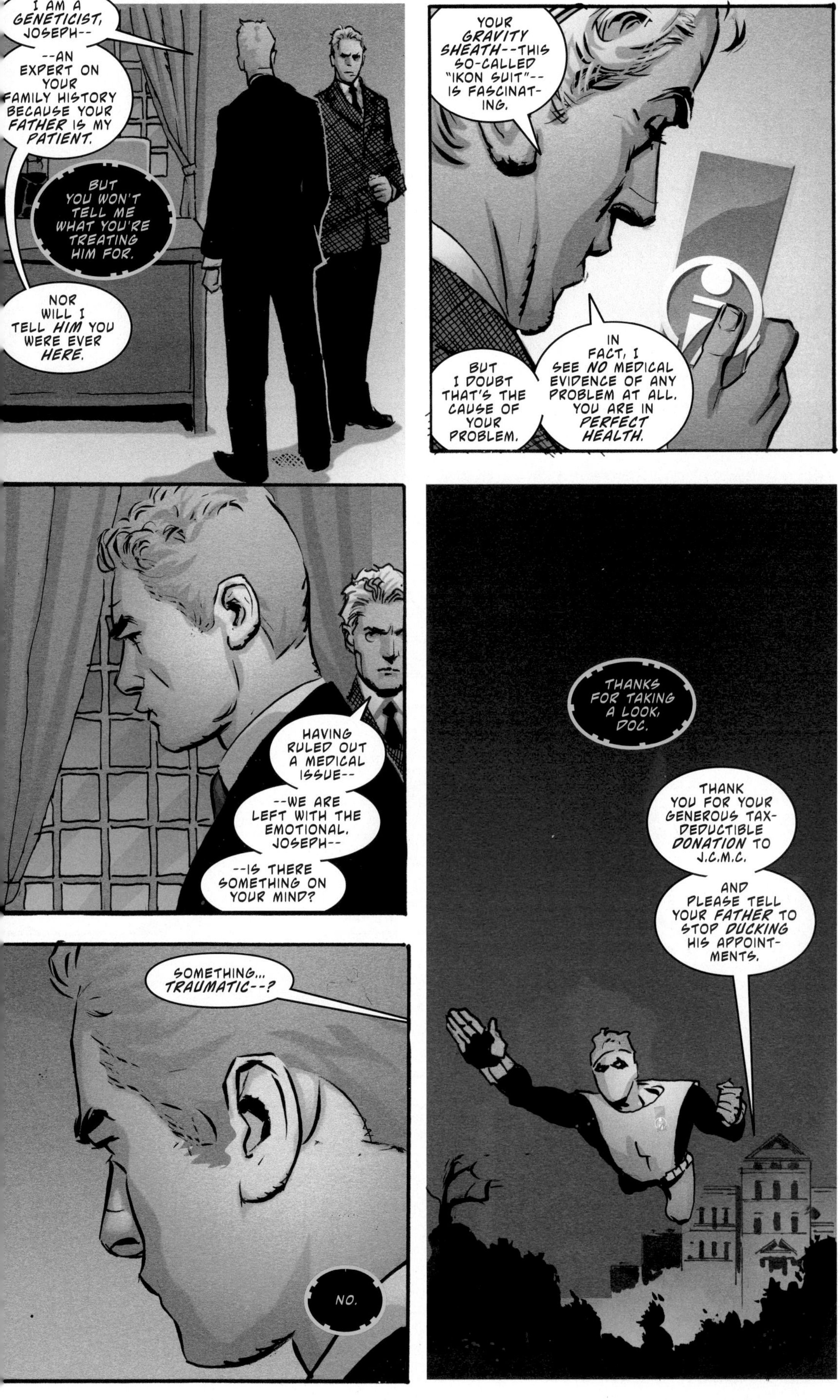
I AM A GENETICIST, JOSEPH--
--AN EXPERT ON YOUR FAMILY HISTORY BECAUSE YOUR FATHER IS MY PATIENT.
BUT YOU WON'T TELL ME WHAT YOU'RE TREATING HIM FOR.
NOR WILL I TELL HIM YOU WERE EVER HERE.
YOUR GRAVITY SHEATH--THIS SO-CALLED "IKON SUIT"--IS FASCINATING.
BUT I DOUBT THAT'S THE CAUSE OF YOUR PROBLEM.
IN FACT, I SEE NO MEDICAL EVIDENCE OF ANY PROBLEM AT ALL. YOU ARE IN PERFECT HEALTH.
HAVING RULED OUT A MEDICAL ISSUE--
--WE ARE LEFT WITH THE EMOTIONAL, JOSEPH--
--IS THERE SOMETHING ON YOUR MIND?
SOMETHING... TRAUMATIC--?
NO.
THANKS FOR TAKING A LOOK, DOC.
THANK YOU FOR YOUR GENEROUS TAX-DEDUCTIBLE DONATION TO J.C.M.C.
AND PLEASE TELL YOUR FATHER TO STOP DUCKING HIS APPOINTMENTS.

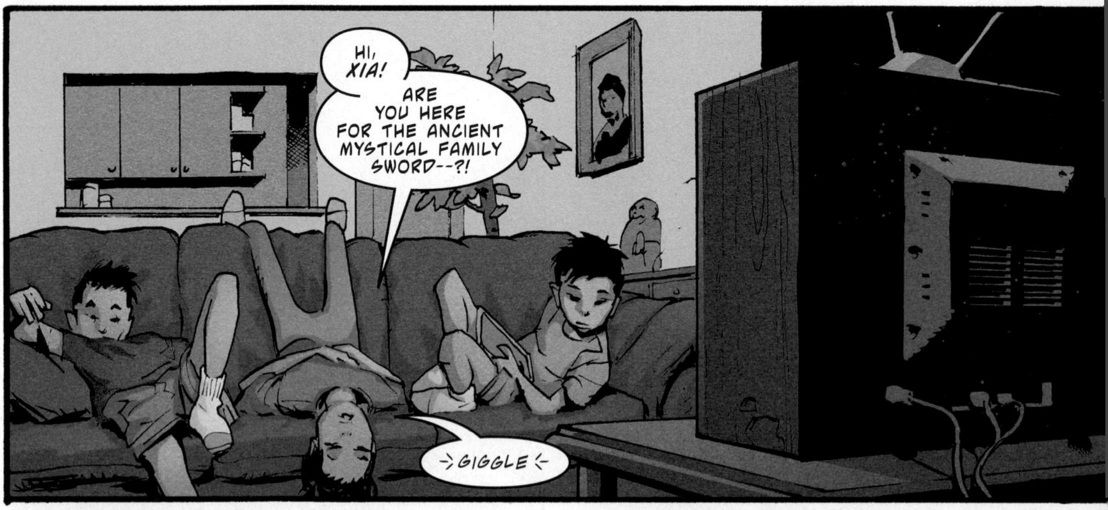
HI, XIA!
ARE YOU HERE FOR THE ANCIENT MYSTICAL FAMILY SWORD--?!
GIGGLE

"Xia"

MINNEAPOLIS

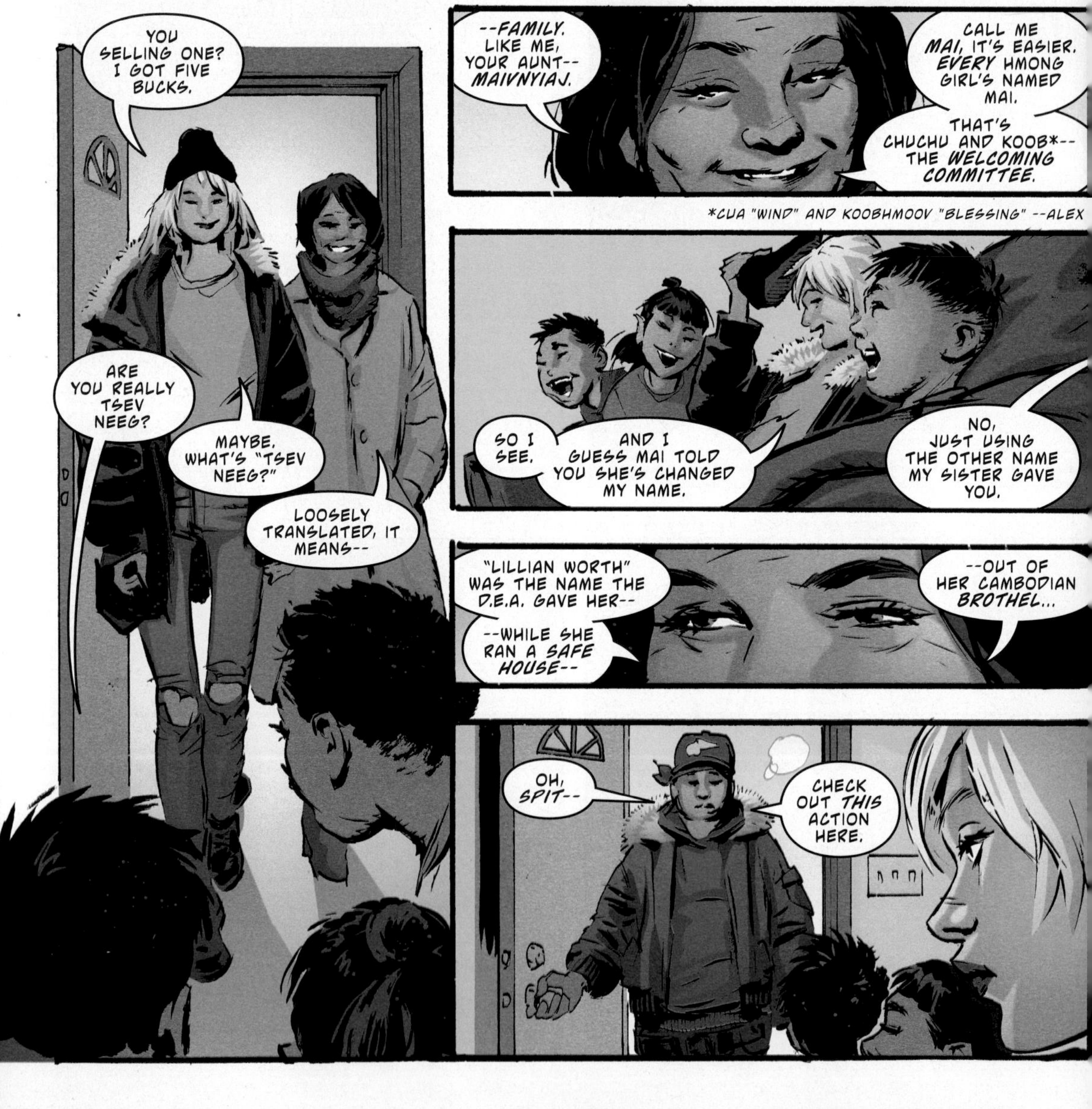
YOU SELLING ONE? I GOT FIVE BUCKS.
ARE YOU REALLY TSEV NEEG?
MAYBE. WHAT'S "TSEV NEEG?"
LOOSELY TRANSLATED, IT MEANS--
--FAMILY. LIKE ME, YOUR AUNT-- MAIVNYIAJ.
CALL ME MAI, IT'S EASIER. EVERY HMONG GIRL'S NAMED MAI.
THAT'S CHUCHU AND KOOB*-- THE WELCOMING COMMITTEE.
*CUA "WIND" AND KOOBHMOOV "BLESSING" --ALEX
SO I SEE.
AND I GUESS MAI TOLD YOU SHE'S CHANGED MY NAME.
NO, JUST USING THE OTHER NAME MY SISTER GAVE YOU.
"LILLIAN WORTH" WAS THE NAME THE D.E.A. GAVE HER--
--WHILE SHE RAN A SAFE HOUSE--
--OUT OF HER CAMBODIAN BROTHEL...
OH, SPIT--
CHECK OUT THIS ACTION HERE.

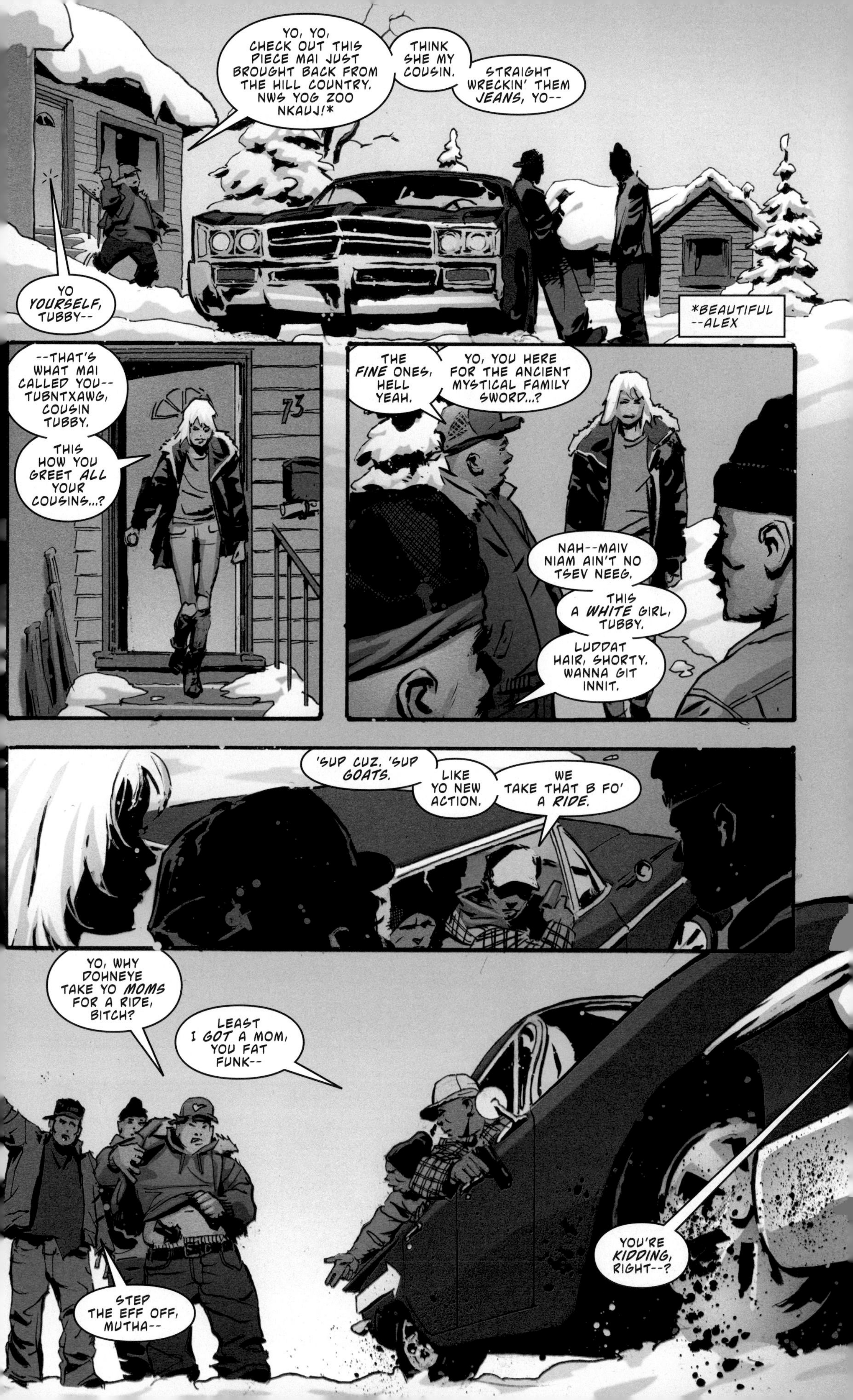
YO, YO, CHECK OUT THIS PIECE MAI JUST BROUGHT BACK FROM THE HILL COUNTRY. NWS YOG ZOO NKAUJ!*
THINK SHE MY COUSIN.
STRAIGHT WRECKIN' THEM JEANS, YO--
YO YOURSELF, TUBBY--
*BEAUTIFUL --ALEX
--THAT'S WHAT MAI CALLED YOU-- TUBNTXAWG, COUSIN TUBBY.
THIS HOW YOU GREET ALL YOUR COUSINS...?
73
THE FINE ONES, HELL YEAH.
YO, YOU HERE FOR THE ANCIENT MYSTICAL FAMILY SWORD...?
NAH--MAIV NIAM AIN'T NO TSEV NEEG.
THIS A WHITE GIRL, TUBBY.
LUDDAT HAIR, SHORTY. WANNA GIT INNIT.
'SUP CUZ. 'SUP GOATS.
LIKE YO NEW ACTION.
WE TAKE THAT B FO' A RIDE.
YO, WHY DOHNEYE TAKE YO MOMS FOR A RIDE, BITCH?
LEAST I GOT A MOM, YOU FAT FUNK--
STEP THE EFF OFF, MUTHA--
YOU'RE KIDDING, RIGHT--?

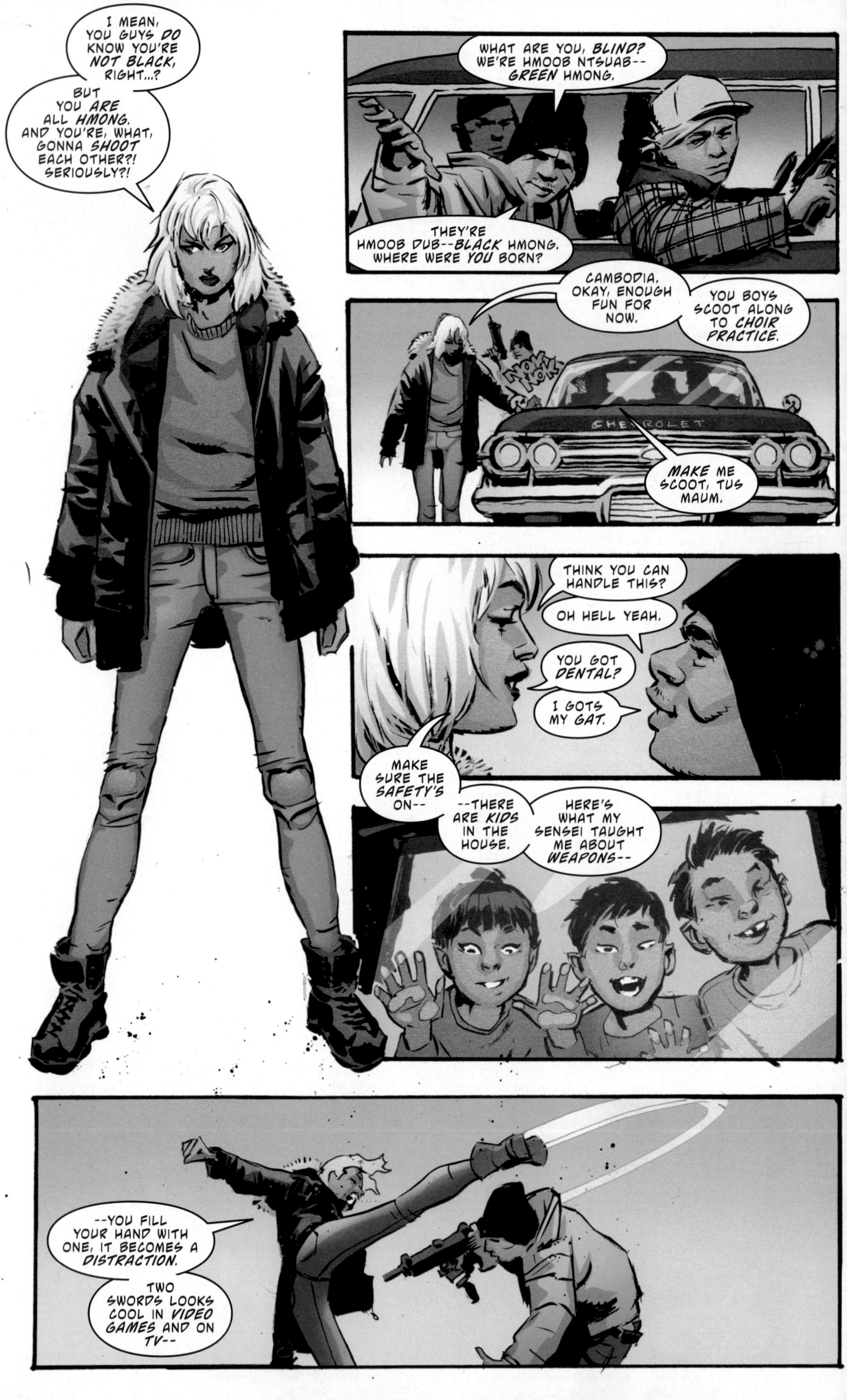

I MEAN, YOU GUYS DO KNOW YOU'RE NOT BLACK, RIGHT...?
BUT YOU ARE ALL HMONG. AND YOU'RE, WHAT, GONNA SHOOT EACH OTHER?! SERIOUSLY?!
WHAT ARE YOU, BLIND? WE'RE HMOOB NTSUAB-- GREEN HMONG.
THEY'RE HMOOB DUB--BLACK HMONG. WHERE WERE YOU BORN?
CAMBODIA. OKAY, ENOUGH FUN FOR NOW.
YOU BOYS SCOOT ALONG TO CHOIR PRACTICE.
NOK NOK
CHEVROLET
MAKE ME SCOOT, TUS MAUM.
THINK YOU CAN HANDLE THIS?
OH HELL YEAH.
YOU GOT DENTAL?
I GOTS MY GAT.
MAKE SURE THE SAFETY'S ON--
--THERE ARE KIDS IN THE HOUSE.
HERE'S WHAT MY SENSEI TAUGHT ME ABOUT WEAPONS--
--YOU FILL YOUR HAND WITH ONE, IT BECOMES A DISTRACTION.
TWO SWORDS LOOKS COOL IN VIDEO GAMES AND ON TV--

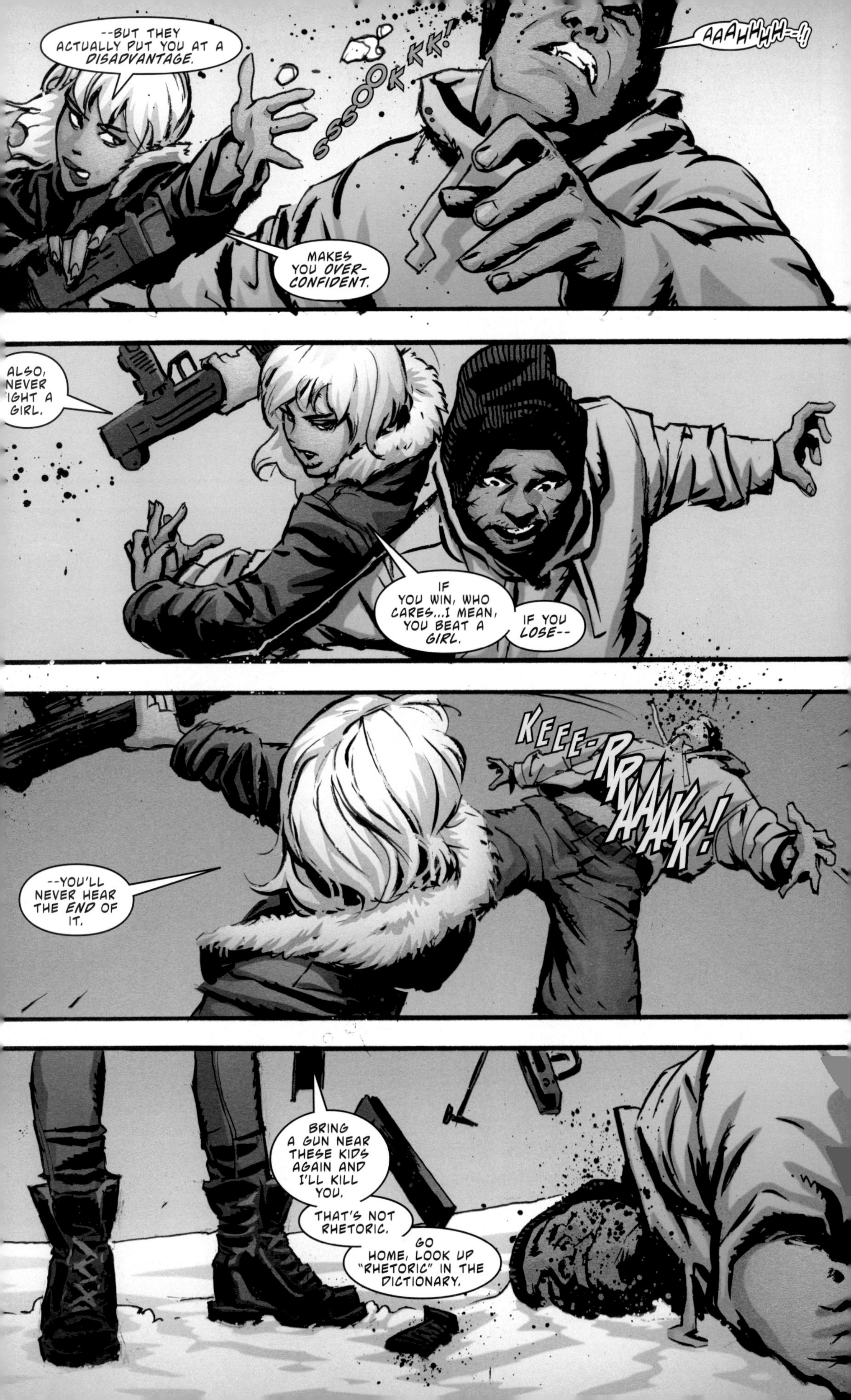
--BUT THEY ACTUALLY PUT YOU AT A DISADVANTAGE.
SSSOOKKK!
AAAHHHH--!!
MAKES YOU OVER-CONFIDENT.
ALSO, NEVER FIGHT A GIRL.
IF YOU WIN, WHO CARES...I MEAN, YOU BEAT A GIRL.
IF YOU LOSE--
KEEE-RRAAAKK!
--YOU'LL NEVER HEAR THE END OF IT.
BRING A GUN NEAR THESE KIDS AGAIN AND I'LL KILL YOU.
THAT'S NOT RHETORIC.
GO HOME, LOOK UP "RHETORIC" IN THE DICTIONARY.

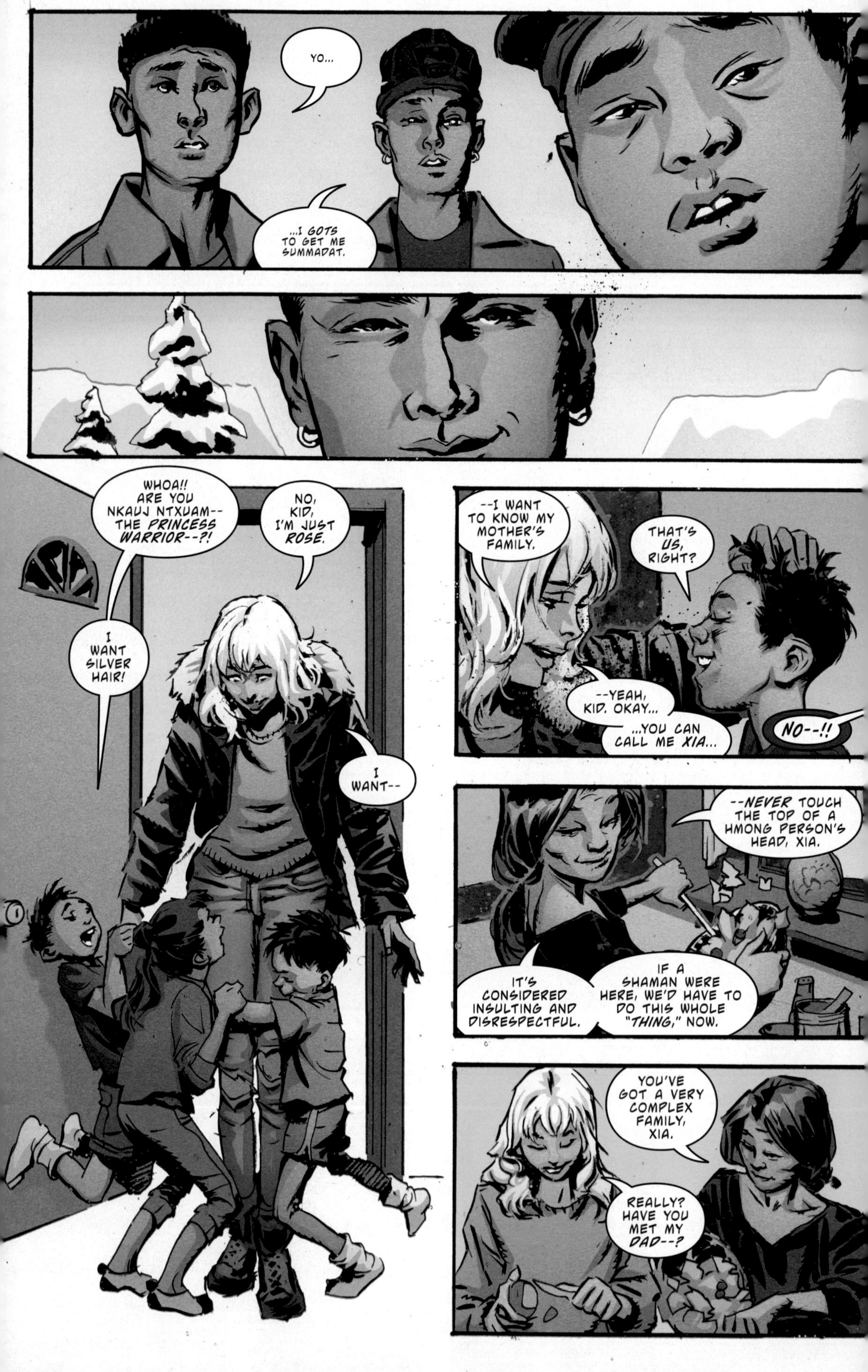
YO...
...I GOTS TO GET ME SUMMADAT.
WHOA!! ARE YOU NKAUJ NTXUAM-- THE PRINCESS WARRIOR--?!
NO, KID, I'M JUST ROSE.
I WANT SILVER HAIR!
I WANT--
--I WANT TO KNOW MY MOTHER'S FAMILY.
THAT'S US, RIGHT?
--YEAH, KID. OKAY...
...YOU CAN CALL ME XIA...
NO--!!
--NEVER TOUCH THE TOP OF A HMONG PERSON'S HEAD, XIA.
IT'S CONSIDERED INSULTING AND DISRESPECTFUL.
IF A SHAMAN WERE HERE, WE'D HAVE TO DO THIS WHOLE "THING," NOW.
YOU'VE GOT A VERY COMPLEX FAMILY, XIA.
REALLY? HAVE YOU MET MY DAD--?

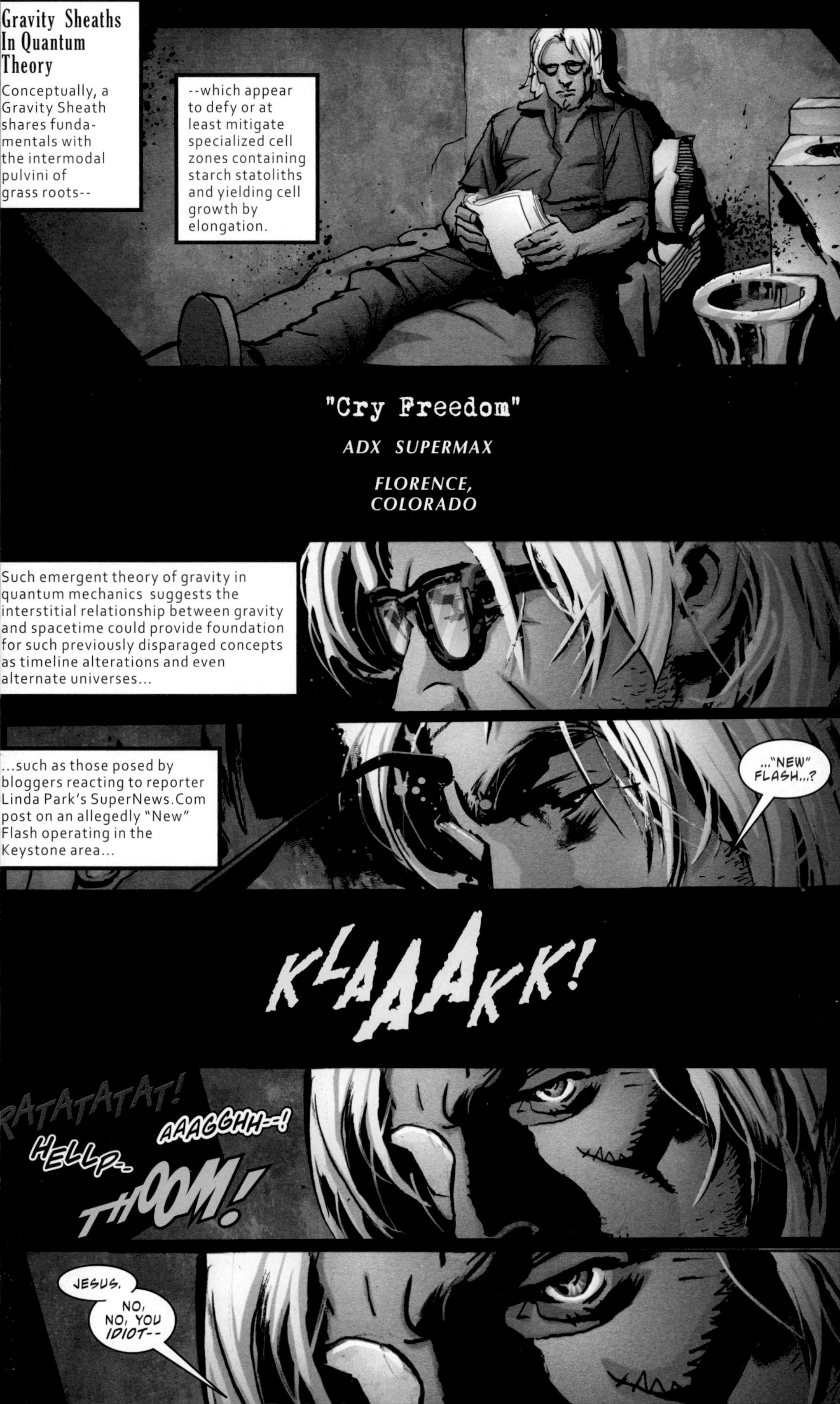
Gravity Sheaths In Quantum Theory
Conceptually, a Gravity Sheath shares funda-mentals with the intermodal pulvini of grass roots--
--which appear to defy or at least mitigate specialized cell zones containing starch statoliths and yielding cell growth by elongation.
"Cry Freedom"
ADX SUPERMAX
FLORENCE, COLORADO
Such emergent theory of gravity in quantum mechanics suggests the interstitial relationship between gravity and spacetime could provide foundation for such previously disparaged concepts as timeline alterations and even alternate universes...
...such as those posed by bloggers reacting to reporter Linda Park's SuperNews.Com post on an allegedly "New" Flash operating in the Keystone area...
..."NEW" FLASH...?
KLAAAKK!
RATATATAT!
AAAGGHH--!
HELLP--
THOOM!
JESUS.
NO, NO, YOU IDIOT--

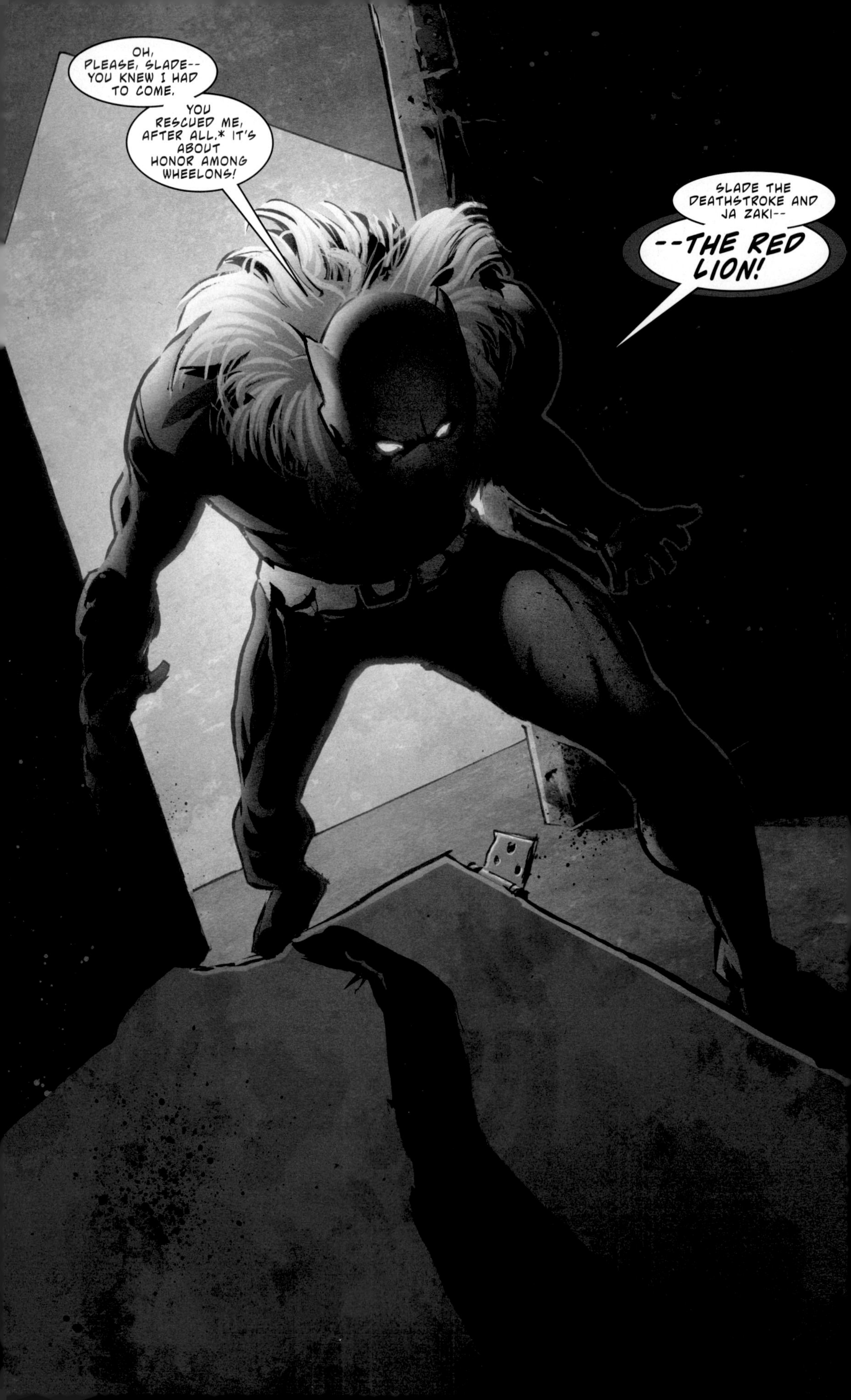
OH, PLEASE, SLADE-- YOU KNEW I HAD TO COME.
YOU RESCUED ME, AFTER ALL.* IT'S ABOUT HONOR AMONG WHEELONS!
SLADE THE DEATHSTROKE AND JA ZAKI--
--THE RED LION!

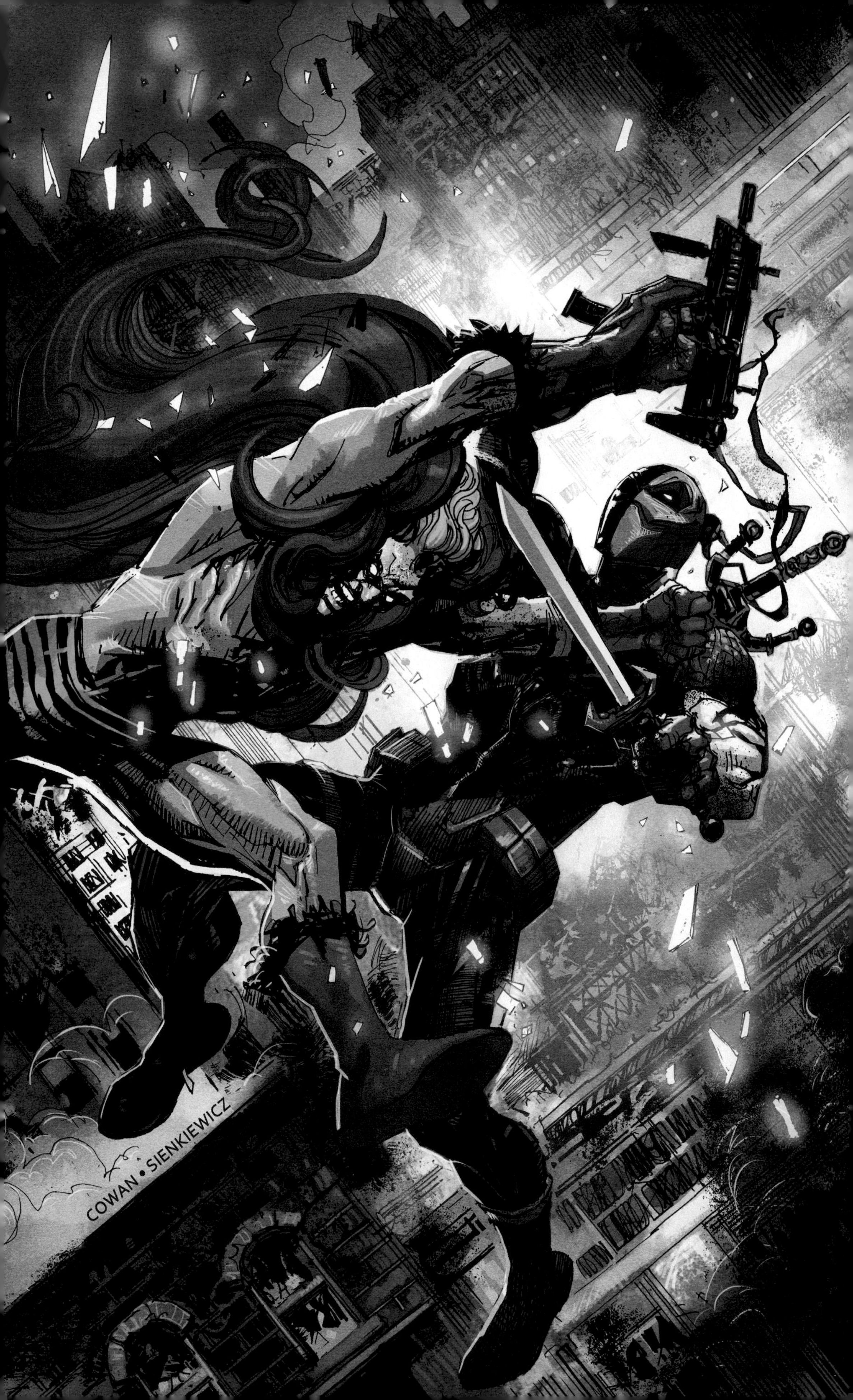
COWAN • SIENKIEWICZ

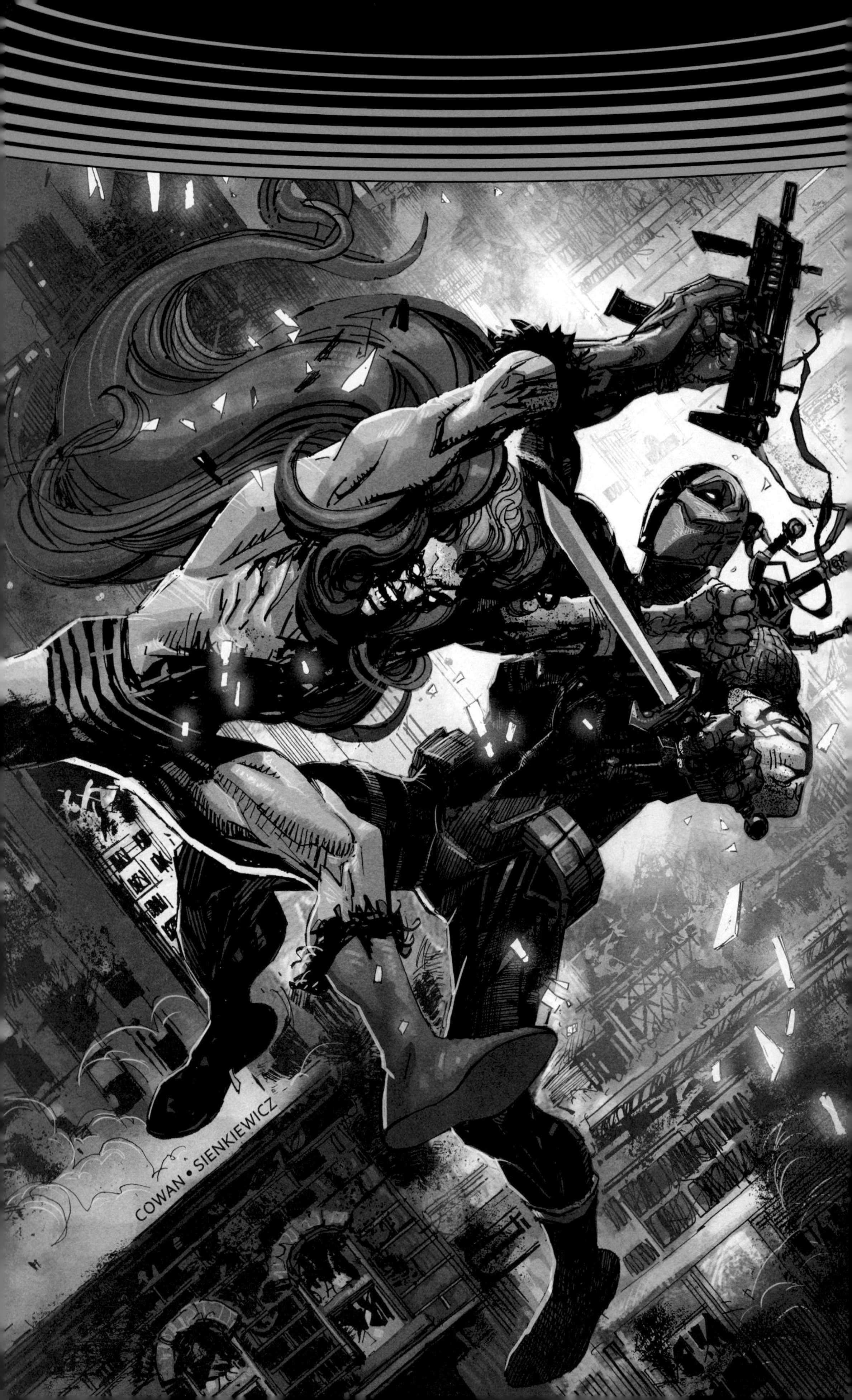
COWAN • SIENKIEWICZ

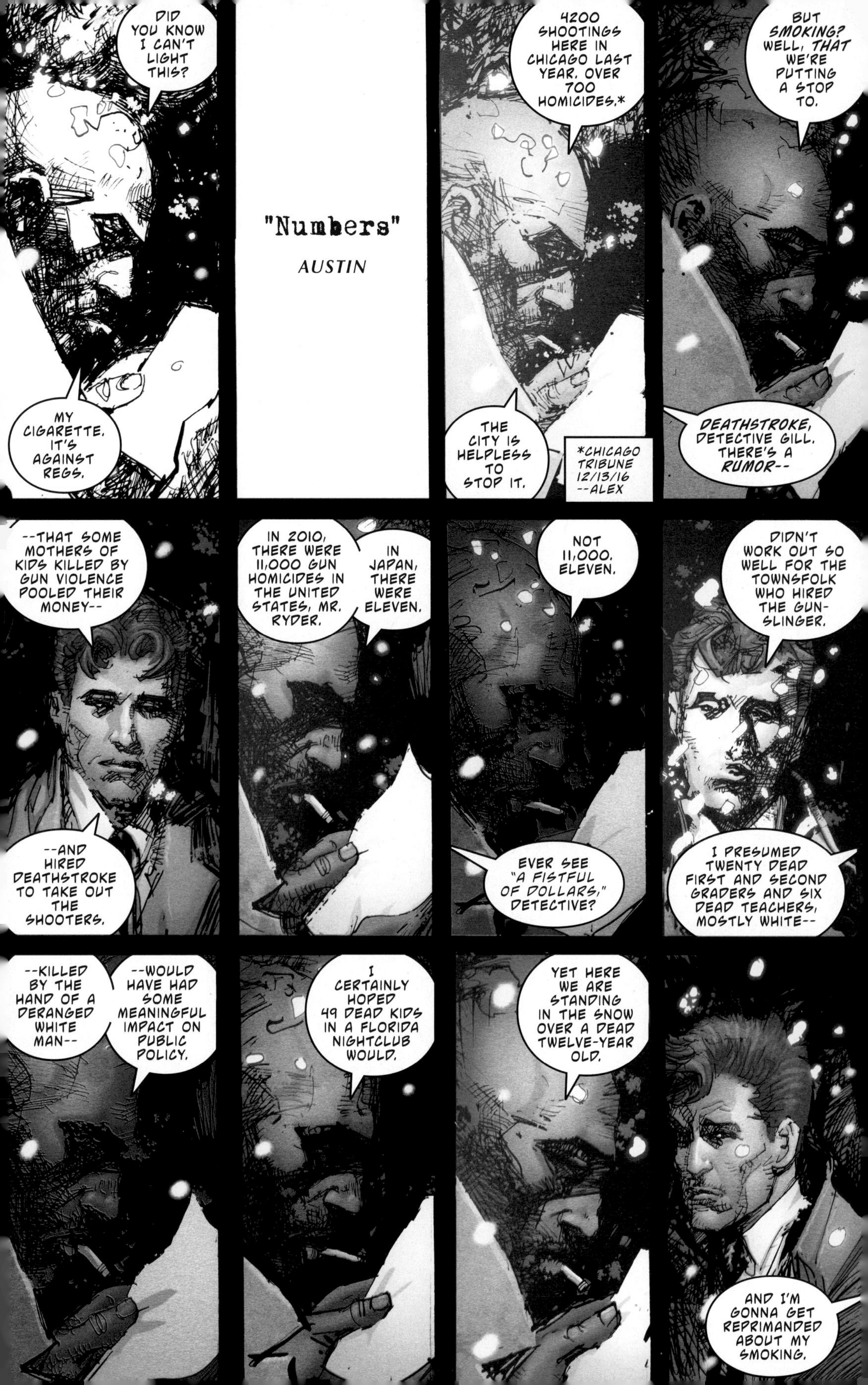
DID YOU KNOW I CAN'T LIGHT THIS?
MY CIGARETTE. IT'S AGAINST REGS.
"Numbers"
AUSTIN
4200 SHOOTINGS HERE IN CHICAGO LAST YEAR. OVER 700 HOMICIDES.*
THE CITY IS HELPLESS TO STOP IT.
*CHICAGO TRIBUNE 12/13/16 --ALEX
BUT SMOKING? WELL, THAT WE'RE PUTTING A STOP TO.
DEATHSTROKE, DETECTIVE GILL. THERE'S A RUMOR--
--THAT SOME MOTHERS OF KIDS KILLED BY GUN VIOLENCE POOLED THEIR MONEY--
--AND HIRED DEATHSTROKE TO TAKE OUT THE SHOOTERS.
IN 2010, THERE WERE 11,000 GUN HOMICIDES IN THE UNITED STATES, MR. RYDER.
IN JAPAN, THERE WERE ELEVEN.
NOT 11,000. ELEVEN.
EVER SEE "A FISTFUL OF DOLLARS," DETECTIVE?
DIDN'T WORK OUT SO WELL FOR THE TOWNSFOLK WHO HIRED THE GUN-SLINGER.
I PRESUMED TWENTY DEAD FIRST AND SECOND GRADERS AND SIX DEAD TEACHERS, MOSTLY WHITE--
--KILLED BY THE HAND OF A DERANGED WHITE MAN--
--WOULD HAVE HAD SOME MEANINGFUL IMPACT ON PUBLIC POLICY.
I CERTAINLY HOPED 49 DEAD KIDS IN A FLORIDA NIGHTCLUB WOULD.
YET HERE WE ARE STANDING IN THE SNOW OVER A DEAD TWELVE-YEAR OLD.
AND I'M GONNA GET REPRIMANDED ABOUT MY SMOKING.

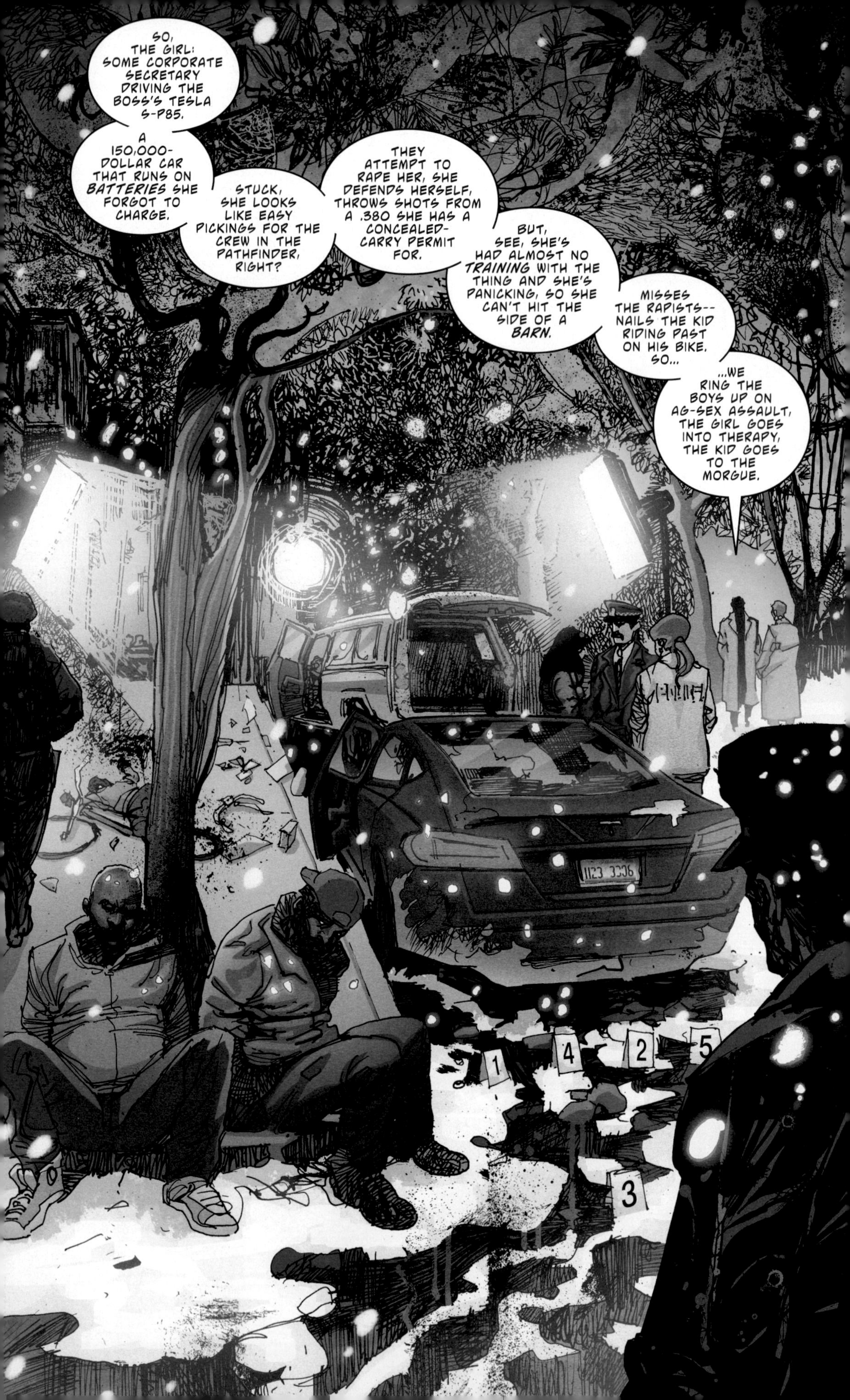
SO, THE GIRL: SOME CORPORATE SECRETARY DRIVING THE BOSS'S TESLA S-P85.
A 150,000-DOLLAR CAR THAT RUNS ON *BATTERIES* SHE FORGOT TO CHARGE.
STUCK, SHE LOOKS LIKE EASY PICKINGS FOR THE CREW IN THE PATHFINDER, RIGHT?
THEY ATTEMPT TO RAPE HER, SHE DEFENDS HERSELF, THROWS SHOTS FROM A .380 SHE HAS A CONCEALED-CARRY PERMIT FOR.
BUT, SEE, SHE'S HAD ALMOST NO *TRAINING* WITH THE THING AND SHE'S PANICKING, SO SHE CAN'T HIT THE SIDE OF A *BARN.*
MISSES THE RAPISTS--NAILS THE KID RIDING PAST ON HIS BIKE. SO...
...WE RING THE BOYS UP ON AG-SEX ASSAULT, THE GIRL GOES INTO THERAPY, THE KID GOES TO THE MORGUE.
1
4
2
5
3

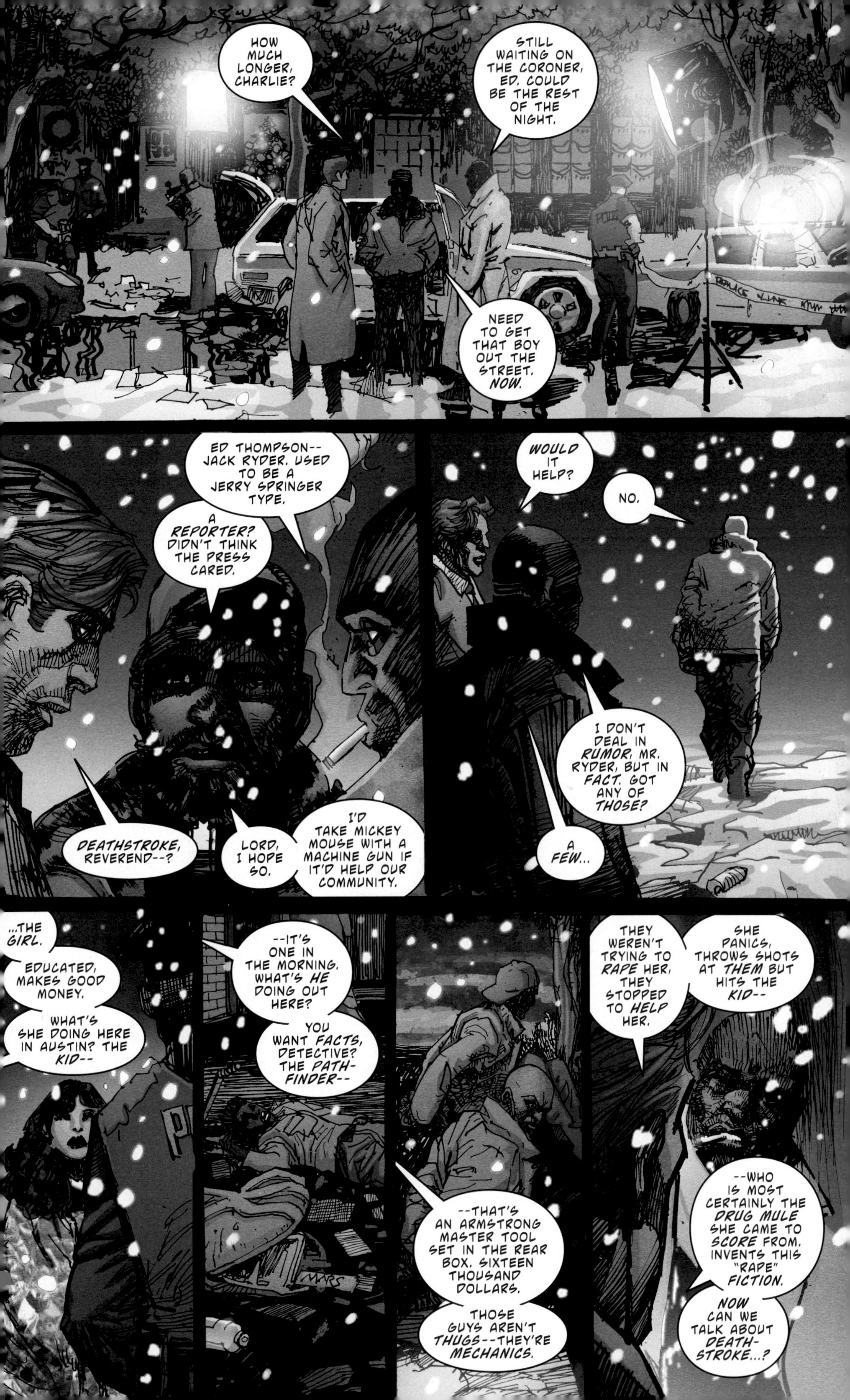
HOW MUCH LONGER, CHARLIE?
STILL WAITING ON THE CORONER, ED. COULD BE THE REST OF THE NIGHT.
NEED TO GET THAT BOY OUT THE STREET. NOW.
ED THOMPSON-- JACK RYDER. USED TO BE A JERRY SPRINGER TYPE.
A REPORTER? DIDN'T THINK THE PRESS CARED.
DEATHSTROKE, REVEREND--?
LORD, I HOPE SO.
I'D TAKE MICKEY MOUSE WITH A MACHINE GUN IF IT'D HELP OUR COMMUNITY.
WOULD IT HELP?
NO.
I DON'T DEAL IN RUMOR, MR. RYDER, BUT IN FACT. GOT ANY OF THOSE?
A FEW...
...THE GIRL.
EDUCATED, MAKES GOOD MONEY.
WHAT'S SHE DOING HERE IN AUSTIN? THE KID--
--IT'S ONE IN THE MORNING. WHAT'S HE DOING OUT HERE?
YOU WANT FACTS, DETECTIVE? THE PATH-FINDER--
--THAT'S AN ARMSTRONG MASTER TOOL SET IN THE REAR BOX. SIXTEEN THOUSAND DOLLARS.
THOSE GUYS AREN'T THUGS--THEY'RE MECHANICS.
THEY WEREN'T TRYING TO RAPE HER, THEY STOPPED TO HELP HER.
SHE PANICS, THROWS SHOTS AT THEM BUT HITS THE KID--
--WHO IS MOST CERTAINLY THE DRUG MULE SHE CAME TO SCORE FROM. INVENTS THIS "RAPE" FICTION.
NOW CAN WE TALK ABOUT DEATH-STROKE...?

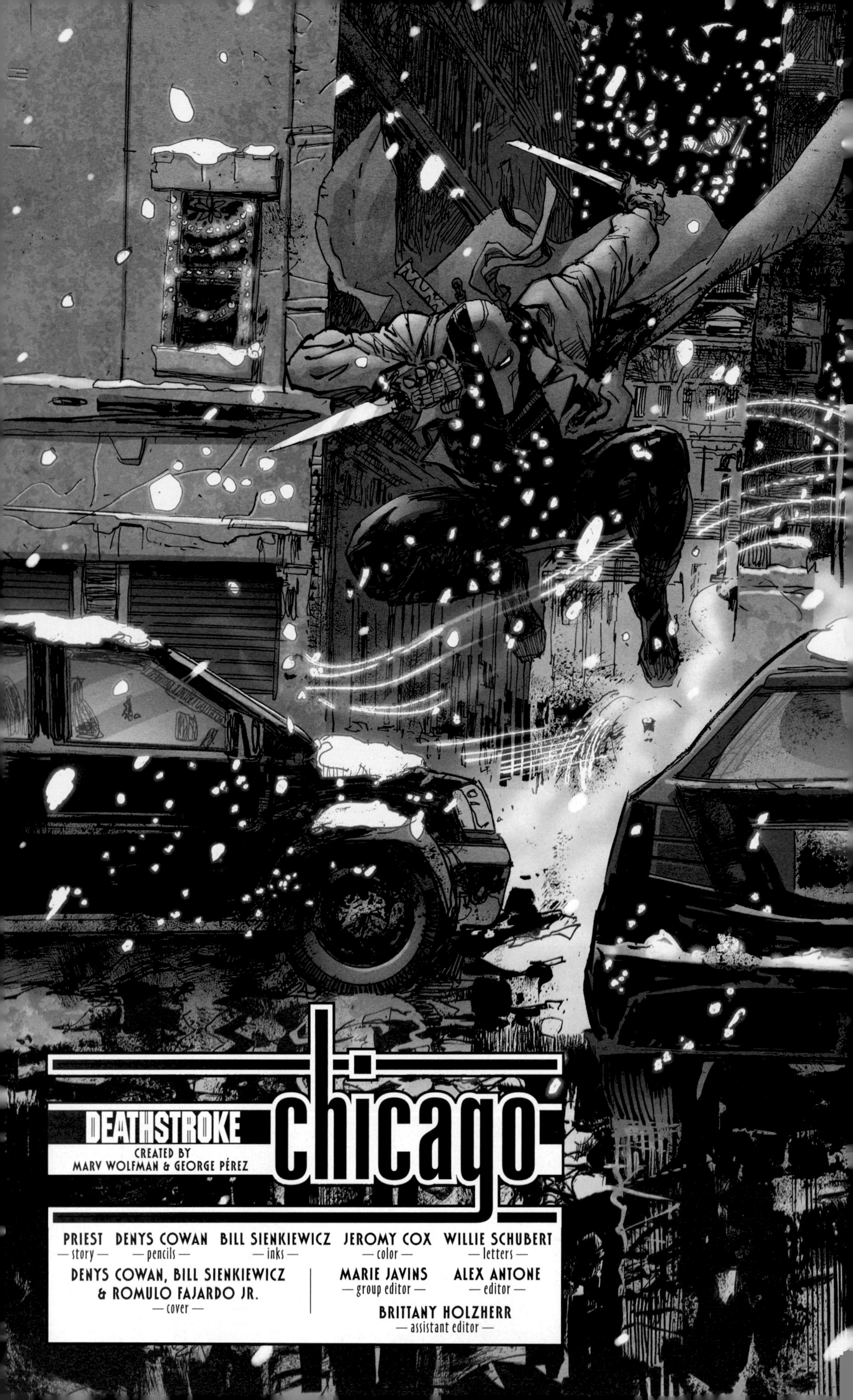

DEATHSTROKE
CREATED BY
MARV WOLFMAN & GEORGE PÉREZ

chicago

PRIEST — story —
DENYS COWAN — pencils —
BILL SIENKIEWICZ — inks —
JEROMY COX — color —
WILLIE SCHUBERT — letters —

DENYS COWAN, BILL SIENKIEWICZ & ROMULO FAJARDO JR. — cover —

MARIE JAVINS — group editor —
ALEX ANTONE — editor —
BRITTANY HOLZHERR — assistant editor —

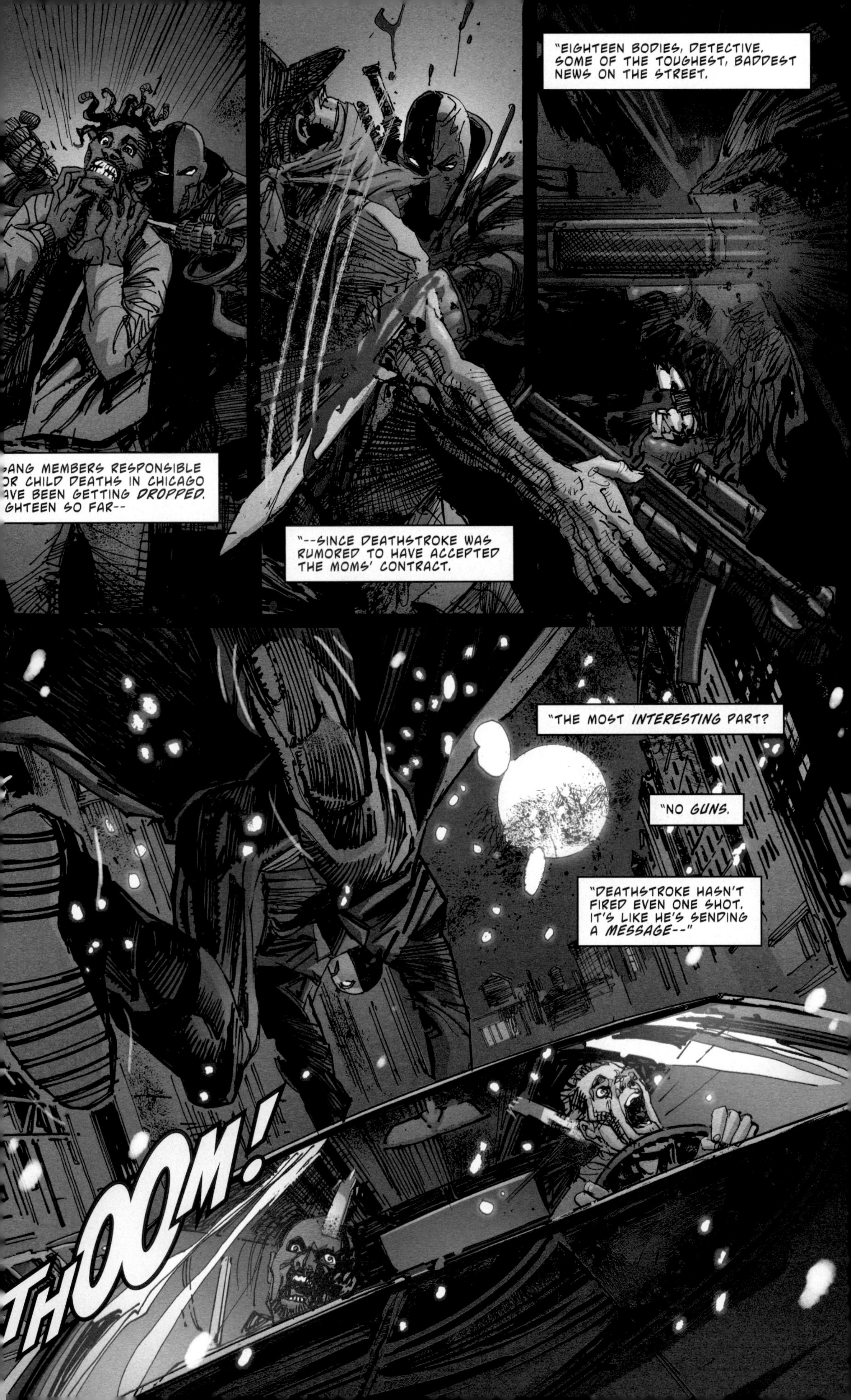
GANG MEMBERS RESPONSIBLE
OR CHILD DEATHS IN CHICAGO
AVE BEEN GETTING *DROPPED*.
GHTEEN SO FAR--
"--SINCE DEATHSTROKE WAS RUMORED TO HAVE ACCEPTED THE MOMS' CONTRACT.
"EIGHTEEN BODIES, DETECTIVE. SOME OF THE TOUGHEST, BADDEST NEWS ON THE STREET.
"THE MOST *INTERESTING* PART?
"NO *GUNS*.
"DEATHSTROKE HASN'T FIRED EVEN ONE SHOT. IT'S LIKE HE'S SENDING A *MESSAGE*--"
THOOM!

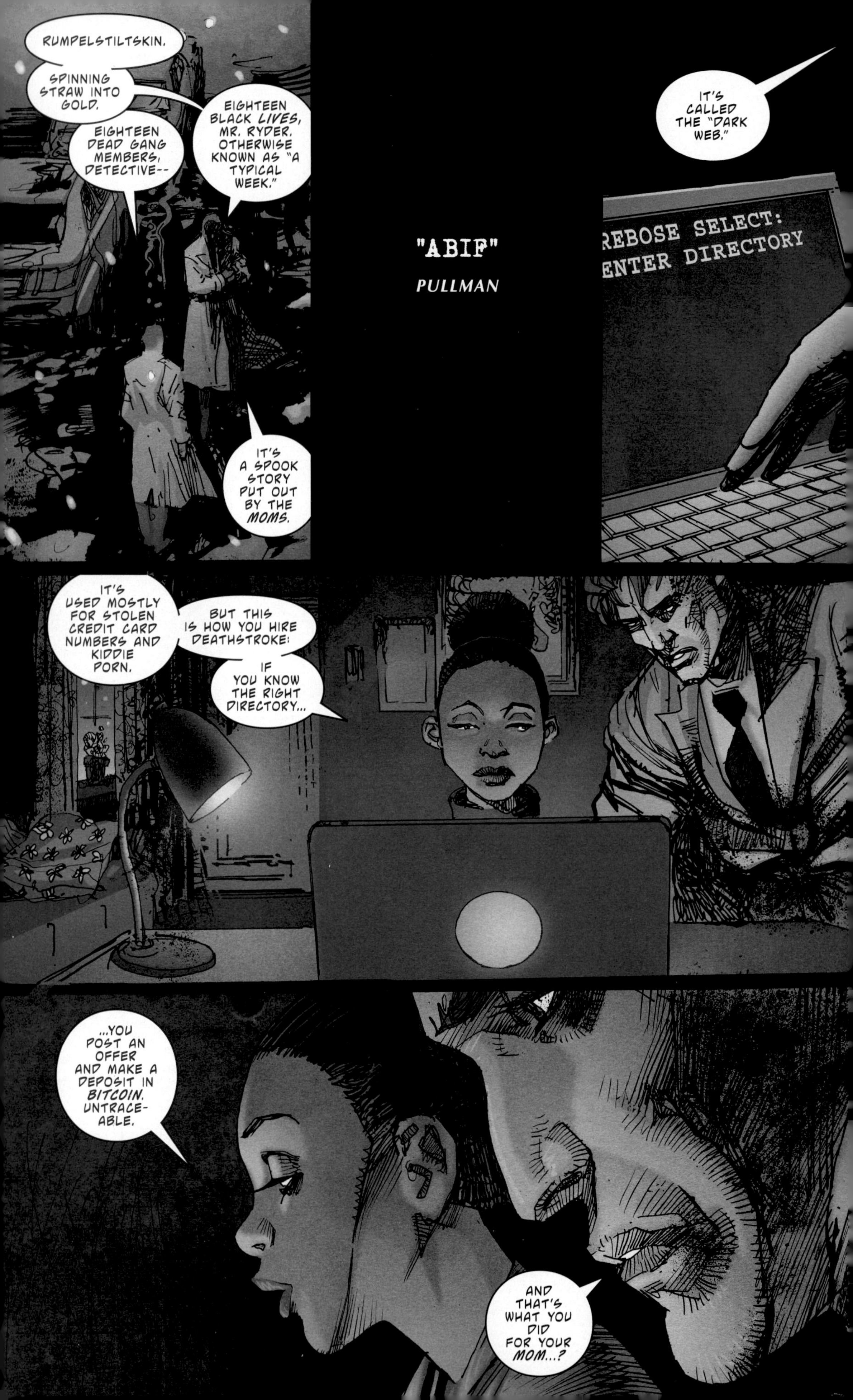
RUMPELSTILTSKIN.
SPINNING STRAW INTO GOLD.
EIGHTEEN DEAD GANG MEMBERS, DETECTIVE--
EIGHTEEN BLACK *LIVES*, MR. RYDER. OTHERWISE KNOWN AS "A TYPICAL WEEK."
IT'S A SPOOK STORY PUT OUT BY THE *MOMS*.
"ABIF"
PULLMAN
IT'S CALLED THE "DARK WEB."
REBOSE SELECT:
ENTER DIRECTORY
IT'S USED MOSTLY FOR STOLEN CREDIT CARD NUMBERS AND KIDDIE PORN.
BUT THIS IS HOW YOU HIRE DEATHSTROKE:
IF YOU KNOW THE RIGHT DIRECTORY...
...YOU POST AN OFFER AND MAKE A DEPOSIT IN *BITCOIN*. UNTRACE-ABLE.
AND THAT'S WHAT YOU DID FOR YOUR *MOM*...?

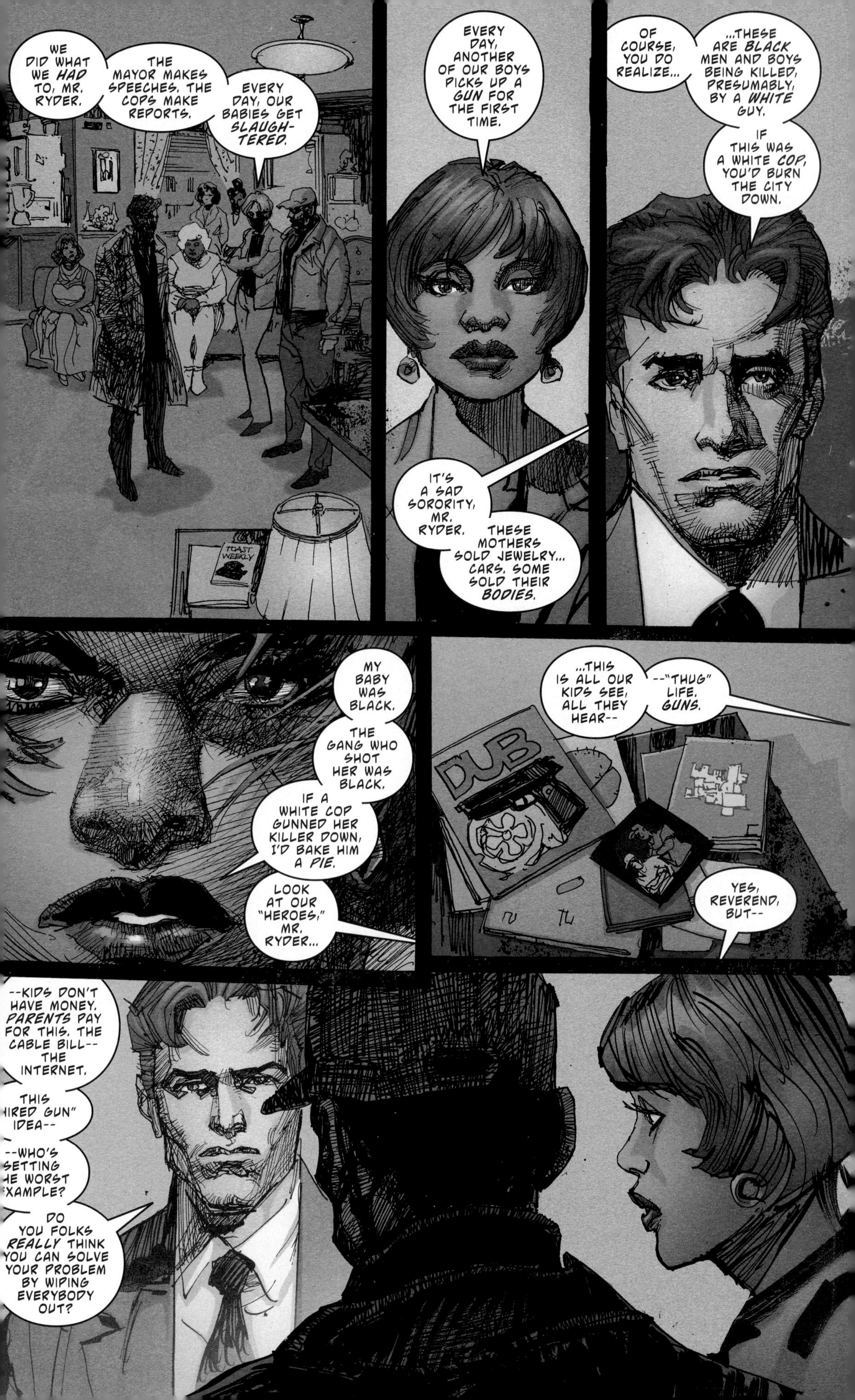
WE DID WHAT WE HAD TO, MR. RYDER.
THE MAYOR MAKES SPEECHES. THE COPS MAKE REPORTS.
EVERY DAY, OUR BABIES GET SLAUGHTERED.
TOAST WEEKLY
EVERY DAY, ANOTHER OF OUR BOYS PICKS UP A GUN FOR THE FIRST TIME.
IT'S A SAD SORORITY, MR. RYDER.
THESE MOTHERS SOLD JEWELRY... CARS. SOME SOLD THEIR BODIES.
OF COURSE, YOU DO REALIZE...
...THESE ARE BLACK MEN AND BOYS BEING KILLED, PRESUMABLY, BY A WHITE GUY.
IF THIS WAS A WHITE COP, YOU'D BURN THE CITY DOWN.
MY BABY WAS BLACK.
THE GANG WHO SHOT HER WAS BLACK.
IF A WHITE COP GUNNED HER KILLER DOWN, I'D BAKE HIM A PIE.
LOOK AT OUR "HEROES," MR. RYDER...
...THIS IS ALL OUR KIDS SEE, ALL THEY HEAR--
--"THUG" LIFE. GUNS.
DUB
YES, REVEREND, BUT--
--KIDS DON'T HAVE MONEY. PARENTS PAY FOR THIS. THE CABLE BILL-- THE INTERNET.
THIS HIRED GUN" IDEA--
--WHO'S SETTING HE WORST EXAMPLE?
DO YOU FOLKS REALLY THINK YOU CAN SOLVE YOUR PROBLEM BY WIPING EVERYBODY OUT?

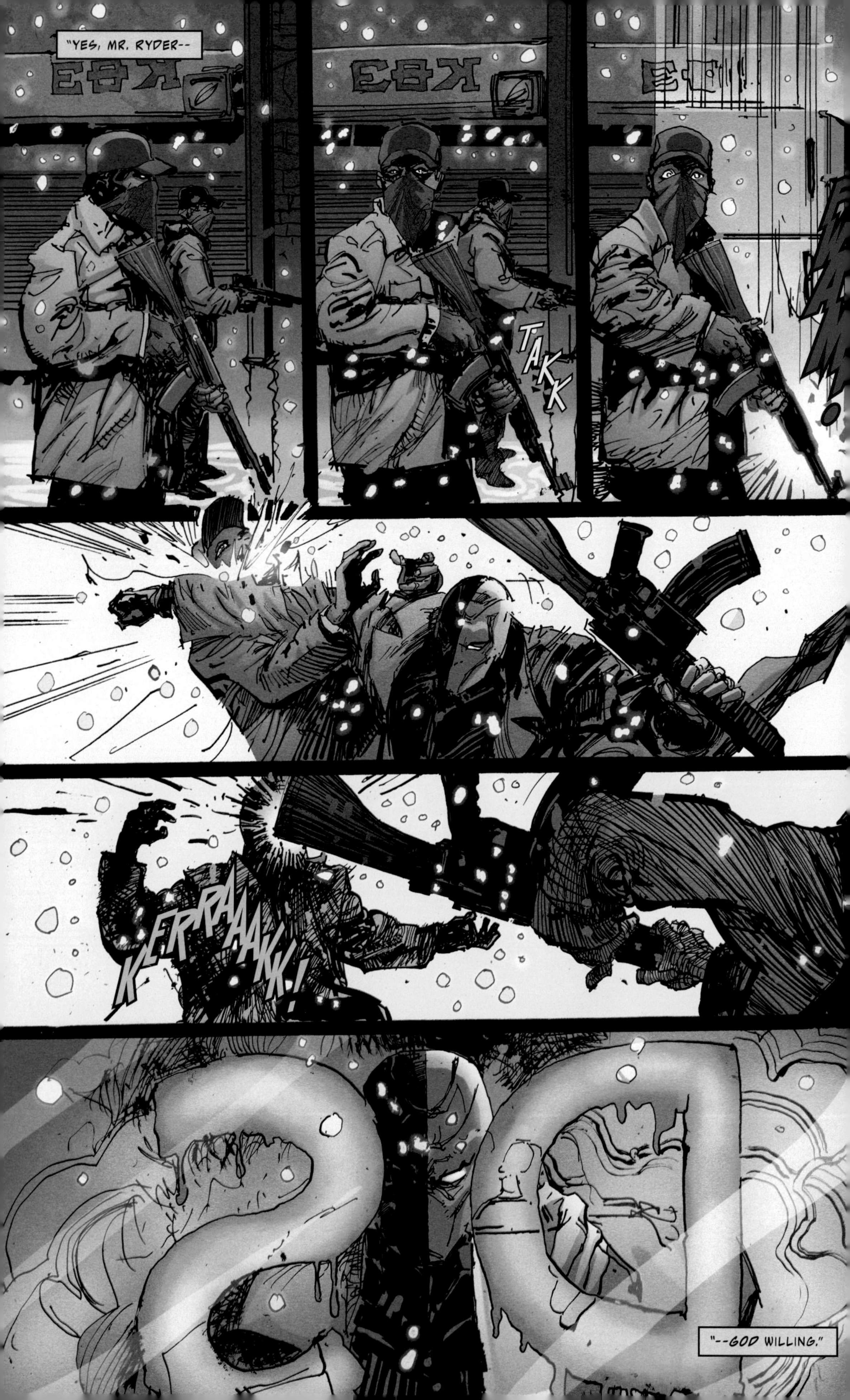
"YES, MR. RYDER--
TAKK
KERRRAAAKK!
"--GOD WILLING."

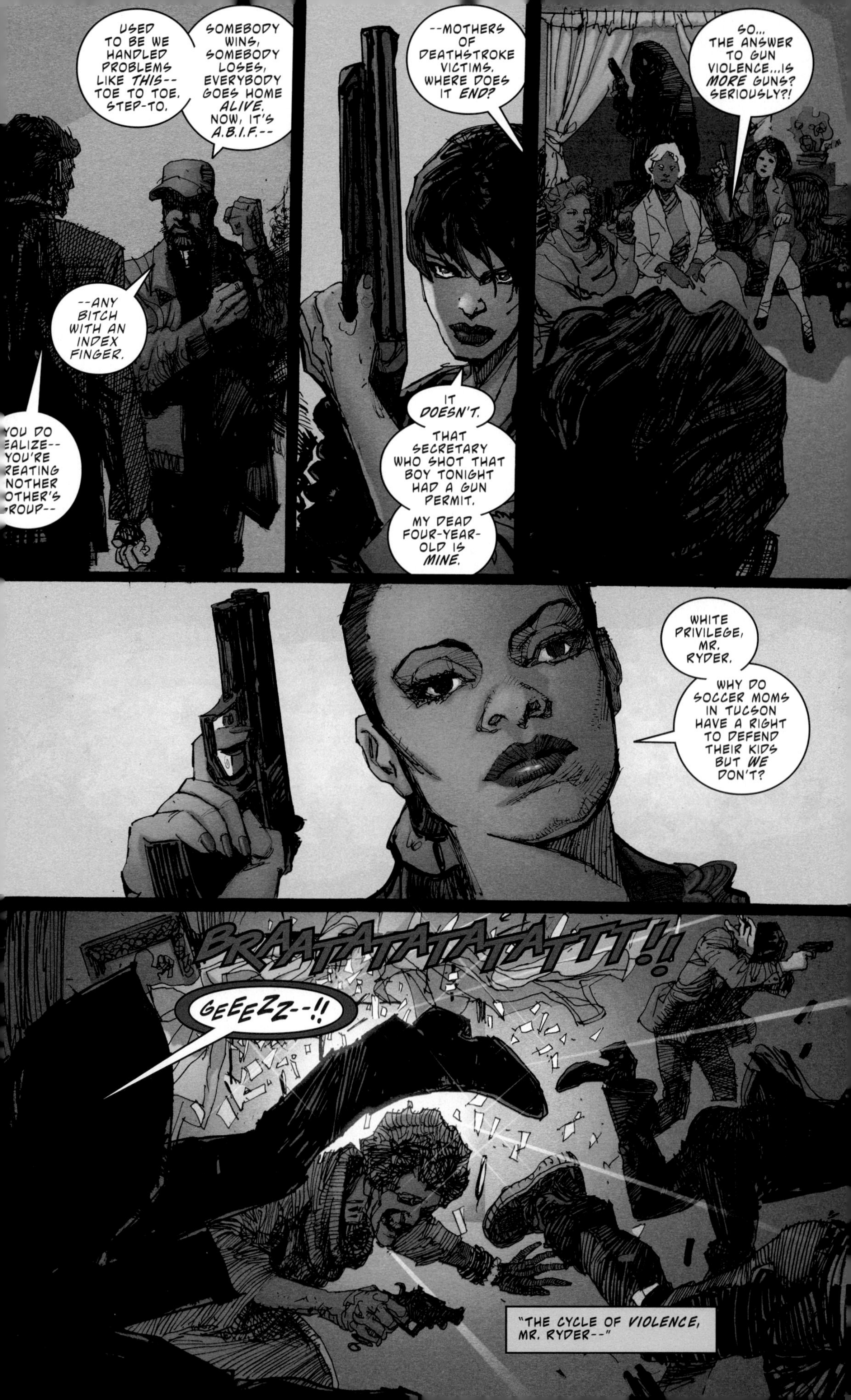
USED TO BE WE HANDLED PROBLEMS LIKE *THIS*-- TOE TO TOE. STEP-TO.
SOMEBODY WINS, SOMEBODY LOSES, EVERYBODY GOES HOME *ALIVE*. NOW, IT'S A.B.I.F.--
--ANY BITCH WITH AN INDEX FINGER.
YOU DO EALIZE-- YOU'RE REATING NOTHER OTHER'S ROUP--
--MOTHERS OF DEATHSTROKE VICTIMS. WHERE DOES IT *END?*
IT *DOESN'T*.
THAT SECRETARY WHO SHOT THAT BOY TONIGHT HAD A GUN PERMIT.
MY DEAD FOUR-YEAR-OLD IS *MINE*.
SO... THE ANSWER TO GUN VIOLENCE...IS *MORE* GUNS? SERIOUSLY?!
WHITE PRIVILEGE, MR. RYDER.
WHY DO SOCCER MOMS IN TUCSON HAVE A RIGHT TO DEFEND THEIR KIDS BUT *WE* DON'T?
BRAATATATATATTT!!
GEEEZZ--!!
"THE CYCLE OF *VIOLENCE*, MR. RYDER--"

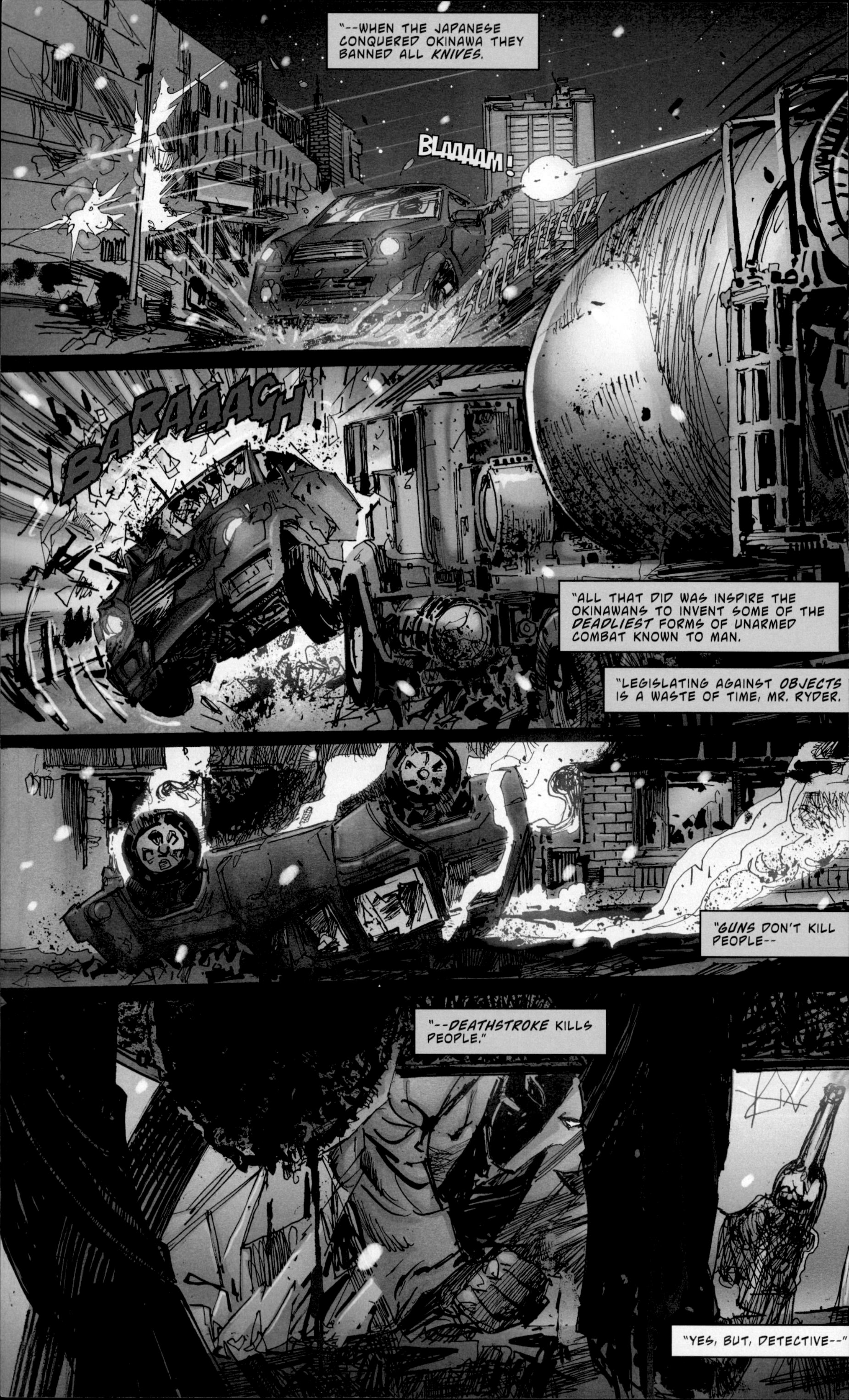
"--WHEN THE JAPANESE CONQUERED OKINAWA THEY BANNED ALL KNIVES.
BLAAAAM!
SCREEEEEEECH!
BARAAAGH
"ALL THAT DID WAS INSPIRE THE OKINAWANS TO INVENT SOME OF THE DEADLIEST FORMS OF UNARMED COMBAT KNOWN TO MAN.
"LEGISLATING AGAINST OBJECTS IS A WASTE OF TIME, MR. RYDER.
"GUNS DON'T KILL PEOPLE--
"--DEATHSTROKE KILLS PEOPLE."
"YES, BUT, DETECTIVE--

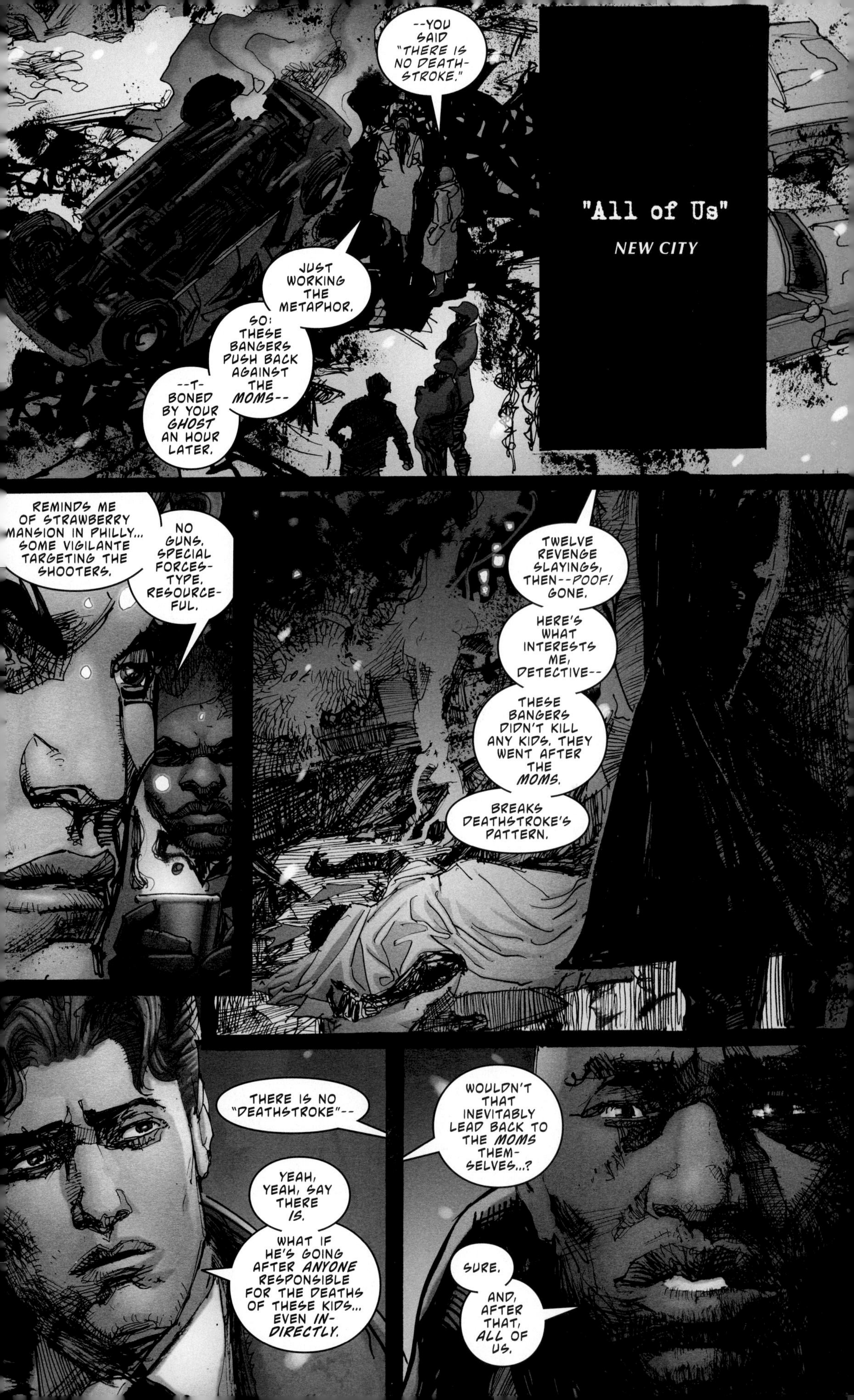
--YOU SAID "THERE IS NO DEATH-STROKE."
"All of Us"
NEW CITY
JUST WORKING THE METAPHOR.
SO: THESE BANGERS PUSH BACK AGAINST THE MOMS--
--T-BONED BY YOUR GHOST AN HOUR LATER.
REMINDS ME OF STRAWBERRY MANSION IN PHILLY... SOME VIGILANTE TARGETING THE SHOOTERS.
NO GUNS. SPECIAL FORCES-TYPE. RESOURCE-FUL.
TWELVE REVENGE SLAYINGS, THEN--POOF! GONE.
HERE'S WHAT INTERESTS ME, DETECTIVE--
THESE BANGERS DIDN'T KILL ANY KIDS. THEY WENT AFTER THE MOMS.
BREAKS DEATHSTROKE'S PATTERN.
THERE IS NO "DEATHSTROKE"--
YEAH, YEAH, SAY THERE IS.
WHAT IF HE'S GOING AFTER ANYONE RESPONSIBLE FOR THE DEATHS OF THESE KIDS... EVEN IN-DIRECTLY.
WOULDN'T THAT INEVITABLY LEAD BACK TO THE MOMS THEM-SELVES...?
SURE.
AND, AFTER THAT, ALL OF US.

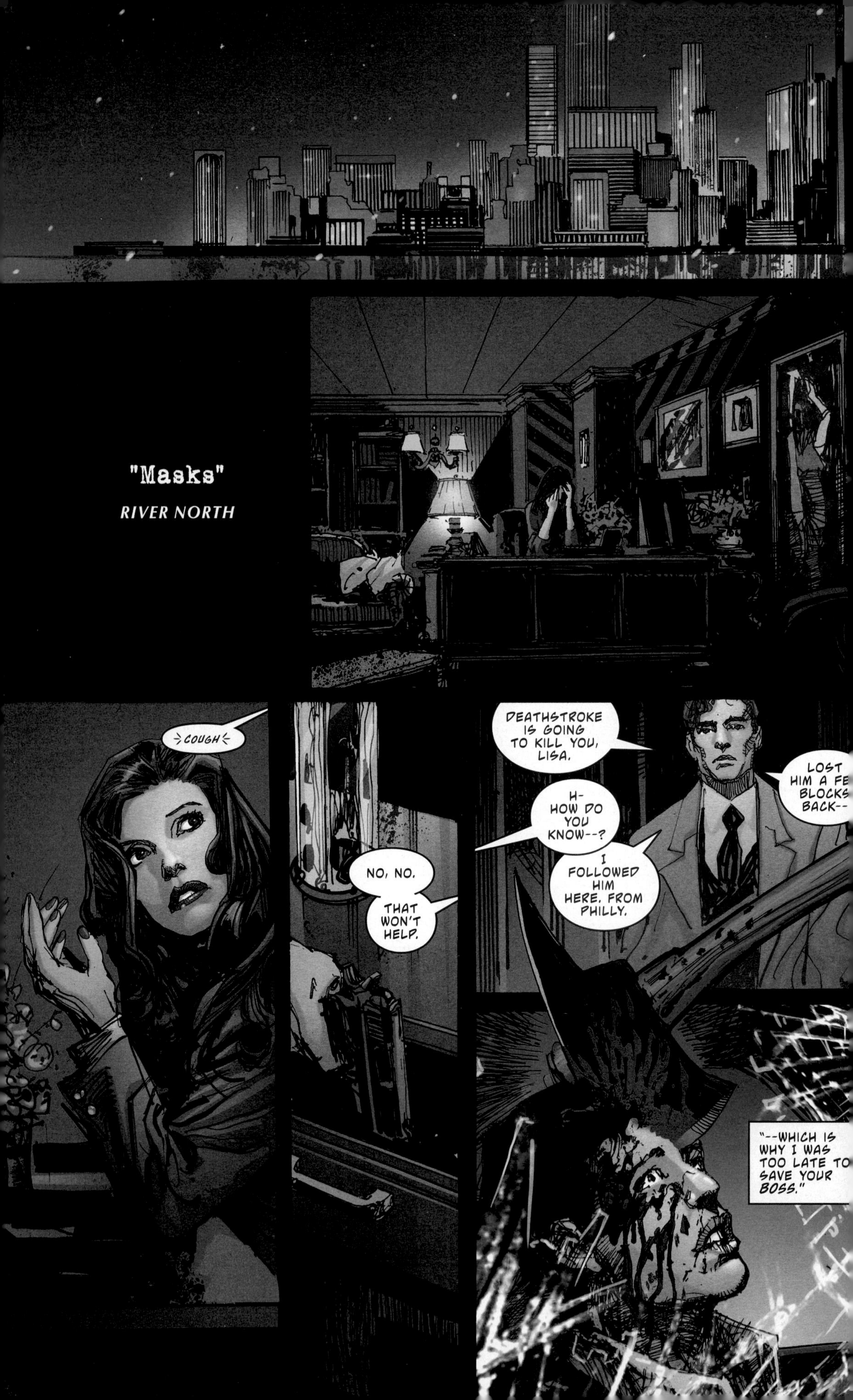
"Masks"
RIVER NORTH
COUGH
NO, NO.
THAT WON'T HELP.
DEATHSTROKE IS GOING TO KILL YOU, LISA.
H- HOW DO YOU KNOW--?
I FOLLOWED HIM HERE. FROM PHILLY.
LOST HIM A FE BLOCKS BACK--
"--WHICH IS WHY I WAS TOO LATE TO SAVE YOUR BOSS."

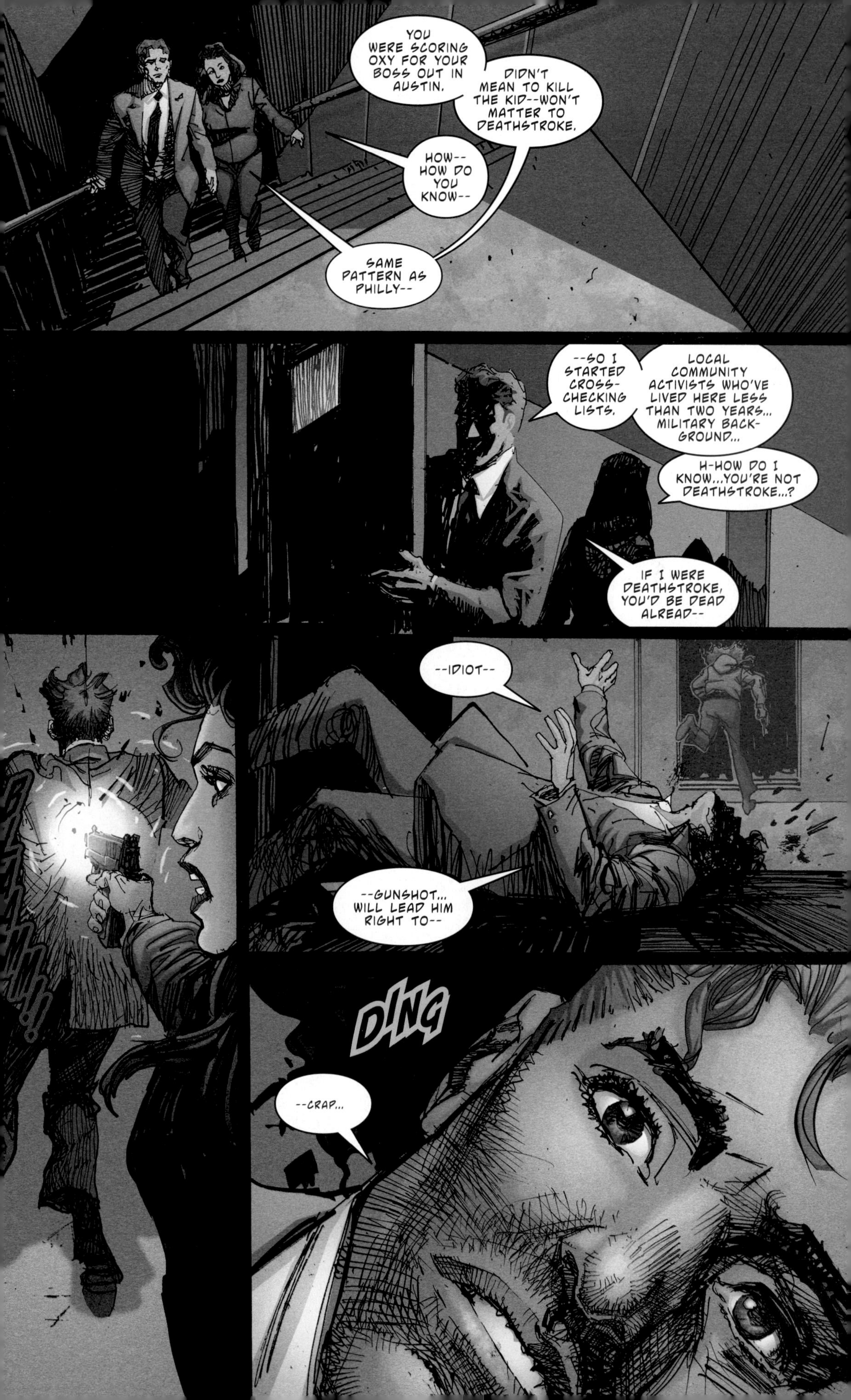

YOU WERE SCORING OXY FOR YOUR BOSS OUT IN AUSTIN.
DIDN'T MEAN TO KILL THE KID--WON'T MATTER TO DEATHSTROKE.
HOW--HOW DO YOU KNOW--
SAME PATTERN AS PHILLY--
--SO I STARTED CROSS-CHECKING LISTS.
LOCAL COMMUNITY ACTIVISTS WHO'VE LIVED HERE LESS THAN TWO YEARS... MILITARY BACK-GROUND...
H-HOW DO I KNOW...YOU'RE NOT DEATHSTROKE...?
IF I WERE DEATHSTROKE, YOU'D BE DEAD ALREAD--
--IDIOT--
--GUNSHOT... WILL LEAD HIM RIGHT TO--
DING
--CRAP...

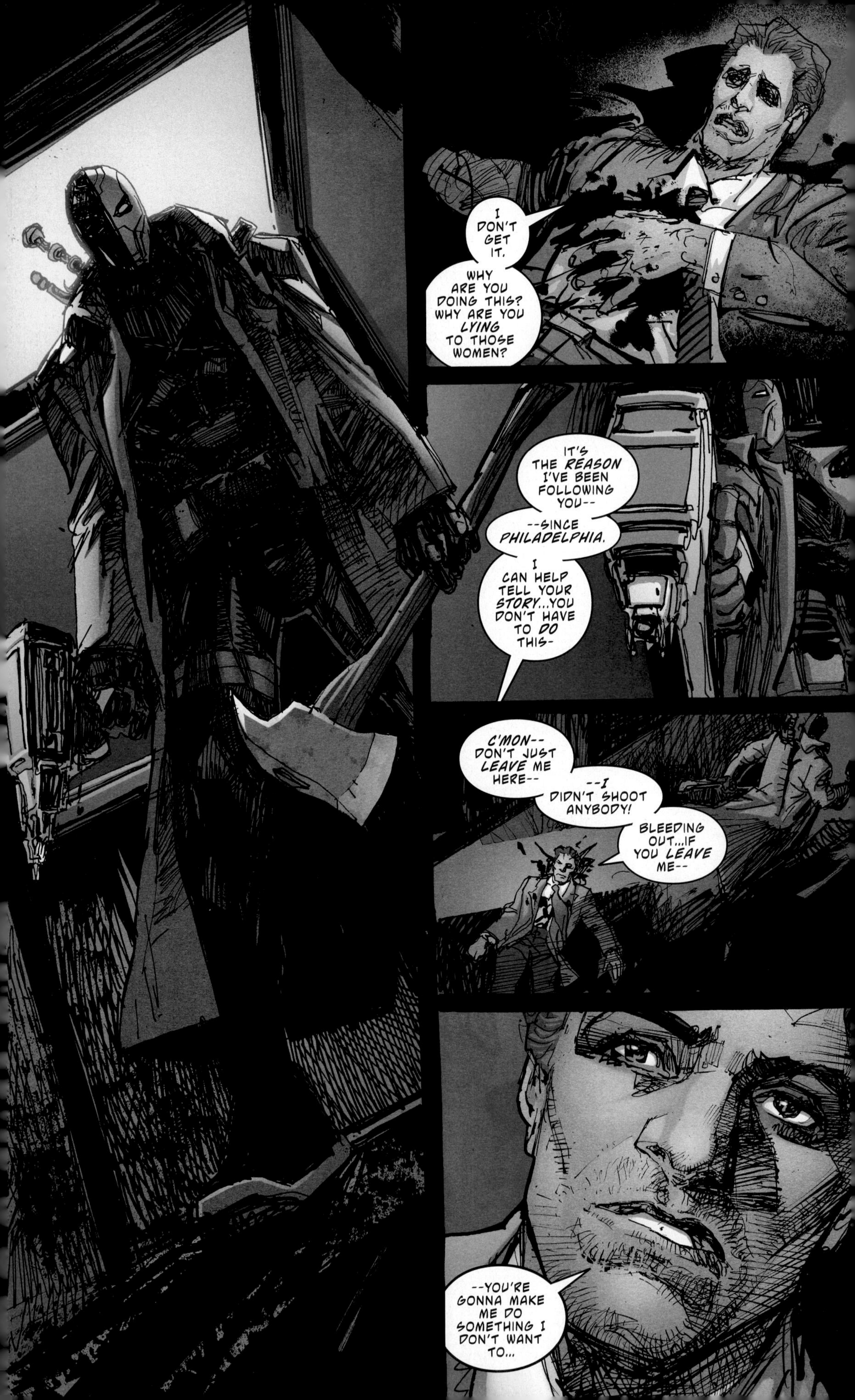
I DON'T GET IT.
WHY ARE YOU DOING THIS? WHY ARE YOU LYING TO THOSE WOMEN?
IT'S THE REASON I'VE BEEN FOLLOWING YOU--
--SINCE PHILADELPHIA.
I CAN HELP TELL YOUR STORY...YOU DON'T HAVE TO DO THIS-
C'MON-- DON'T JUST LEAVE ME HERE--
--I DIDN'T SHOOT ANYBODY!
BLEEDING OUT...IF YOU LEAVE ME--
--YOU'RE GONNA MAKE ME DO SOMETHING I DON'T WANT TO...

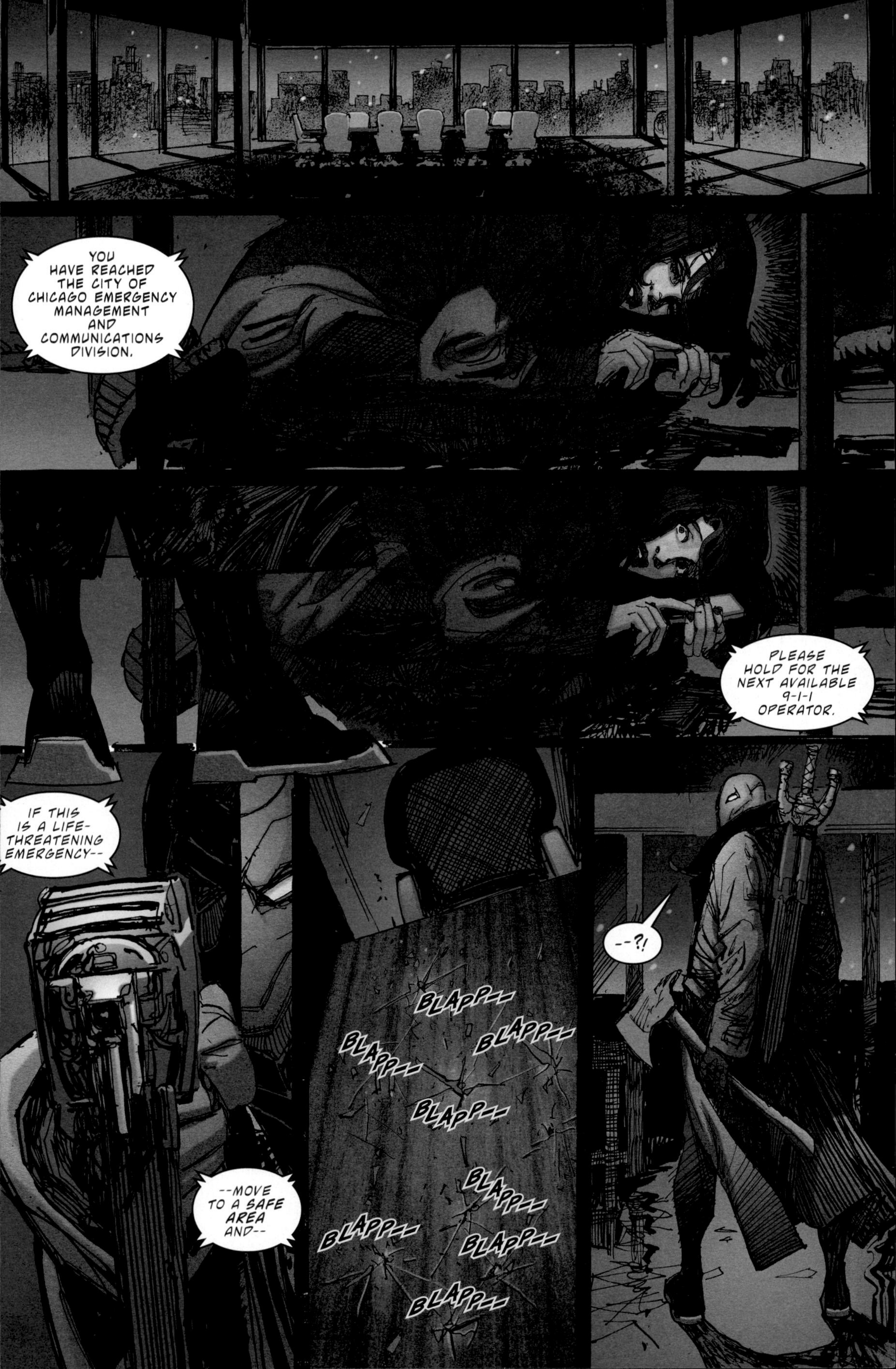
YOU HAVE REACHED THE CITY OF CHICAGO EMERGENCY MANAGEMENT AND COMMUNICATIONS DIVISION.
PLEASE HOLD FOR THE NEXT AVAILABLE 9-1-1 OPERATOR.
IF THIS IS A LIFE-THREATENING EMERGENCY--
--MOVE TO A SAFE AREA AND--
BLAPP--
BLAPP--
BLAPP--
BLAPP--
BLAPP--
BLAPP--
BLAPP--
BLAPP--
--?!

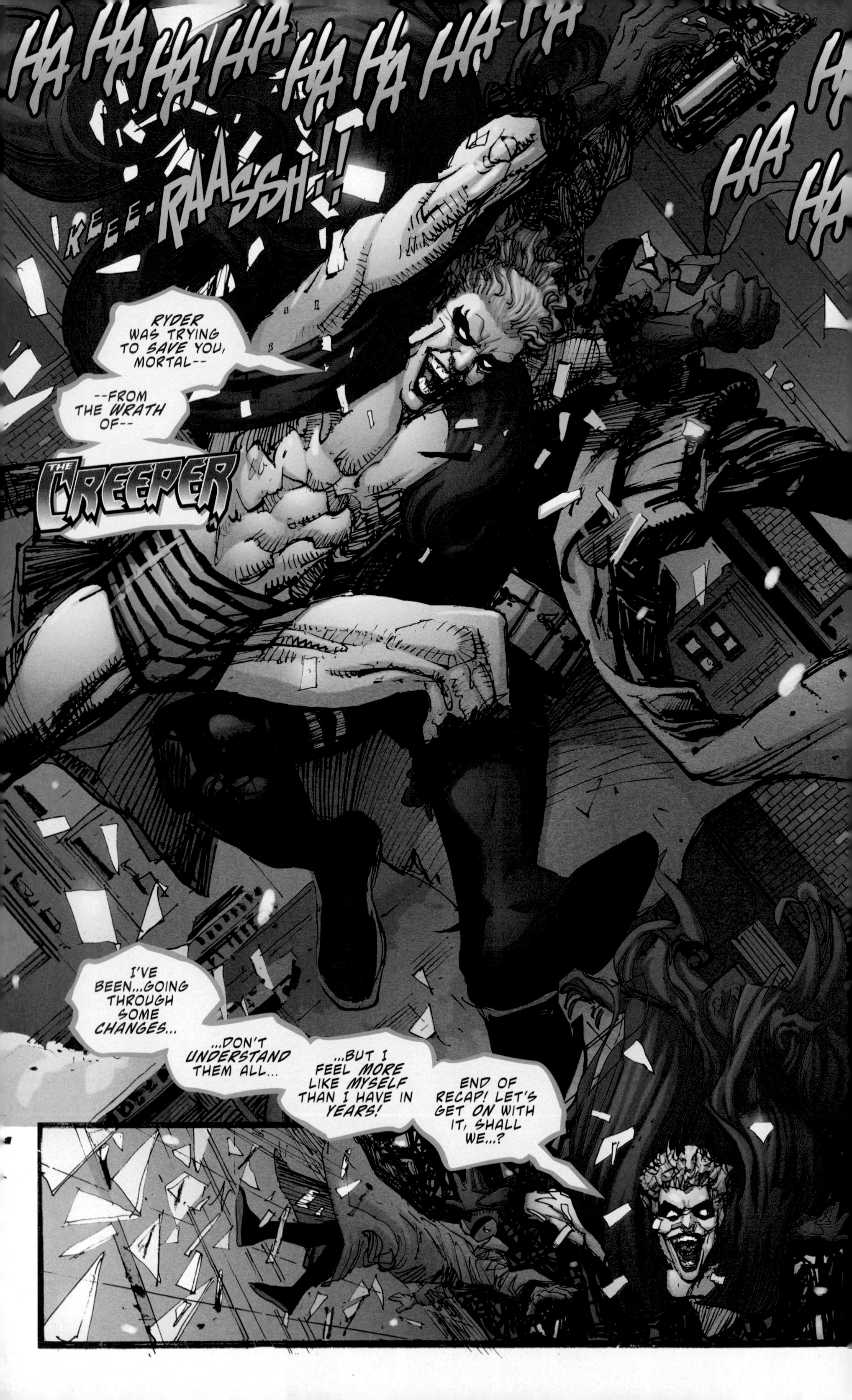
HA HA HA HA HA HA HA HA HA
KREEE-RAASSH!!
HA HA HA HA
RYDER WAS TRYING TO SAVE YOU, MORTAL--
--FROM THE WRATH OF--
THE CREEPER
I'VE BEEN...GOING THROUGH SOME CHANGES...
...DON'T UNDERSTAND THEM ALL...
...BUT I FEEL MORE LIKE MYSELF THAN I HAVE IN YEARS!
END OF RECAP! LET'S GET ON WITH IT, SHALL WE...?

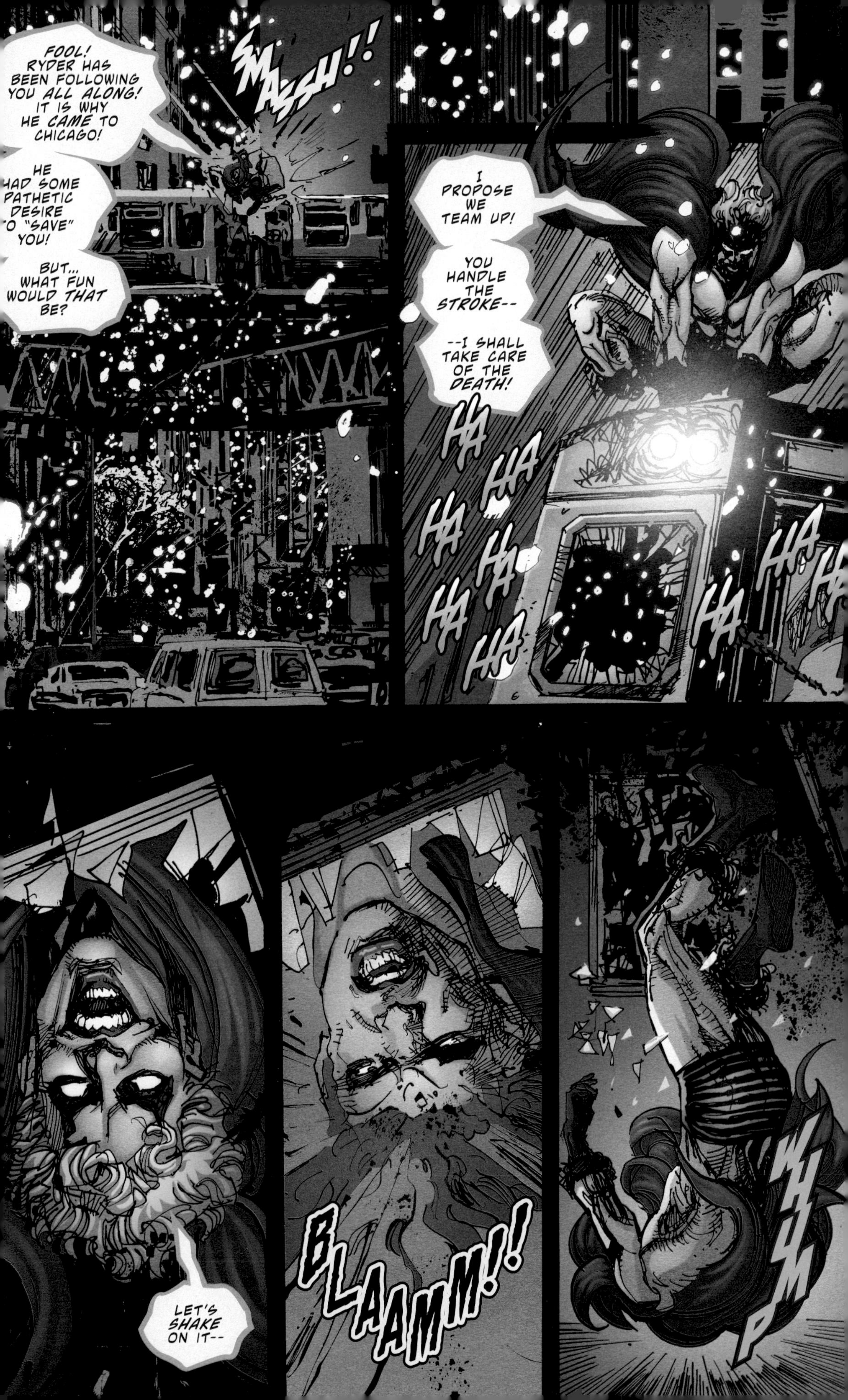
FOOL! RYDER HAS BEEN FOLLOWING YOU ALL ALONG! IT IS WHY HE CAME TO CHICAGO!
HE HAD SOME PATHETIC DESIRE TO "SAVE" YOU!
BUT... WHAT FUN WOULD THAT BE?
SMASSH!!
I PROPOSE WE TEAM UP!
YOU HANDLE THE STROKE--
--I SHALL TAKE CARE OF THE DEATH!
HA HA HA HA HA HA HA HA HA HA HA
LET'S SHAKE ON IT--
BLAAMM!!
WHUMP

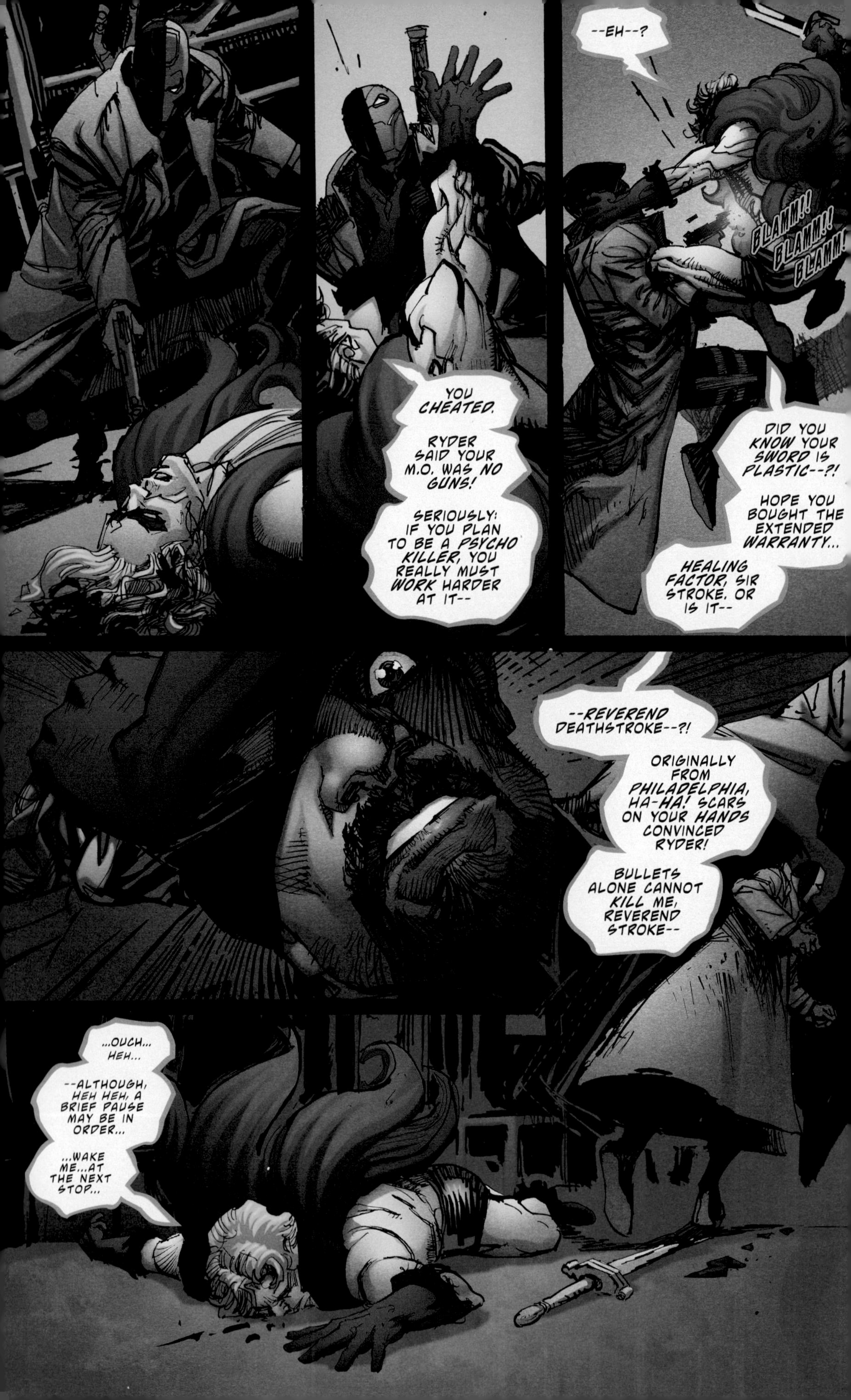
YOU CHEATED.
RYDER SAID YOUR M.O. WAS NO GUNS!
SERIOUSLY: IF YOU PLAN TO BE A PSYCHO KILLER, YOU REALLY MUST WORK HARDER AT IT--
--EH--?
BLAMM!! BLAMM!! BLAMM!
DID YOU KNOW YOUR SWORD IS PLASTIC--?!
HOPE YOU BOUGHT THE EXTENDED WARRANTY...
HEALING FACTOR, SIR STROKE. OR IS IT--
--REVEREND DEATHSTROKE--?!
ORIGINALLY FROM PHILADELPHIA, HA-HA! SCARS ON YOUR HANDS CONVINCED RYDER!
BULLETS ALONE CANNOT KILL ME, REVEREND STROKE--
...OUCH... HEH...
--ALTHOUGH, HEH HEH, A BRIEF PAUSE MAY BE IN ORDER...
...WAKE ME...AT THE NEXT STOP...

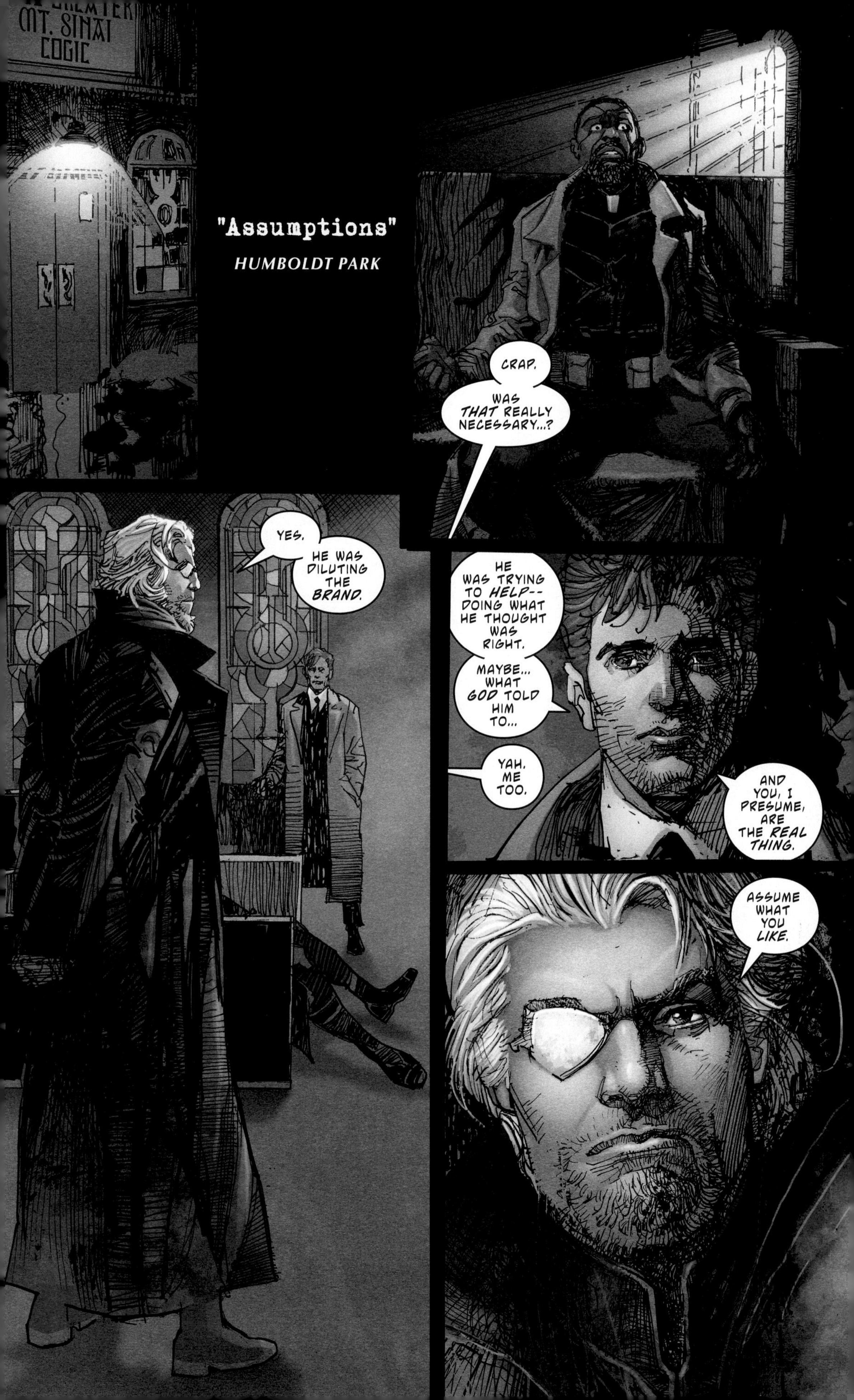
MT. SINAI
COGIC
"Assumptions"
HUMBOLDT PARK
CRAP.
WAS *THAT* REALLY NECESSARY...?
YES.
HE WAS DILUTING THE *BRAND*.
HE WAS TRYING TO *HELP*-- DOING WHAT HE THOUGHT WAS RIGHT.
MAYBE... WHAT *GOD* TOLD HIM TO...
YAH. ME TOO.
AND YOU, I PRESUME, ARE THE *REAL THING*.
ASSUME WHAT YOU *LIKE*.

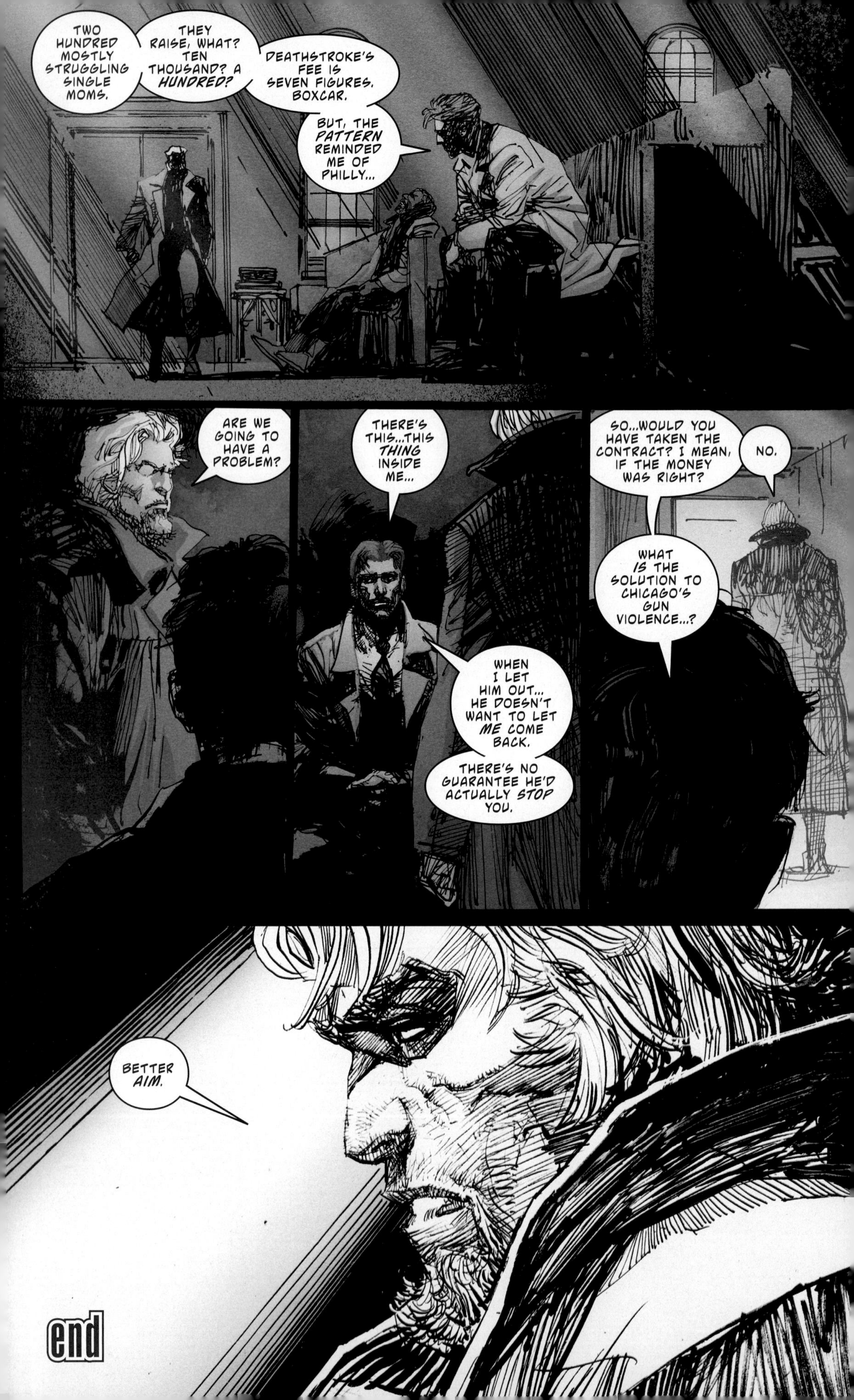
TWO HUNDRED MOSTLY STRUGGLING SINGLE MOMS.
THEY RAISE, WHAT? TEN THOUSAND? A HUNDRED?
DEATHSTROKE'S FEE IS SEVEN FIGURES, BOXCAR.
BUT, THE PATTERN REMINDED ME OF PHILLY...
ARE WE GOING TO HAVE A PROBLEM?
THERE'S THIS...THIS THING INSIDE ME...
WHEN I LET HIM OUT... HE DOESN'T WANT TO LET ME COME BACK.
THERE'S NO GUARANTEE HE'D ACTUALLY STOP YOU.
SO...WOULD YOU HAVE TAKEN THE CONTRACT? I MEAN, IF THE MONEY WAS RIGHT?
NO.
WHAT IS THE SOLUTION TO CHICAGO'S GUN VIOLENCE...?
BETTER AIM.
end

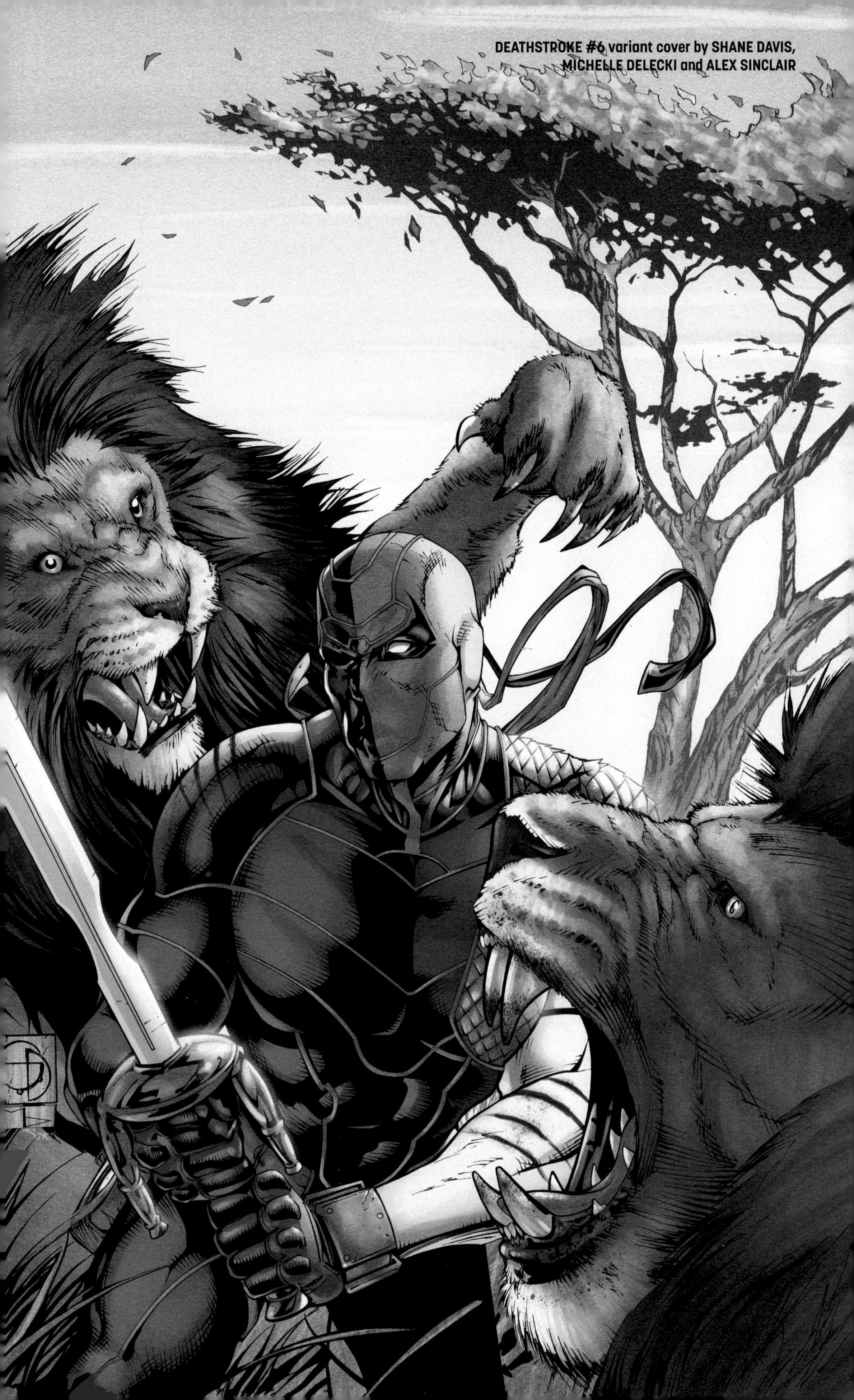

DEATHSTROKE #6 variant cover by SHANE DAVIS,
MICHELLE DELECKI and ALEX SINCLAIR

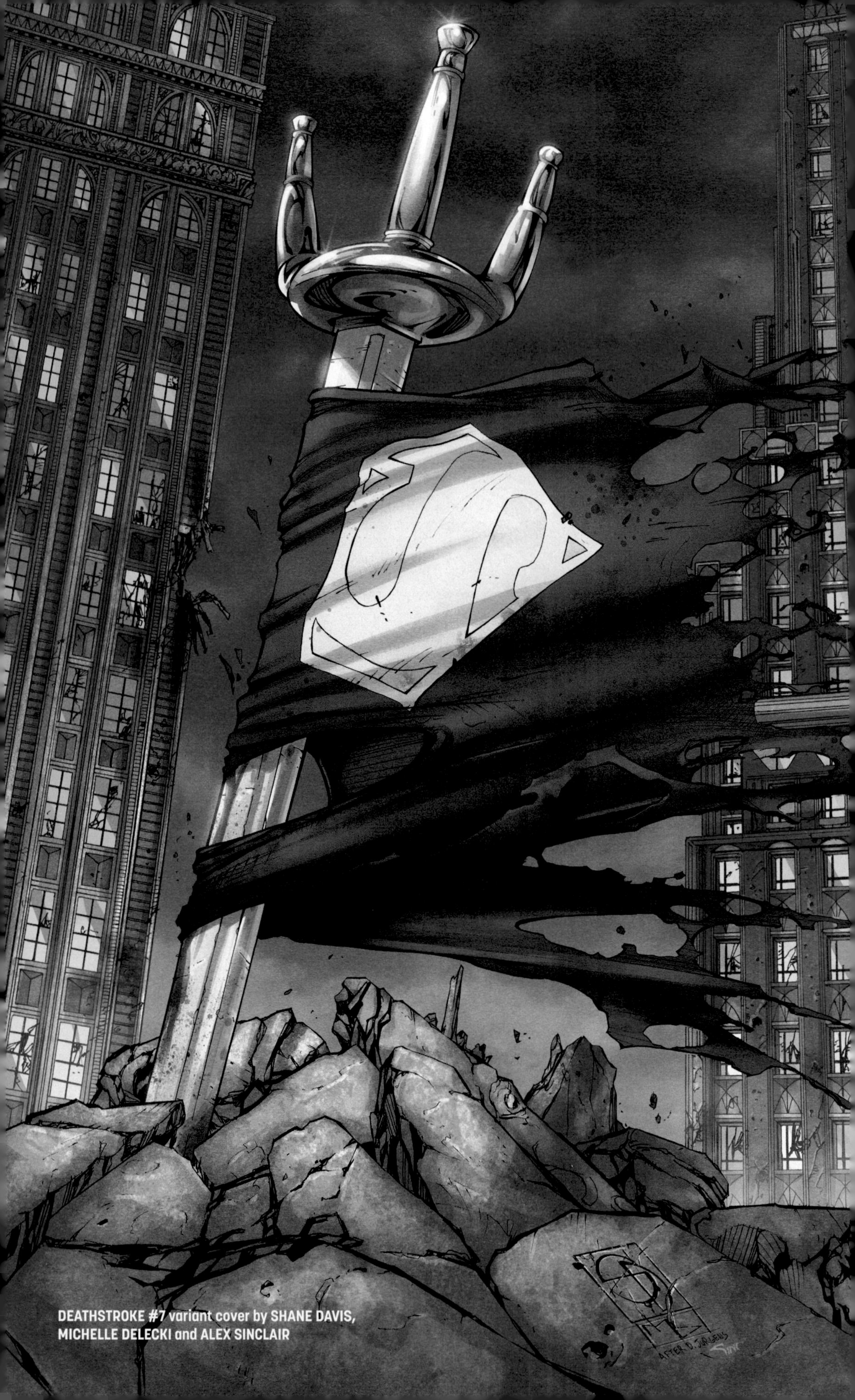
AFTER D. JURGENS

DEATHSTROKE #7 variant cover by SHANE DAVIS,
MICHELLE DELECKI and ALEX SINCLAIR

DEATHSTROKE #8 variant cover by SHANE DAVIS, MICHELLE DELECKI and ALEX SINCLAIR

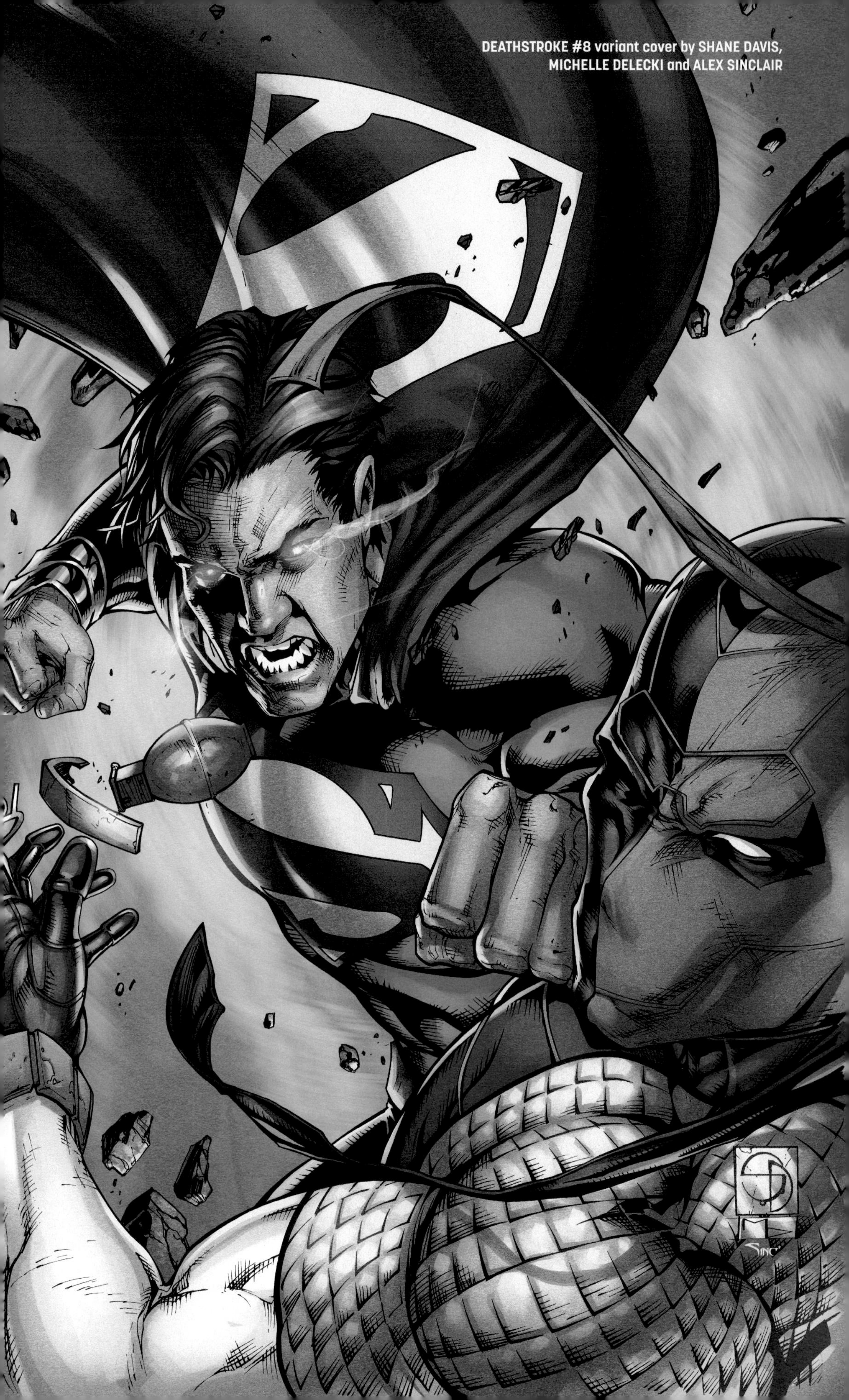

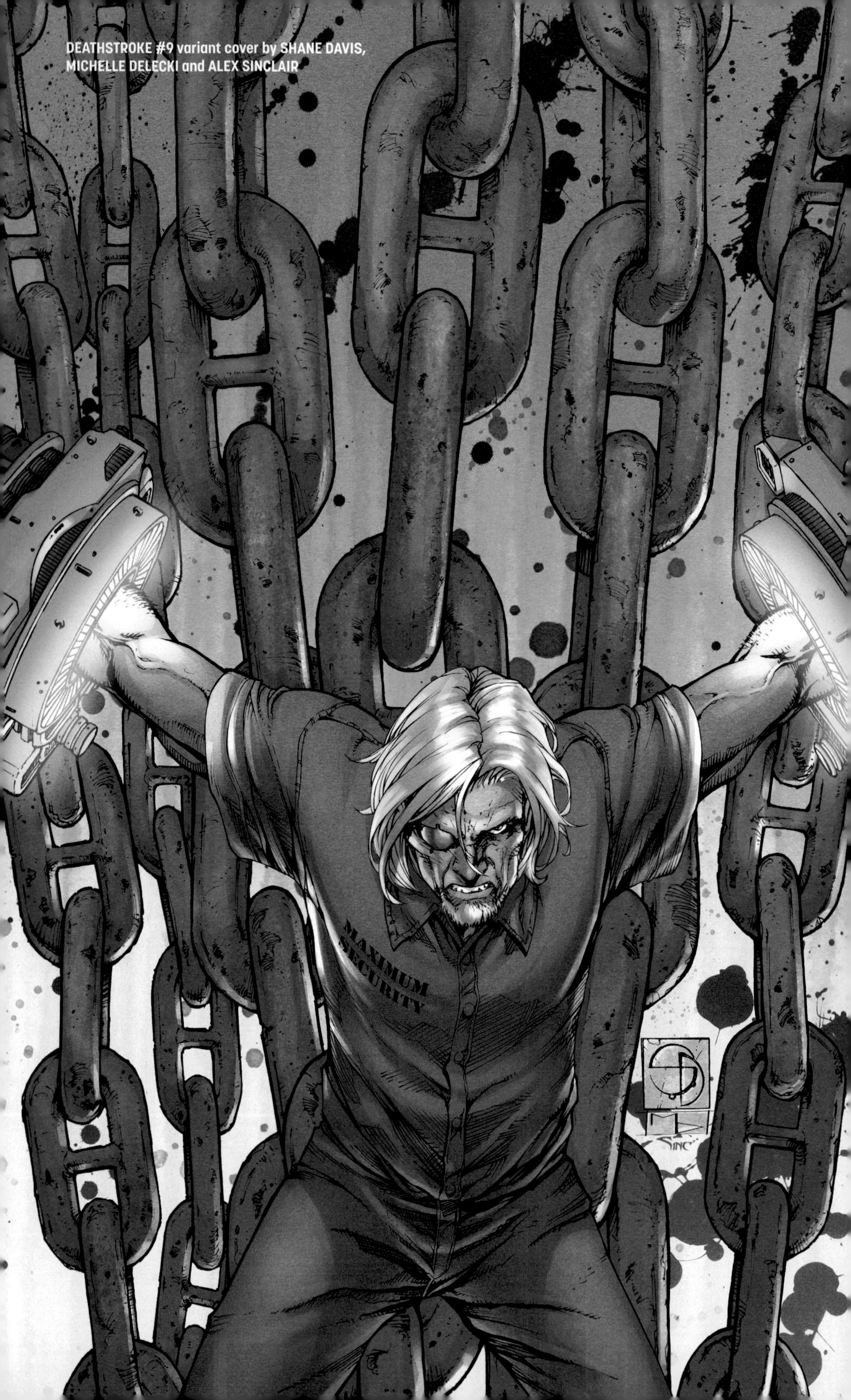
MAXIMUM
SECURITY

DEATHSTROKE #9 variant cover by SHANE DAVIS, MICHELLE DELECKI and ALEX SINCLAIR

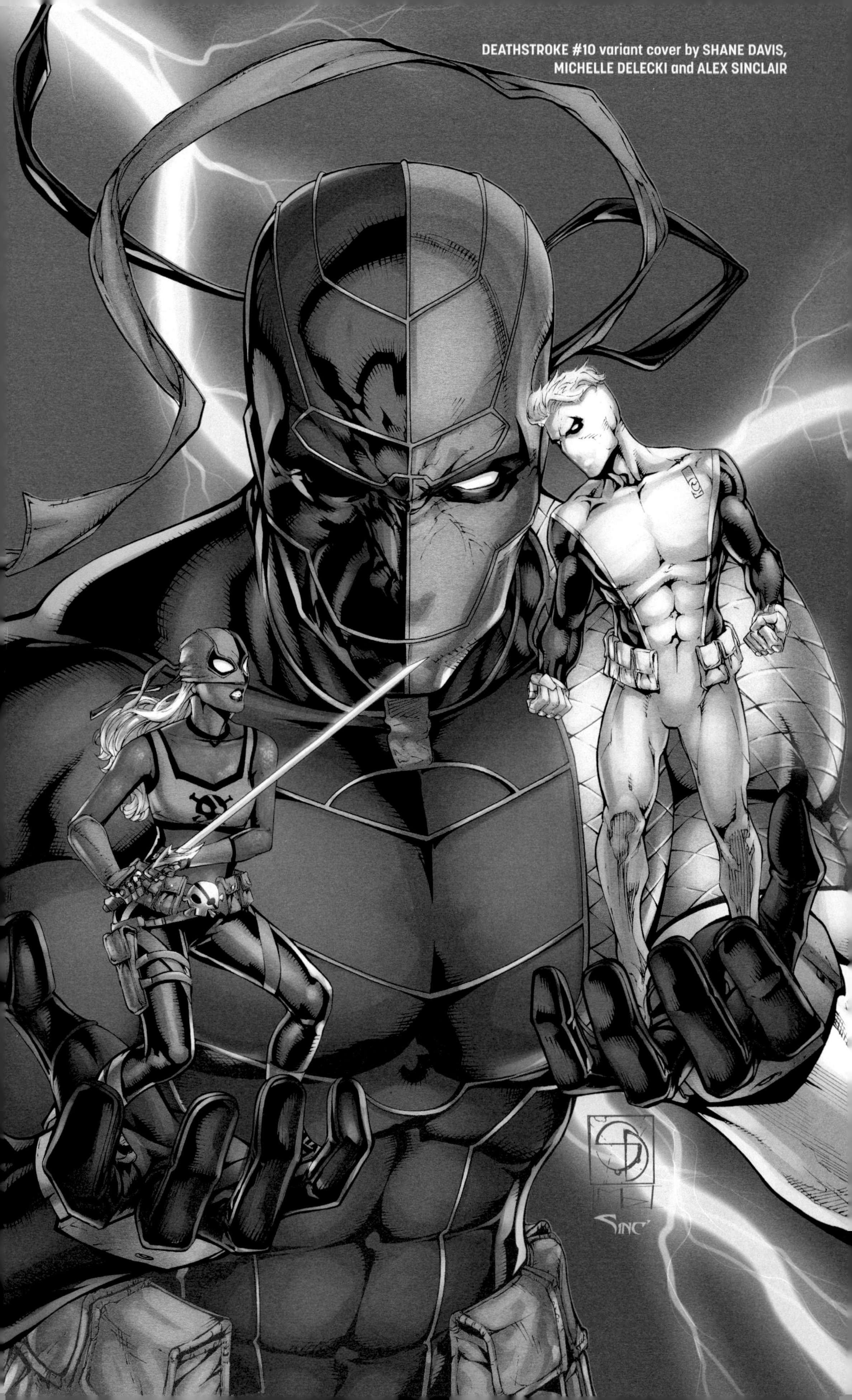
SINC'

DEATHSTROKE #10 variant cover by SHANE DAVIS,
MICHELLE DELECKI and ALEX SINCLAIR

DEATHSTROKE #11 variant cover by SHANE DAVIS,
MICHELLE DELECKI and ALEX SINCLAIR

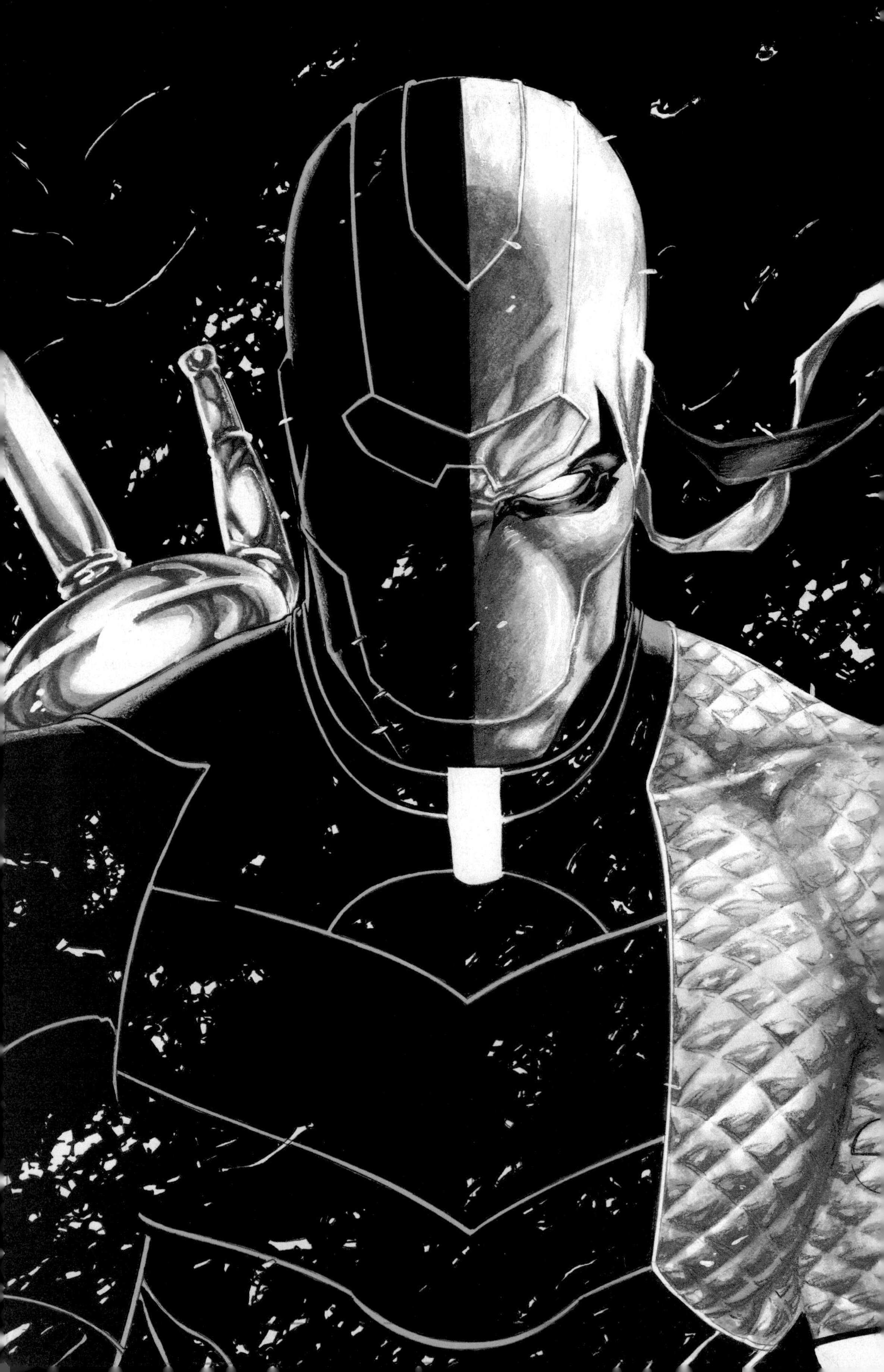

"It's nice to see one of the best comics of the late '80s return so strongly."
– Comic Book Resources

"It's high energy from page one through to the last page." **– BATMAN NEWS**

DC UNIVERSE REBIRTH

SUICIDE SQUAD

VOL. 1: THE BLACK VAULT

ROB WILLIAMS
with JIM LEE and others

VOL.1 THE BLACK VAULT

ROB WILLIAMS • JIM LEE • PHILIP TAN • JASON FABOK • IVAN REIS • GARY FRANK

THE HELLBLAZER VOL. 1:
THE POISON TRUTH

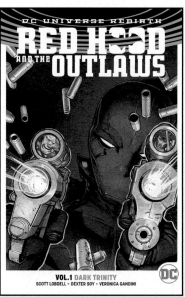

RED HOOD AND THE OUTLAWS VOL. 1:
DARK TRINITY

HARLEY QUINN VOL. 1:
DIE LAUGHING

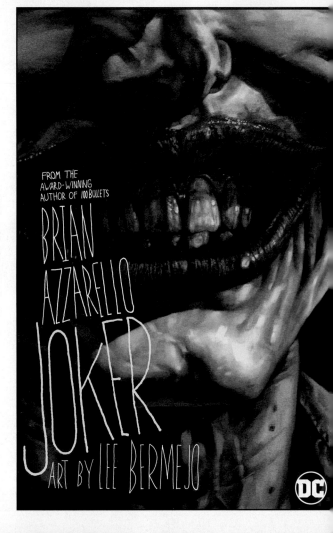